GOLD

C1 Advanced

NEW EDITION

CONTENTS

Exam information

The *Cambridge C1 Advanced Certificate, formerly known as Cambridge English: Advanced (CAE)* is an examination at level C1 of the Common European Framework of Reference for Languages (CEFR). There are four papers, each testing a different skill in English. There are five grades: *A, B* and *C* are pass grades; *D* and *E* are fail grades.

Reading and Use of English (1 hour 30 minutes)

The Reading and Use of English test is divided into eight parts. Parts 1–4 test use of English and parts 5–8 test reading comprehension. Be sure to use your time wisely: the Use of English section is worth 36 marks and the Reading section is worth 42 marks. There is one mark given for each correct answer in Parts 1–3 and in Part 8, up to two marks for each correct answer in Part 4 and two marks for each correct answer in Parts 5–7.

Part 1 Multiple-choice cloze	Focus	Vocabulary/Lexico-grammatical
	Task	You read a text with eight gaps and choose the best word for each gap from a choice of four options (A, B, C or D).
Part 2 Open cloze	Focus	Grammar/Lexico-grammatical
	Task	You read a text with eight gaps and think of an appropriate word to fit in each gap.
Part 3 Word formation	Focus	Vocabulary
	Task	You read a text with eight gaps. You are given the stems of the missing words in capitals at the end of the lines with the gaps. You have to change the form of each word to fit the context.
Part 4 Key word transformation	Focus	Grammar, vocabulary and collocations
	Task	There are six sentences. You are given a sentence and a 'key word'. You have to complete a second gapped sentence using the key word. The second sentence has a different grammatical structure but must have a similar meaning to the original.
Part 5 Multiple-choice	Focus	Detail, opinion, attitude, main idea, text organisation, purpose
	Task	There are six four-option multiple-choice questions. You read a long text and choose the correct option (A, B, C or D) based on the information in the text.
Part 6 Cross-text multiple matching	Focus	Attitude, opinion, comparing and contrasting points of view across texts
	Task	You read four short texts on a related topic. You have to decide which text expresses a similar/different opinion to the idea mentioned in each question.
Part 7 Gapped text	Focus	Text structure, cohesion and coherence
	Task	You read a long text from which six paragraphs have been removed and put before the text. You have to decide where in the text each paragraph (A–G) should go. There is one paragraph you do not need to use.
Part 8 Multiple matching	Focus	Specific information, detail, attitude, opinion
	Task	You read ten questions or statements about four to six short texts, or a text which has been divided into sections. You have to decide which section or text contains the information relating to each question or statement.

Writing (1 hour 30 minutes)

The Writing test is divided into two parts. You have to complete one task from each part. Each part carries equal marks, so you should not spend longer on one than another.

Part 1	Focus	Content, communicative achievement , organisation, language
	Task	Part 1 is compulsory and there is no choice of questions. You have to write an essay of 220–260 words on a given topic using the notes provided.
Part 2	Focus	Content, communicative achievement, organisation, language
	Task	Part 2 has four tasks to choose from: an email/letter, a report, a proposal or a review. You have to write 220–260 words using the prompts provided.

Listening (approximately 40 minutes)

There are four parts in the Listening test, with a total of thirty questions. You write your answers on the question paper and then you have five minutes at the end of the exam to transfer them to an answer sheet. In each part, you will hear the recording(s) twice. The texts may be monologues or exchanges between interacting speakers. There will be a variety of accents.

Part 1 Multiple choice	Focus	Attitude, agreement, opinion, gist, detail
	Task	You hear three short conversations. You have to answer six multiple-choice questions – two questions for each conversation – by choosing the correct option (A, B or C).
Part 2 Sentence completion	Focus	Specific information, opinion
	Task	You hear a monologue. You complete eight sentences using words from the recording.
Part 3 Multiple choice	Focus	Attitude, opinion
	Task	You hear a conversation. You answer six multiple-choice questions by choosing the correct option.
Part 4 Multiple matching	Focus	Gist, attitude, main point
	Task	You hear five short monologues on a related topic. You have to match five statements (A–F) in Task 1 and Task 2 to each speaker. There is one statement in each task you do not need to use. The two tasks must be completed simultaneously.

Speaking (Approximately 15 minutes)

You take the Speaking test with one or two other candidates. There are two examiners. One is the 'Interlocutor' who speaks to you and the other is the 'assessor' who just listens.

Part 1 Interview	Focus	General interaction and social language skills
	Task	The Interlocutor asks each of you questions about yourself.
Part 2 Long turn	Focus	Comparing, contrasting, speculating
	Task	The Interlocutor gives you three pictures and asks you to answer the questions on the task card by discussing two of the pictures. You have to speak for one minute. Then you answer a question briefly about the other candidate's pictures.
Part 3 Collaborative task	Focus	Expressing and justifying opinions, negotiating a decision, suggesting, agreeing/disagreeing, etc.
	Task	You are given a task to discuss with another candidate, based on the prompts on the task card. Then you discuss a second question on the same topic for a minute and make a decision together.
Part 4 Discussion	Focus	Expressing and justifying opinions, agreeing/disagreeing, etc.
	Task	The Interlocutor asks you questions related to the topic in Part 3. You discuss them with the other candidate.

For more information see the **Writing reference** (page 166) the **Exam focus** (page 178) and the **General marking guidelines** (page 184).

Where we live

Interview (Part 1)
Talking about yourself

▶ **EXAM** FOCUS p.182

1 **Discuss the questions.**

1 What did you like most about the area where you grew up?
2 What are the advantages and disadvantages of living abroad for a short time?
3 If you could live in another country, where would you choose? Why?

2 ▶ 01 **Listen to two candidates talking to an examiner and answer the questions.**

1 Which of the questions in Activity 1 does the examiner ask?
2 Which of the candidates, Karl or Elena, provides responses of an appropriate length?

EXAM TIP

Don't just give single-word answers to the examiner's questions. Try to use introductory phrases like *Well, … , Actually, … , Now I come to think of it, … .*

3 **Look at responses to the questions Karl and Elena were asked. How could you make the responses longer and more interesting?**

1 Spain.
2 I'm a student.
3 The weather.
4 My friends.

4 **Work in pairs. Turn to page 134 and do the activities.**

5 **How would you evaluate your own performance? Use the General marking guidelines on page 185 to help you. Can you suggest any ways in which the other students you worked with could improve?**

Multiple-choice cloze (Part 1)

▶ **EXAM** FOCUS p.178

6 Look at the title of the article about lottery winners' dream homes. What would you expect a lottery winner's dream home to be like?

7 Read the first sentence of the article and look at the example (0). The correct answer is B. Look at the two reasons why the other alternatives are wrong and match them to the incorrect alternatives A, C and D.

1 usually plural
2 usually preceded by an adjective

8 Read the whole article. For questions 1–8, decide which answer (A, B, C or D) best fits each gap. Use the criteria in Activity 7 to help you.

Lottery winners' dream homes:
not what you'd expect

Not many of us are in a **(0)** B, position to go hunting for the perfect home with a massive cheque in our back pockets. Lottery winners Barbara and Ray Wragg were when they became the **(1)** .... winners of a £7 million prize. Rather than buying a huge mansion with a swimming pool, they **(2)** .... for a relatively ordinary five-bedroom house instead. The Wraggs are not **(3)** .... Most of us dream of living somewhere other than where we are but dreams are essentially different from reality in that they do not **(4)** .... into account things like work and study obligations or **(5)** .... to friends and family. A common dream is to own a wood cabin in the middle of a forest, something most of us could **(6)** .... but few would actually want. Although the cottage in the woods or the rock star mansion is what we **(7)** .... about, the reality is that the ideal home is a warm, comfortable place where we can be near our **(8)** .... ones and escape.

	A	B	C	D
0	condition	position	circumstance	situation
1	exclusive	only	unique	individual
2	chose	decided	elected	opted
3	unusual	uncommon	unfamiliar	unlikely
4	consider	bear	take	weigh
5	proximity	vicinity	immediacy	locality
6	permit	let	allow	afford
7	aspire	hope	fantasise	wish
8	esteemed	loved	liked	fond

9 How closely does the place you live in now correspond to your ideal home?

1 Discuss. What are the advantages and disadvantages of living in a small town or village as opposed to a big city?

2 ▶ 02 Listen to a woman talking about moving to a remote village. Does she mention any of the things you talked about?

Verbs in perfect and continuous forms

▶ **GRAMMAR** REFERENCE p.149

3 Work in pairs. Discuss the difference in meaning between the underlined phrases in the pairs of sentences.

1 A <u>We've been discussing</u> where we should move to look for work. We can't seem to agree.

  B <u>We've discussed</u> where we should move to look for work. We agree that Ireland is the best choice.

2 A <u>I'll have walked</u> from one end of the island to the other by Christmas day.

  B <u>I will have been walking</u> twenty kilometres a day for nearly a month by then.

3 A When I was offered the job, <u>I had already spent a lot of time wondering about leaving the city</u>.

  B When I was offered the job, <u>I had been spending a lot of time wondering</u> about leaving the city.

4 Choose the correct verb form in each sentence. In which sentences are both forms possible? Then listen to the recording again. Which form does the speaker use in each case?

1 For years *I had told/I had been telling* all my friends that I wanted to get away from the hustle and bustle of London.

2 *I had, in fact, always been/I had, in fact, always been being* a real city person.

3 By the beginning of next month *I will have lived/I will have been living* here for exactly a year.

4 *I've looked back, retraced my steps and come/I've been looking back, retracing my steps and coming* to understand just how great a change it has been.

5 *I've spent/I've been spending* hours exploring the glorious countryside by bicycle and on foot and *have discovered/been discovering* a taste for silence and solitude.

6 By the time the first year comes to an end almost all my London friends *will have been/have been* here to stay.

Stative verbs

▶ **GRAMMAR** REFERENCE p.150

LANGUAGE TIP

Some verbs have stative and dynamic meanings. They can only be used in continuous forms with a dynamic meaning, e.g. *I'm **feeling** unwell. Feel* = 'experience a feeling or emotion'. Compare this with the stative meaning, e.g. *I **feel** we should give him a chance. Feel* = 'have an opinion'.

5 Divide the stative verbs in the box into five groups according to their meanings: emotions, knowledge, possession, communication, senses.

agree   believe   belong   care   deny   hear   know like   love   own   possess   promise   smell   taste understand

6 Complete the sentences with the correct form of the verb in brackets.

1 I .... (*think*) that living in a small village would be a bit boring.

2 I .... (*think*) of spending a week in Ireland in early June.

3 I .... (*see*) a friend of mine for dinner tonight.

4 I .... (*see*) your point, but I think cities can be very lonely places.

5 The judges .... (*taste*) the cakes at the moment to decide who will win.

6 This sauce .... (*taste*) a bit strange.

7 Imagine that you have won the lottery and have been living in your dream home for a year now. Tell other students what changes there have been in your life over the last year.

Multiple matching (Part 4)

▶ **EXAM** FOCUS p.182

> ### EXAM TIP
> Don't worry if you don't understand every word and expression the speakers use. As long as you understand the general message, you should be able to answer the questions.

1 **Look at the exam tasks and answer the questions. Compare your answers with a partner.**

1 Have you ever moved house for any of the reasons in Task 1?

2 What advantages does the place you live in now have over other places you've lived in? Are any of these advantages mentioned in Task 2?

Task 1

For questions 1–5, choose from the list (A–H) the reason each speaker gives for moving house.

A I'd finished studying.
B I needed more space.
C I'd won the lottery.
D I wanted to downsize.
E I had no choice.
F I hated city life.
G I wanted a change of lifestyle.
H I'd saved enough money.

Speaker 1	1
Speaker 2	2
Speaker 3	3
Speaker 4	4
Speaker 5	5

Task 2

For questions 6–10, choose from the list (A–H) what each speaker likes about the place where they live.

A the amount of storage space
B the entertainment facilities nearby
C the cosy atmosphere
D the chance to work from home
E the local community
F the overall dimensions
G the view
H the cost of living there

Speaker 1	6
Speaker 2	7
Speaker 3	8
Speaker 4	9
Speaker 5	10

2 ▶ 03 **Do the exam tasks in Activity 1. You will hear five short extracts in which people are talking about the places where they live. While you listen you must complete both tasks.**

3 **What kind of neighbour do you imagine each of the speakers is?**

Vocabulary

expressions with *space* and *room*

4 **Decide if it is possible to complete the sentences with *space*, *room* or both words.**

1 That chest of drawers takes up too much .... We ought to get rid of it.

2 I don't think I've got enough .... in my suitcase for these boots.

3 Could you make .... for people to get past, please?

4 It was such a popular event that there was standing .... only by the time we got there.

5 There isn't really enough .... here to do aerobics.

6 I like cities with plenty of open ....

7 That was delicious but if I have any more, I won't have any .... for dessert.

8 The only explanation she gave for breaking up with him was that she needed more ....

5 **Work in pairs. Turn to page 144 and do the activity.**

Multiple choice (Part 5)

▶ **EXAM** FOCUS p.179

1 **Work in pairs and discuss the questions.**

1 How well do you know your way around your town or city?

2 What do you do to help you navigate in a town or city you don't know well?

3 Have you ever got completely lost?

2 **Read the title and the first paragraph of the newspaper article. Will the rest of the text be about a) futuristic cities in movies b) aerial photography or c) our relationship with contemporary cities? Read the rest of the article to see if you were right.**

EXAM TIP

Don't answer questions using your own beliefs or experience. Always look for evidence in the text.

3 **Read the article again. For questions 1–6, choose the answer (A, B, C or D) which you think fits best according to the text.**

1 What point is the writer making about aerial views of cities?

A They are used too frequently in cinema photography.

B They reveal interesting patterns not seen at ground level.

C They are an indicator of how perceptions of cities have changed.

D They make us feel insignificant.

2 What does the writer suggest about GPS?

A It has made us entirely reliant on technology.

B It can stop us noticing what is actually around us.

C It has made it necessary for architects to work remotely.

D It is so complex that few of us understand how it works.

3 The writer uses the word 'hybrid' in line 47 to suggest that

A we find our cities have become very similar.

B we have negative and positive views of our cities.

C we see our cities as performing two different functions.

D we experience our cities in more than one way.

4 What does the writer feel about Friedman's prediction today?

A It is remarkably accurate.

B There may be some evidence to support it.

C It will soon be a reality.

D It is how he sees European cities.

5 What is the writer's opinion of George Leonidas Leslie?

A He was extremely thorough in his approach.

B He was not really an architect.

C He was not as bad as the police thought.

D He deserved what happened to him in the end.

6 What does 'them' in line 105 refer to?

A The authorities who control our cities.

B The rules about building designs.

C The criminals who study cities.

D The buildings architects create.

4 **Work in pairs and discuss the questions.**

1 Do you have favourite parts of your town or city?

2 What are your most vivid memories of cities you have visited?

5 **Match the underlined words in the article to meanings 1–8.**

1 visit **5** exploration

2 disinterest **6** structure

3 accomplishment **7** boundaries

4 playfully **8** meet

6 **Write one sentence for each of the words in Activity 5. Compare your sentences with a partner.**

THE ENDLESS CITY

In almost every Hollywood action movie today there will be an aerial tracking shot of the city, the skyscrapers or favelas below massing into a complex abstract geometry. From a helicopter, an airship or perhaps a drone, we get a·view that establishes context – the background against which the smaller stories of individuals intersect and also, in a way, a character in itself. It represents a new conception of the city, the perspective of a god, a superhero or a disembodied soul.

You might argue that this is a result of the pervasive influence of GPS. We now navigate not by using landmarks or streets but through the mysteries of quantum mechanics and satellite communication, a weirdly excessive feat of technology that beams our coordinates up into space and then affirms our existence in the form of a moving dot. In architecture, the phenomenon of seeming to engage with the city from a distance has been archly termed 'Google Earth urbanism': the dropping of a building or a development into a context understood through digital mapping by a designer in another country, and inevitably lacking in the texture of the actual place.

Interactive maps have provoked a fundamental change in the way we engage with our environment. At the same time, the streets themselves are becoming increasingly homogenous and globalised – from Vancouver to Singapore via Manchester, it can seem as though the same glass façade systems, backlit corporate signage and coffee shops mark our routes. Add to this our increasing detachment from our surroundings — the barriers of headphones, telephone conversations and social media on the move – and we realise that the cities in which we live are a hybrid of visceral and virtual reality.

The history of cities is peppered with inventions that change our perception of them – street lights, plate glass, skyscrapers, elevators, and so on. Ease of travel and urban sprawl has raised questions about parameters: where does one metropolis end and another begin? In the 1970s, the architect Yona Friedman suggested that by the early 21st century we would perceive almost the whole of northern Europe, from London to Paris, Amsterdam to Hamburg, as essentially one continuous city, much as the Boston–Washington Corridor (arguably a linear city of 50 million people) could today be seen.

Geoff Manaugh, a U.S.-based architecture writer, suggests that it is criminals who are the most astute readers of the contemporary urban fabric, working out exactly where its weaknesses lie through an intimate understanding of how it is made. He tells the wonderful story of George Leonidas Leslie, an architect who arrived in New York in 1869, as the modern metropolis was being built. Leslie had come not to contribute to the city's architecture but, in Manaugh's words, 'to rob the place blind'. His methods were remarkable. He would use his architectural credentials to talk to safe manufacturers and bank builders, and to fire officers with whom blueprints and plans of new buildings had been deposited. He would build entire replica rooms and vaults in a warehouse in Brooklyn, recreating the interiors of the houses of the wealthy, their safes and the vaults of banks. He would break into houses and vaults for reconnaissance, testing routes, stealing nothing and leaving, just so he could visualise them better. The New York police reckoned that for a decade or so Leslie might have been responsible for an astonishing 80 percent of all bank robberies in the city, including the $3 million Manhattan Savings Institution heist of 1878, although it was that robbery that led to his being murdered by one of his own crew.

The city is always adapting and being reshaped in surprising ways. Authority dictates the rules for their construction, then criminals subvert those mechanisms to turn them back on their designers. Even as we increasingly rely on Google Maps and travel apps, we are still able to make mental connections in our heads and build our version of the city through the places we frequent and the associations and memories we make. There is the overhead tracking shot but there is also the city of bits, the landscape we construct in our minds – for whatever purposes. We live in the city but the city also lives inside us.

Compound words

1 **Work in pairs and discuss the questions.**

1 What attracts visitors to your town or city?

2 Describe a landmark in your city or country for someone who has never visited it.

3 Are your city or town's landmarks well known to people who have never been there?

2 **Read the extract from an article about branding cities. Does your town or city have any of the characteristics mentioned in the extract?**

CITY BRANDS

Does your city have a famous <u>landmark</u>, a rich cultural tradition or is it home to a major industry, a <u>world-renowned</u> hotel or even a distinctive way of getting around like London's black cabs or Amsterdam's barges? Perhaps it's a mecca for <u>theatre-goers</u>, musicians or party animals. Or maybe it's just a nice place to be. <u>Top-brand</u> cities seem to have it all. They boast lists as long as your arm of iconic buildings, museums and galleries, they are also home to gourmet restaurants, glorious parks, <u>purpose-built</u> sports stadiums and all sorts of places to see and be seen.

For cities and towns less favourably endowed, the first step in establishing a brand is to identify assets and find a way of communicating these, usually by means of a logo and slogan. But getting the logo and slogan right is no mean feat. Under no circumstances should visitors be led to believe a city can promise something it cannot deliver.

No one is impressed if a place calls itself <u>sun-soaked</u> but is in fact <u>wind-swept</u>, wet and cold, or claims to 'never sleep' when <u>bylaws</u> oblige all bars and restaurants to close by midnight.

3 **Look at the underlined compound words. Which words do not combine a noun and adjective?**

LANGUAGE TIP

Compound words are two or more words joined to form a new word. They can be written as one word without a hyphen, e.g. *keyboard*, as two separate words, e.g. *post office* or hyphenated, e.g. *self-esteem*. Compound adjectives usually have a hyphen, e.g. *world-renowned* but if the compound begins with an adverb, the hyphen isn't necessary, e.g. *happily married*.

4 **Match compound adjectives 1–6 to the nouns A–F.**

1	long-standing	A	job
2	run-down	B	man
3	cut-price	C	airline tickets
4	drop-down	D	menu
5	middle-aged	E	friendship
6	part-time	F	area

5 **Complete the compound adjectives in these sentences with the words in the box.**

air built far high highly interest life mass

1 If your apartment isn't ....-conditioned, summers can be pretty unbearable.

2 A lot of the ....-produced goods we buy today would once have taken weeks of careful work to make.

3 She has a lot of ....-fetched ideas about the origins of the universe but no one takes them seriously.

4 Mary was one of the .... regarded members of staff.

5 Apartments in ....-rise buildings often have wonderful views

6 Their baby needed a ....-saving transplant operation.

7 They were able to get an ....-free loan to pay for their new computer.

8 This area of the city has become so ....-up over the last few years it's hard to find any open spaces.

6 **Write sentences with the compound adjectives and nouns from Activity 5. Compare your sentences with a partner.**

 1 Work in pairs and discuss. What is meant by 'The past is a foreign country. They do things differently there.'?

 2 Read an extract from a blog about a visit to a childhood home. Summarise the main reasons the writer found the visit unsatisfactory.

https://MyBlog/Memory Lane

A trip down memory lane?

When I was a child we lived in a lovely old house in a village. It backed onto a perfect sandy beach where my sister and I spent many happy afternoons. I have often thought about that house, and wished I could go back. A few weeks ago my sister discovered that it had been turned into a bed and breakfast and that it was possible to stay there. We were both very excited and made a booking, imagining a blissful weekend reliving our childhood. But it didn't turn out like that.

The problem is that the past was probably not as wonderful as we imagine. **(1)** Nor do things stay the same even if they were wonderful. The people who ran the bed and breakfast had almost completely destroyed everything that I had loved about that house. It had been painted turquoise and they'd cut down the trees I used to climb. **(2)** Provided they get planning permission, they will build a wall that will block the view of the beach. That too has changed, but **(3)** whether or not you think it has improved will depend on your personal tastes. **(4)** Whereas once it was a deserted stretch of white sand, it is now covered in sun beds, beach umbrellas and people! The author J. P. Hartley said 'The past is a foreign country. They do things differently there.' If only I could visit that country and find our old house as it once was! But **(5)** as long as it is being run by the current owners, I won't be going back.

Conjunctions

▶ **GRAMMAR** REFERENCE p.150

3 Match the underlined conjunctions (1–5) in the blog extract to their functions.

1 making a contrast
2 giving a condition
3 adding information

LANGUAGE TIP

Be careful to use the correct word order with *nor*. It is followed by a verb and then the subject. *As* is also used in this way.

*I wasn't happy, **nor was I** sad.*

*Buying a car is expensive, **as is insurance**.*

4 Choose the correct alternative in each sentence.

1 Living in the inner city does not mean you are completely cut off from nature, *as yet/nor* does it mean you will be less active than you would be if you lived in the country.

2 Although there have been efforts to create pedestrian malls and make the inner city more attractive to businesses, *as yet/nor* these measures have not borne fruit.

3 *As yet/As long as* people continue to find living in large houses surrounded by gardens desirable, it will be difficult to persuade them to move back to the inner city.

4 In the city door-to-door recycling collections are made weekly, *whether/whereas* those who live in the countryside often have to take their own rubbish to recycling centres.

5 People don't understand the benefits of inner-city living. *Provided/Whereas* they are shown the potential advantages, they will begin to move back from the suburbs.

6 Despite cars being environmentally unfriendly, many people will refuse to walk or cycle, *nor/as long as* they continue to live too far from the centre of the city.

5 Match the underlined phrases with *as* in the sentences to the meanings in the box.

current regarding since starting until now while

1 As time begins to run out, the need to take action is increasingly urgent.

2 As for people who refuse to accept that infrastructure outside the city centre represents a huge financial burden, I can only say they need to look at the figures.

3 The government as yet has not invested sufficiently in campaigns to raise awareness of the benefits of using public transport.

4 The situation as it is seems alarming but there is cause for optimism.

5 As the government has failed to solve the problem, it's up to local communities to take action.

6 As from next Monday, anyone caught using a car in the pedestrianised zone will be given an automatic fine.

Essay (Part 1)

using the task input to help you plan

▶ **WRITING** REFERENCE p.168

1 ▶ 04 Work in pairs and listen to a podcast about a way to improve contact between neighbours. How would people react to a scheme like this where you live?

2 Work in pairs and imagine that you have been asked to write an essay on promoting greater contact between neighbours.

1 Brainstorm ideas, including the ones in the podcast and your own ideas.

2 Think of points for and against your ideas.

3 Choose three ideas and include a comment for or against each one.

3 Look at a good and a poor plan for an essay about moving to the suburbs and then turn to the checklist on page 166. What is wrong with plan B?

Plan A

Introduction: Say why the move to the suburbs has been such a big problem.

Solution 1: Invest in urban renewal schemes in the centre of the city.

+ It will attract businesses that had moved out to the shopping malls.

- Money should be spent on schools and hospitals, not prettying up the centre of town.

Solution 2: Offer incentives for moving back to the centre.

+ If there are financial and lifestyle benefits, people will come back.

- Unless life in the suburbs is made harder for them, no one will bother to make the move.

Conclusion: Say which solution I believe will be most effective.

Plan B

Introduction: Explain why we have to get people to move back to the city centre.

Paragraph 1: Why I think the government should invest more.

Paragraph 2: People should realise that infrastructure for suburban living is too costly.

Conclusion: If all these things are done, people will move back.

---

4 Write a plan for the essay in Activity 2. Show it to other students. Can they suggest improvements to your plan?

5 Read points 1–3 and use them to help you write another plan for the task below.

1 Think of what specific ideas might be connected to each of the three methods the government could use (investment, education and taxes).

2 Use the opinions expressed to give you a clue.

3 For each opinion expressed, think of a comment for or against to balance the opinion.

Your class has attended a panel discussion on what methods governments should use to discourage the use of private cars in the centre of the city. You have made the notes below.

Methods governments could use to discourage the use of private cars in the city centre

- investment
- education
- taxes

Some opinions expressed in the discussion

'Make businesses pay parking levies for their employees and they'll move out of the city centre.'

'Improve the public transport system, then people won't need their cars.'

'If people understood how much better pedestrianised city centres are, they wouldn't want to bring their cars in.'

Write an essay for your tutor, discussing **two** of the methods in your notes. You should **explain which method you think is more important** for governments to consider, **giving reasons** to support your opinion.

You may, if you wish, make use of the opinions expressed in the discussion but you should use your own words as far as possible. Write your **essay** in **220–260** words in an appropriate style.

EXAM TIP

Don't copy phrases from the input in Part 1. Use your own words.

6 Write a draft of the essay in Activity 5. Show it to two other students and see if they agree that you have covered all the points in the checklist on page 166.

1 Complete the sentences with the present simple or continuous form of the verb in brackets.

1 I .... (*smell*) smoke. Is there something burning?

2 The soup is almost ready. Dad .... (*taste*) it to see if it's hot enough.

3 I .... (*see*) Josh on Friday evening but perhaps you and I could get together on Saturday.

4 Look at the cat! He .... (*smell*) the roses!

5 We .... (*think*) of renting a small plot of land to grow our own vegetables.

6 This tea .... (*taste*) of mangoes.

2 Complete the second sentence so that it has a similar meaning to the first sentence, using the word in brackets.

1 The new fridge won't go through the kitchen door
There .... get the fridge through the kitchen door. (*room*)

2 Susan doesn't complain about the cold winters unless it rains a lot.
Susan doesn't complain about the cold winters .... a lot. (*provided*)

3 Nigel started doing his ironing two hours ago.
Nigel .... two hours. (*for*)

4 In February next year it will be twenty years since I went to live in Australia.
Next February, I .... in Australia for twenty years. (*will*)

5 I'll go home for Christmas provided I have finished the project by then.
I'll go home for Christmas .... finished the project by then. (*long*)

6 I love hiking, as does Stefano.
Stefano loves hiking .... too. (*and*)

3 Read the article and decide which answer (A, B, C or D) best fits each gap.

	A		B		C		D	
1	draw		create		make		come	
2	reverse		back		rear		underside	
3	led		brought		produced		saw	
4	history		past		ages		time	
5	holding		storing		bearing		exhibiting	
6	seems		looks		resembles		reminds	
7	appealed		charmed		attracted		enticed	
8	get		bring		set		put	

Weekly Herald

The logo that *everyone* loves

It was 1977 and the American graphic designer Milton Glaser had been asked to **(1)** .... up with a logo for New York State. He pulled a red crayon from his pocket and began to sketch on the **(2)** .... of an envelope: first an I, then the simple outline of a heart, followed by two letters, N and Y. Glaser's doodle **(3)** .... to the development of one of the most successful advertising campaigns of all **(4)** .... It was so successful, in fact, that the torn envelope **(5)** .... his original idea is now in a permanent collection in a museum. The upbeat message of Glaser's design, which **(6)** .... the kind of joyful graffiti that a young lover might carve into a tree, **(7)** .... to New Yorkers as well as tourists. Glaser himself acknowledges that it seems strange that a logo could have such an impact but it seems his design really did **(8)** .... about a change in people's attitudes at a time when the city had been going through difficult times.

2 The art of conversation

Long turn (Part 2)
giving opinions

▶ **EXAM** FOCUS p.183

1 Work in pairs. What would be the worst thing about being stuck somewhere without a phone or internet access?

2 ▶ 05 Listen to four students giving their opinion about the statements. Do they agree (A) or disagree (D) with them?

1 I feel anxious if I don't receive a message every few minutes.
2 It's important to respond to messages immediately.
3 There are some things you should always communicate face-to-face.
4 I find it easier to express myself online than face-to-face.

3 Listen again and complete the expressions for giving opinions you hear. Compare your answers with a partner.

1 Generally ...., I …
2 I'm sure some people would .... that …
3 The .... I see it …
4 I think that .... without saying.
5 I wouldn't go that .... but …
6 I think it's .... to say …

4 Work in pairs and discuss which of the statements in Activity 2 you agree/disagree with. Use some of the expressions for giving opinions.

5 Look at the exam task. How many things does the examiner ask the candidate to do?

> Look at the pictures. They show people using their phones. I'd like you to compare two of the pictures and say why people might be communicating in this way and how effective this form of communication might be.

EXAM TIP

Don't focus on factual descriptions of the pictures. Make sure you answer the examiner's questions.

6 ▶ 06 Listen to a candidate doing the task and answer the questions. Does the candidate

1 use a variety of expressions?
2 compare the pictures?
3 follow the examiner's instructions?
4 give too much factual information?

7 Work in pairs. Turn to page 134 and do Task 1. Then turn to page 140 and do Task 2.

Review of narrative tenses
past simple, past continuous, past perfect

▶ **GRAMMAR** FOCUS p.151

8 **Read the text quickly. What problem is the writer describing?**

1 being unable to avoid checking her phone at night
2 receiving unwanted messages during the night
3 being expected to work late at night

9 **Read the first two paragraphs again. Match the underlined examples (1–8) to the tenses (A–H).**

A the past simple for describing past actions or states
B the past simple for a finished event that happened at a specific time
C the past continuous for describing two actions that were in progress at the same time
D the past continuous for describing a repeated action or habit
E the past continuous for describing something that was in progress at a particular time
F the past perfect for referring to a time before another time in the past
G the past perfect continuous for describing a repeated action that happened before another event in the past
H *would* for describing a past habit

LANGUAGE TIP

It's not necessary to use the past perfect with *before/after*.

I turned the light off before I went to sleep.

---

10 **Complete the rest of the text with the correct form of the verbs in brackets.**

Nocturnal smartphone addiction is a national epidemic – and it needs to stop.
For me, it started when my daughter **(1)** was born in 2013. She **(2)** was waking several times in the night to feed and I found it impossible to get back to sleep between feeds. **(3)** I'd never experienced sleep problems and I'm ashamed to say that while my baby **(4)** was feeding, I was messaging friends who were in the same situation. It helped to know that I **(5)** wasn't alone. **(6)** I'd also use the time to catch up on my emails. Sometimes after the baby had woken up again for the next feed, I'd realise that **(7)** I'd been surfing aimlessly for two hours.

Now my daughter's three years old but when I wake in the small hours I automatically reach for my phone. Last night for example, at 3a.m., while my husband and daughter **(8)** were sleeping peacefully, I decided to check if anyone had replied to my last tweet.

I can think of only one time when I **(9)** .... (*learn*) important information by checking an email in the middle of the night. This was when the hotel I **(10)** .... (*book*) for a conference the next day **(11)** .... (*email*) me at midnight to cancel because their kitchen **(12)** .... (*flood*). In a panic I **(13)** .... (*communicate*) the news immediately to everyone. I **(14)** .... (*plan*) this event for months, so of course I spent the rest of the night worrying, needlessly as it turned out, because in the morning the hotel **(15)** .... (*call*) to say they **(16)** .... (*manage*) to find a nearby hotel for our conference.

11 **Work in pairs. Do you agree that 'nocturnal smartphone addiction is a national epidemic – and it needs to stop'? Discuss with a partner and say why/why not.**

12 **Complete the paragraph using the narrative forms in Activity 9.**

Last night I woke up suddenly because my phone was ringing ….

Multiple choice (Part 1)

▶ **EXAM** FOCUS p.181

1 Answer the questionnaire and compare your answers with a partner. Then turn to page 147 to see if you agree with the results.

Are you an introvert?

1 Do you often ignore messages from friends on your phone?

2 Do you prefer online relationships to face-to-face ones?

3 Do you prefer listening to talking?

4 Do you dread going to parties where you don't know many people?

5 Do you feel uncomfortable speaking in front of groups of people?

6 Do you immediately put in earphones and start listening to music when you're in a public place in case anyone tries to talk to you?

EXAM TIP

Read the question and options for each extract carefully before you listen. Don't expect to hear exactly the same words used in the options and the recording – often, these will be paraphrases.

2 ▶ 07 You will hear three different extracts. For questions 1–6, choose the answer (A, B or C) which fits best according to what you hear. There are two questions for each extract.

Extract 1

You hear two friends discussing a book about personality types.

1 How did the book make the man feel?

  A unsure what makes him an introvert

  B positive about his personality

  C relieved that his behaviour is normal

2 They agree that the book

  A contains too much detailed research.

  B is written in an academic style.

  C presents an unbalanced argument.

Extract 2

You hear two friends discussing online friendships.

3 What do they agree about the way social networking sites are used?

  A Too much personal information is provided.

  B People aren't honest enough.

  C There is very little privacy.

4 What is the man's attitude to his online friendships?

  A He's irritated by online friends' lack of sensitivity.

  B He's unsure about why he still maintains online relationships.

  C He's worried about losing online friendships.

Extract 3

You hear two people talking about why they decided to stay offline for a month.

5 How did the woman feel after the first week offline?

  A content to be able to focus on other things

  B disturbed by the isolation

  C used to the lack of contact

6 Why would the man recommend the experience?

  A It changed his attitude to online friendships.

  B It made him realise that he was addicted to the internet.

  C It helped him to be self-disciplined.

3 Listen to Extract 1 again and look at question 1. Are there any paraphrases in the recording for *unsure* or *relieved*? Which words in the recording are summarised by the word *normal*?

4 Match phrases A–E from the recording to the correct answers to questions 2–6 in Activity 2.

A … everyone presents a certain cultivated image of themselves online, which isn't always totally accurate.

B … so not worth devoting so many pages to them.

C … it was weird – almost like being invisible.

D I've had to learn to be strict with myself.

E What gets me is people who insist on going on and on about their perfect life.

Word formation (Part 3)

▶ **EXAM** FOCUS p.179

1 What do these emojis mean? Which ones do you use?

2 What part of speech is missing in the sentences? Complete the questions with the correct form of the word in capitals and then discuss them with a partner.

COMMUNICATE

1 Apart from being excellent ...., what other characteristics should politicians have?

2 Do you think shy people are necessarily ....?

3 Do you agree that chatting online is a great form of ....?

3 Read the text. What problems with the over-30s' use of emojis are mentioned? Do you agree with the writer's opinion?

4 Read the text again. For questions 1–8, use the word given in capitals at the end of some of the lines to form a word that fits in the gap in the same line.

5 Check your answers by answering the questions about each missing word.

1 Is it an adjective, an adverb, a noun or a verb?

2 Should it be singular or plural?

3 Does it need a negative prefix?

4 If it is a verb, is it past or present?

EXAM TIP

Read the whole of each sentence through carefully to make sure it makes sense with the form of the word you have written – don't just read line by line.

Should people over 30 ever use emojis?

When using emojis, the over-30s seem to have a weird **(0)** attachment to the idea of communicating something specific. | **ATTACH**

My parents' use of emojis is **(1)** .... because it's so literal. | **EMBARRASS**

They haven't realised that the humour of emojis lies in selecting ones which are **(2)** .... or random, and not literally | **EXPECT**

translating words into pictures. Using emojis literally can also lead to **(3)** .... because it's almost impossible to be subtle. | **UNDERSTAND**

The over-30s' attempts to use emojis are also always a little too **(4)** .... and obvious. What they fail to comprehend is | **ENTHUSIASM**

that emojis should always be used slightly **(5)** .... | **IRONY**

People over 30 never quite get this right because the effort involved is so painfully evident to the reader. My generation understands instinctively that you never give the **(6)** .... | **IMPRESS**

that you have spent actual time browsing for something **(7)** .... and relevant, or that you have | **MEANING**

given it any thought at all. An **(8)** .... emoji is one that seems casual and spontaneous. | **EFFECT**

Gapped text (Part 7)

▶ **EXAM** FOCUS p.180

1 Work in pairs and discuss. Who do you have the best conversations with? What do you talk about?

2 Look at the title and read the article quickly, ignoring the missing paragraphs. How useful did the writer find the class on how to have a conversation?

3 Read the first two paragraphs of the article again carefully and look at the words in bold. What information do you think the missing paragraph will contain?

1 some information about the teacher
2 some background information
3 some information about the other participants

4 Read paragraphs A–G and look at the words in bold. Which one contains the right kind of information for the first gap?

EXAM TIP

Read each paragraph, followed by each possible missing paragraph A–G, to see which one fits best in the gap. Think about meaning, reference words, grammar, etc. Check that the option you choose also fits with the paragraph that follows.

5 Six paragraphs have been removed from the article. Choose from the paragraphs A–G the one which fits each gap (1–6). Use the words in bold to help you. There is one extra paragraph which you do not need to use.

6 Work out the meanings of the underlined words in paragraphs A–F from the context. Compare your answers with a partner.

7 Work in pairs and discuss the questions.

1 Do you think you would enjoy a class like this?
2 How would you answer the 'opener' questions in the fifth paragraph? What do you think of them?
3 What do you think of the six ways to have a better conversation in paragraph B? How similar are they to Cicero's rules in paragraph G?
4 Do you think technology is having a negative effect on the quality of your conversations? Give examples.

A
These aims seemed disappointingly unambitious to me. I had hopes of becoming a witty and intellectual conversationalist. But none of my new friends shared this desire. It was the simple act of talking and listening and learning that my classmates sought.

B
Some useful advice **followed** on the 'six ways to have a better conversation'. These, according to the school, are:
(1) Be curious about others.
(2) Take off your mask.
(3) Empathise with others.
(4) Get behind the job title.
(5) Use adventurous openings.
(6) Have courage.

C
Haynes **went on** to explain that the Enlightenment was the age of conversation, when ladies and gentlemen in English dining rooms and French salons could become famous through eloquence alone.

D
Then we were told to break off into pairs and answer the question: Which three words describe your conversations with (a) friends, (b) family and (c) colleagues? My partner said *banter*, *sarcastic* and *sporadic* were the words he would use to describe all three types of conversation. Before I had a chance to share my three words, it was time for a **break**.

E
There was general unease about how email, instant messaging and texting had crept into the space formerly occupied by conversation. 'What was the point,' asked a **young man**, 'of asking how someone's day was when you've been emailing them from the office?'

F
After **this** enjoyable burst of roleplay Haynes put up a slide that said: *What conversation are you not having?* and then it was all over. Once the class structure had been dismantled, conversation seemed to dwindle.

G
The basics of **this** were first described by the ancient Roman writer Cicero, which can be summarised as follows: speak clearly, do not interrupt, be courteous, never criticise people behind their backs, stick to subjects of general interest, do not talk about yourself and, above all, never lose your temper.

HOW TO HAVE A CONVERSATION

Is conversation a dying art, struck down by text, email and messaging? And do we really need to be taught how to talk to each other? I enrolled in a class at the School of Life, an academy of 'self-help', to find out. The topic was *How to have a* **conversation**.

1

I had arrived about twenty minutes early but the rest of the class was already there. **One woman** kindly invited me into her circle. She was finding it hard to have meaningful relationships. Technology was partly to blame: 'Sometimes you feel the smartphone is like a third person,' she said. **Another new acquaintance** agreed and described how immediate access to Google had blocked off avenues of conversation with her boyfriend. 'Before we would argue about this or that but now we just look it up on Wikipedia,' she said.

2

My classmates also spoke of more personal reasons for their attendance. An IT worker in her fifties had found that her conversations with her husband 'wandered' and wanted to learn ways to become a better partner. A man in his late twenties said he wanted to have fewer rows with his girlfriend.

3

Our discussion was interrupted by the arrival of our teacher, Cathy Haynes. Haynes flicked to the first slide in her PowerPoint presentation and we sat attentively as she talked about how the nature of conversation had changed over the past 300 years.

4

After an enjoyable ten minutes spent chatting to my classmates and discovering more about their motives for joining the class, we were told to retake our seats. Haynes continued her PowerPoint presentation, asking us to reflect on a René Magritte painting, a comedy sketch and a book about marriage. All of these examples were meant to encourage us to stop seeing conversations as a means to an end and to avoid stereotyping the other person.

5

Then it was time to put some of these ideas into practice. In groups, we had to try out ideas for unusual openings. A man in his early twenties, who joked that he had thought of this before, suggested as a chat-up line: 'Tell me something I want to know.' A more challenging opener came from another group member: 'If you were coming to the end of your life, what would you have wanted to have achieved?'

6

Despite our excellent teacher, I suspect the class was too abstract to be useful. Nearly three-quarters of the session were spent listening to theories of conversation. Genuine discussions were stopped in mid-flow, with the class asked to return its attention to the presentation. There was a touching eagerness to share ideas but frustration grew as our time ran out. What I suspect my classmates had hoped to find was that most basic thing: human connection. But I doubt the class had made this any more achievable.

1 Work in pairs and discuss which of the statements you agree with.

1 You should never raise your voice during a discussion.
2 People who shout the loudest tend to get heard.
3 How you say something is as important as what you say.
4 Gossip is never harmless.

Communication collocations

2 Match the nouns in the box to the verbs *make*, *have*, *give* and *hold*. Make one or two collocations for each noun.

a chat (x1) (a) conversation (x2) a debate (x2)
a discussion (x2) a gossip (x1) a presentation (x1)
a speech (x2) a statement (x2) a talk (x2)

3 Choose the correct alternative in each sentence.

1 He delivered an interesting *debate/speech* at the conference.
2 We had to make polite *talk/conversation* with the director of the company.
3 Most people hate making small *talk/gossip* at parties.
4 The *discussion/speech* was led by the CEO.
5 His controversial ideas have stimulated a lot of *debate/talk*.
6 It was difficult to keep the *chat/conversation* going because the connection kept breaking up.
7 How to improve the system is a matter for *debate/conversation*.
8 They were deep in *gossip/conversation* and didn't notice the restaurant had closed.

Adjectives: ways of speaking

4 ▶ 08 Listen and answer the questions. Then compare your ideas with a partner.

1 Do you agree with the information given?
2 What are your impressions of each speaker?
3 Which person is the easiest to understand?
4 Which accent do you prefer?
5 Which person do you think sounds the most trustworthy and authoritative?

5 Work in pairs. Look at the adjectives in the box and answer the questions.

deep flat harsh high-pitched husky lively
mellow monotonous nasal soft soothing
squeaky warm wobbly

1 Which seven adjectives have a positive meaning?
2 Which three adjectives have a similar meaning to 'mellow'?
3 Which are attractive in a man or a woman?
4 Which do you think match the voices of the speakers in Activity 4?

6 Work in pairs and discuss the questions.

1 How important do you think someone's voice is?
2 Do you think it's possible to fall in love with someone from the sound of their voice?
3 Which celebrities do you agree have attractive voices?

7 Complete the sentences with words from Activity 5.

1 She speaks in such a mellow and .... manner that it makes me feel drowsy.
2 Most people find a .... tone the most annoying because it sounds like the person is complaining all the time.
3 Actresses with deep, ... voices are considered to be very attractive.
4 You can often tell if someone is nervous by their .... voice.
5 I don't think he means to but he always sounds bored because he speaks in such a .... monotone.
6 Some languages sound soft and soothing, while others can sound .... – as if people are arguing all the time.

8 Which of the adjectives in Activity 5 can be used to describe:

1 a colour?   3 a person?
2 a landscape?   4 an actor's performance?

Defining and non-defining relative clauses

▶ **GRAMMAR** REFERENCE p.152

1 Work in pairs. Decide whether the sentences contain a defining or non-defining relative clause.

1 Our maths teacher, who's been at the school for twenty years, is leaving.

2 That's the cafe where we used to meet.

3 He's having problems with his new car, which he's really annoyed about.

4 The girl whose brother is a professional football player scored the winning goal.

LANGUAGE TIP

That and *which* can often be used interchangeably in defining relative clauses. *That* rather than *which* is usually used after quantifiers such as *everything, something, all.*

*Something **that** most people find annoying …*

2 Complete the sentences with the words in the box. In some sentences more than one option is possible.

that   when   where   which   who   whom   whose

1 The man .... was speaking loudly on his mobile phone was a journalist.

2 I will never forget .... I was when I heard the news.

3 The person with .... I have most in common is my sister.

4 The man .... phone I found sent me £100!

5 The time .... I spent without internet access was terribly hard.

6 My mobile phone, ... I lost on the train last week, had all my contacts in it.

7 It was early in the morning .... I received a call from my aunt in Australia.

8 I had to take an urgent call, ... was why I walked out of the restaurant.

9 I pressed 'call back' without knowing .... number it was.

10 I've no idea .... it was that just called me.

3 Match sentences 1–2 to meanings A–B.

1 She listened to the second message in her voicemail, which was in English.

2 She listened to the second message in her voicemail which was in English.

A Message number 1 was in another language. She listened to message number 2, which was in English.

B She had received lots of phone messages; the fifth and eleventh messages were in English. She listened to message number 11.

4 Read the article quickly. What problems can your voice cause?

Is **your voice** holding you back?

A University of California study found that when it comes to first impressions, it was visual impact **(1)** *which/who* was the most important consideration, followed by vocal impact. On the telephone, **(2)** *whose/where* appearance is irrelevant, the sound of your voice accounts for a full 83 percent of how others judge you.

Clearly, your voice is a key communication tool. Many professionals **(3)** *which/who* have the talent and motivation to move ahead find common speaking problems block their success. Take the advertising executive, for example, **(4)** *whom/whose* soft, breathy voice makes her otherwise inspired presentation seem weak and lifeless, or the talented IT consultant with a strong regional accent **(5)** *which/whose* people find difficult to understand.

How you use your voice can make others view you as trustworthy and likeable – or insecure, boring or even dishonest. In fact, **(6)** *when/why* trying to get their message across, people pay little, if any, attention to the effect their voices have on other people. Instead, it's the content **(7)** *which/who* they are much more concerned about.

So the reason **(8)** *when/why* you failed to land that dream job may have been because people were more focused on how you sounded rather than on what you had to say.

5 Read the article again and choose the correct alternatives.

6 Can you think of a politician or a person in the public eye who has an unpleasant voice? Compare your ideas with a partner.

Proposal (Part 2)

organising your ideas

▶ **WRITING** REFERENCE p.174

1 **Which statement refers to a proposal and which refers to a report?**

1 This looks to the future, giving specific plans for a particular situation.

2 This makes recommendations that are based on a current situation.

2 **Look at the exam task and the tips for writing a proposal. Then read a candidate's answer. The candidate has not followed one of the tips. Which one?**

You see this announcement on a notice board where you work.

IMPROVE OUR USE OF EMAIL

The Staff Training and Development Department has decided to review the guidelines for the use of email for workplace communication.

The Staff Training and Development Officer invites you to send a proposal outlining any problems with current practice and explaining how it can be improved. A decision will then be made about how the guidelines should be changed.

Write your **proposal** in **220–260** words in an appropriate style.

Tips for writing a proposal

1 Begin by stating the purpose of your proposal.

2 Use an impersonal, semi-formal style.

3 Use clear layout with headings, e.g. Introduction, Problems, Recommendations.

4 Express opinions and make recommendations in the last section of your proposal.

5 Include a final sentence summarising your opinion.

6 Use bullet points but not too many.

Improving workplace communication: a proposal

Introduction

In this proposal I will assess the current situation with regard to the use of email for workplace communication, go on to identify the needs which should be addressed by a staff training programme and conclude by describing this training programme.

Current situation

Feedback from other members of staff suggests that the volume of email messages we receive has become a problem. Many people find that they spend several hours a day responding to these messages. A second but related complaint concerned poorly written emails. Many of us receive messages that cause offence, are difficult to understand or are simply far too long.

Key needs to be addressed

Both the number of email messages we receive and the quality of the messages have a negative impact on our productivity. People feel disinclined to respond to rude, confusing or excessively lengthy messages. This issue must be addressed.

Recommendations

I would suggest the following to the Staff Training and Development Department:

• All members of staff should be encouraged to communicate by phone whenever possible.

• Any information that needs to be communicated to the entire staff should be presented in a face-to-face meeting rather than through email.

• A training course on writing effective email messages should be offered to all staff members.

3 **Look at the exam task and write your answer. Use steps 1–3 to help you.**

EXAM TIP

If you are asked to write about something you haven't experienced directly, use your imagination to generate ideas. You won't be marked down for any ideas as long as they are relevant to the task.

Students at your college have to give a spoken presentation as part of their final assessment and need some help. The school director has invited you to send a proposal outlining any problems students have with presentations and suggesting how these problems could be overcome.

---

1 Begin by brainstorming ideas. Write them down in any order and don't worry about language at this stage.

2 Group your ideas under headings for each section of your proposal.

3 Write a first draft, paying attention to the level of formality of the language.

1 Complete the sentences with the correct form of the word in brackets.

1 That's the total cost of the holiday, ... all meals. (*include*)

2 I'm afraid there's been an .... error. (*administrative*)

3 Texting can be a problem if it becomes an .... (*addict*)

4 .... is a problem which affects many people – they can't decide what to do, so they end up not doing anything. (*decide*)

5 Their music is easy to recognise because the sound is quite .... (*distinction*)

6 The technology museum is very .... – there are lots of gadgets you can try out. (*interact*)

7 Alex is not a very good .... – he often struggles to express himself. (*communicate*)

8 She gave a very inspiring speech which everyone found very .... (*impress*)

2 Decide if it is possible to use both of the alternatives or only one of them.

1 While I *was typing/had been typing* a message to my boyfriend about plans for the weekend, I *got/had got* a message from him saying he *had decided/was deciding* to dump me. I was really shocked because I *hadn't expected/wasn't expecting* this at all and I *felt/had felt* really angry that he *hadn't had/didn't have* the courage to tell me face-to-face.

2 I *had known/knew* Jack for years but *I'd never realised/I never realised* until very recently that *he'd been/he was* a professional footballer. *He'd even played/He even played* in a world cup!

3 Before I *moved/was moving* to London, *I'd been worried/I'd been worrying* about feeling lonely. *I'd been living/I'd lived* at home until then so *I hadn't spent/I hadn't been spending* much time alone.

4 We'd *always planned/were always planning* to travel as soon as *we left/we'd left* university but we *didn't manage/hadn't managed* to save enough money. By the time we *got married/were getting married* though, four years later, *we'd saved/we'd been saving* enough for the trip of a lifetime on our honeymoon.

5 Nina *was working/worked* as a nurse before she *qualified/was qualifying* as a lawyer at the age of thirty-five.

6 I *had hoped/was hoping* to buy my mum a new watch, but when I *went/had gone* to the department store they *said/had said* they *sold/had sold* out of the one she wanted.

3 Complete the article with the correct relative pronouns.

https://News/Talk to yourself

Talk to yourself

Talking to yourself actually helps improve cognitive performance. If you don't believe me, ask a primary schoolteacher. They will know children **(1)** .... are given a task and talk themselves through it. 'Now I'm going to get the blue paint,' they will say. 'That's good,' they add, 'now I want something bright.' Other children will just do their work in silence, **(2)** .... on the surface appears to show greater concentration. But ask the schoolteacher if they know which ones perform better in tests and appear to 'get' things more quickly. They'll tell you, it is the children **(3)** .... verbal reasoning skills are more developed because they talk themselves through a task. Now, evidence from research **(4)** .... was carried out in the USA bears this theory out. Researchers tested the ability of people to find objects in pictures. Those **(5)** .... talked to themselves were able to find the objects more quickly.

4 Choose the correct alternative in each sentence.

1 She had such a *monotonous/high-pitched* voice that students often used to fall asleep in her lectures.

2 I didn't catch what Tom said. He's got a really *soft/harsh* voice.

3 Some women prefer their voice when they have a cold because it sounds *husky/wobbly*.

4 When she gets overexcited, her voice is quite *mellow/squeaky*.

5 The colours in this painting are so *warm/flat* and soothing.

6 I couldn't concentrate on what the actor was saying because his *nasal/lively* tone was so off-putting

3 Ages and stages

Vocabulary
stages of life

1 Work in pairs and discuss what you understand by each quote. Do you agree with them?

> *Youth is wasted on the young.*
> —GEORGE BERNARD SHAW

> *Age isn't how old you are but how old you feel.*
> —GABRIEL GARCÍA MÁRQUEZ

2 Look at the sentences and decide whether the underlined words have a positive or negative connotation.

1 Much as I like him, his rather <u>juvenile</u> sense of humour makes me question his suitability for a job that requires a degree of tact.

2 She has a <u>childlike</u> innocence about her that is rather surprising.

3 Like many actors of his generation, he has retained a <u>youthful</u> demeanour, despite his advancing years.

4 We are both <u>mature</u> enough to discuss this without getting emotional.

5 I may not look my age but I can promise you I'm <u>no spring chicken</u>.

6 He had a lot of fans when he was younger but now he really is a bit <u>over the hill</u>.

3 Which of the words in the box could you use to replace the underlined words and phrases in Activity 2? Which ones have a different connotation?

adolescent adult aging boyish childish elderly infantile old

4 Practise reading the sentences in Activity 2 aloud with a partner. Which words are stressed?

5 Work in pairs. Think of other near synonyms for the words in Activities 2 and 3. Do they have positive, negative or neutral connotations?

6   **Work in pairs and discuss the questions. Give personal examples where relevant.**

1   How much do you think about your future?

2   What kind of sacrifices should people make for their future selves?

3   Do you think it's a good idea for young people to have a life plan?

4   Have your plans for your future changed since you were a child?

7   ▶ 09   **Read the article and say what Chris should do to achieve his goals. Then listen and compare with the advice a life coach gives.**

Commercial executive
Chris Stubbs, 30

'I tend to take each day as it comes and I've never really worried about the future that much. There's a couple I know who have their future all mapped out. They've decided they'll start a family within the next year or so and they even know how they'll finance their future children's education. They're moving to a bigger house soon. In their early fifties they think they'll have enough money to travel around the world for a year. I'm sure that's the way many people believe mature adults should behave and that it's rather childish not to make those sorts of plans, but neither my wife nor I are that great at doing it. We're going to start a family at some point but it never seems to be the right time.

Every so often I think about long-term goals but it's fleeting. Two years from now, I hope I'll have been promoted or found another job. But I need to start thinking about how I'm going to achieve that. I'm worried that I'll be doing exactly the same job in five years' time if I don't start planning ahead. The danger is that by the time I get round to applying for a promotion my employers might think I'm already over the hill. I'll get down to some serious planning tomorrow!'

8   **Work in pairs. How useful would it be to have a life coach?**

Future forms

▶ **GRAMMAR** REFERENCE p.152

9   **Read the article in Activity 7 again and find an example of:**

1   the present continuous for future plans.

2   *going to* for intentions.

3   *will* for predictions.

4   *will* for spontaneous decisions.

5   the future perfect.

6   the future continuous.

10   **Cross out the alternatives that are not possible.**

MyBlog ☆

So tomorrow is the day I've decided **(1)** *I'm going to start/I'll start/I'm starting* planning my future. The first thing **(2)** *I'll do/I'm doing/I'm going to do* is to make a wish list of all the things I hope **(3)** *I'll achieve/I'm achieving/I'm going to achieve*. I need to try and imagine what **(4)** *I do/I'll be doing/I'm going to do* in five years' time. Then **(5)** *I'll be spending/I'm going to spend/I'll have spent* the rest of the morning looking at job websites. **(6)** *I see/I'll see/I'm going to see* what kind of jobs are available. Ideally, **(7)** *I'll stay/I'll be staying/I'll have stayed* with my current employer but if I don't get promoted, I really hope **(8)** *I'll have found/I'm finding/I'll find* another job within two years.

     REPLY

11   **Complete the sentences with the correct form of the verb in brackets.**

1   Two years from now I hope I .... (*do*) my dream job.

2   By the time I'm twenty-five, I expect I .... (*leave*) home.

3   By this time next year, it's likely that I .... (*find*) a new job.

4   Within the next six months, I .... (*pass*) my driving test.

5   It's only a matter of time before I .... (*meet*) the right man.

6   It won't be long until I .... (*find*) the perfect apartment.

7   For the time being I .... (*live*) at home while I save money for my own apartment.

8   I'm sure I .... (*learn*) Arabic in no time.

9   It's about time I .... (*get*) some more up-to-date qualifications.

10   In twenty years I .... (*be*) glad that I took the decision to find my dream job.

LANGUAGE TIP

Some expressions which refer to the future are followed by the present simple/past simple (e.g. *it's only a matter of time before* + present simple, *it's about time* + past simple).

1 Answer the questions. Then compare your answers with other students.

1 Do you keep a diary or have a blog? Why/Why not?

2 What are the main differences between blogs and diaries?

3 What are the potential risks of having a blog or taking part in social media?

Cross-text multiple matching (Part 6)

▶ **EXAM** FOCUS p.180

2 Read extracts A–D from articles about keeping a diary and posting on social media. What risks do the columnists mention?

3 Read the extracts again. Which extracts mention issues 1–4 in the table?

Issue	Extract
1 posting on social media is risky	*A* ...., ...
2 reasons teenagers might not want to keep diaries	.........., ...
3 teenagers' behaviour can seem contradictory	.........., ...
4 reactions of older people when rereading their teenage diaries	.........., ..., ...

4 For questions 1–4, choose from the extracts A–D. The extracts may be chosen more than once.

Which columnist

expresses a similar view to Giannoni on the contents of teenage diaries? **1** ☐

has a different view to the others on disclosing personal feelings on social media? **2** ☐

holds a different opinion to Brooks on which medium is more lasting for diaries? **3** ☐

expresses a similar view to Clarkson on how negative responses to social media posts deter people from keeping diaries? **4** ☐

5 Complete the sentences with the correct form of the underlined words and phrases in the extracts.

1 I thought Tarantino's last film was absolutely .... I hated it.

2 When we feel we have been wronged, ... is always tempting.

3 Sandra has always tried to donate a tenth of what she earns to ....

4 You cannot .... spending so much on entertainment. The money is needed for health care.

5 Unlike Tony, who is always very outspoken, his brother is one of the most .... people I know.

6 She made some really .... but critical comments on my essay.

6 Which of the opinions in the extracts A–D do you agree with? Work in pairs and discuss your answers.

A Aldo Giannoni

Diaries are a safer place for expressing adolescent angst than social media, though as adults, we can find rereading diaries we kept as teenagers a profoundly uncomfortable experience. It's disconcerting to find that they are nothing more than records of the childish hopes and ambitions we've now outgrown. Thankfully, a conventional diary is wonderfully impermanent. It can be quickly and completely destroyed if the writer so chooses, something that can't be said of our digital footprint. The frequently <u>uncharitable</u> responses to narcissistic displays on social media are hardly surprising. If found, a diary too will be read and its contents certainly made fun of in much the same way but the reluctant diarist should remember that diaries are not intended to be found. A blog, a Facebook, Twitter or Instagram post is there for others to see, often with outcomes we cannot control.

B Belinda Clarkson

Though they're perfectly happy to post all sorts of details about their personal lives on Facebook and to <u>retaliate</u> when so-called friends predictably insult or ridicule them, the prospect of somebody finding and reading similar outpourings in a secret diary is enough to put many teenagers off the idea of keeping one. While those fears might be well founded, discovery is not the main threat diaries pose to us. They can actually induce writers to tell themselves something they didn't want to know. It might be an admission of jealousy, a confession of a secret infatuation or even an outpouring of pent-up resentment and rage. Threatening as this might be, there is real power in writing these sorts of things down and when reread we might gain <u>insights</u> into how we have changed over time. I'm not convinced, though, that the dangers of expressing ourselves on social media outweigh the benefits. Sometimes through letting others know we are suffering we elicit genuine support and understanding.

C Cecile Brooks

We tend to make the assumption that diaries are essentially private documents while social media are public. But there are those who keep a diary intending it to be a durable record that at some future date will be read. This may be not because they wish to bare their souls as so many teenagers do but because they have experiences, views or even information that they consider might be of value to others. Blogs and social media in general serve this purpose too, though they are in many senses more ephemeral. We tend not to go back and read them again while a published diary is there for posterity. But for the truly private and personal, a diary is a good place to write without <u>reticence,</u> for your eyes only and without fearing others' unreasonable reactions.

D Darius Prol

Diaries with locks and keys have retained their popularity among teenage girls, despite the fact that they happily keep what amounts to digital diaries through posts on Facebook and the like. Posts on such sites are publications intended to produce a response even if it is just approval or disapproval. Attracting disapproval in the extreme form of cyber bullying along with the <u>justifiable</u> fear that what is out there will remain forever stops many teenagers expressing their feelings even in a diary. But the diary, for all its old-fashioned sentimentality, can, and should, be a place for such honesty. People who reread their teenage diaries are understandably <u>appalled</u> to discover how little space they gave to what really matters and how much time they dedicated to the boy or girl on the bus who might or might not have fancied them. But at least diaries are truly private places where such things can be expressed.

1 Work in small groups. Make a list of five things you think all adults should be able to do.

2 Look at a similar list from a blog. Tick (✓) the things that you can do. Add two more items from your list in Activity 1.

PROFILE | PHOTOS | UPDATES ☰

Things every adult should be able to do.

1 Perform CPR and the Heimlich Manoeuvre
One day it may be your partner or child who needs your help.

2 Do basic cooking
I find it appalling that so many young people live on pot noodles and toast. Learn to cook – you might even enjoy it.

3 Speed-read
The average person reads a couple of thousand words a day and the average student reads a lot more. Sometimes you need to get the gist superfast. Speed-reading can take the pressure off.

4 Use tools like hammers, screwdrivers and saws
Learn basic carpentry and it could end up saving you money. Why buy bookshelves if you can build them yourself?

5 Make a simple budget
It's no fun being in debt. A simple budget is the key.

6 Look good in front of a camera
It's amazing how many people don't know how to find their most beguiling smile.

Introductory *it*

▶ **GRAMMAR** REFERENCE p.153

3 Look at the four uses of the introductory *it* and find more examples of each one in the list in Activity 2.

1 to avoid beginning a sentence with an infinitive or gerund
It's always good to have a chance to catch up with old friends.

2 to emphasise a relative clause (cleft sentence)
It was James who left the lights turned on in the building, not me.

3 when the subject of a clause is another clause
It's shocking how many people don't bother to recycle their rubbish.

4 in the structure: subject + verb + *it* + adjective + infinitive/clause
I found it embarrassing to have to tell her how I felt.

LANGUAGE TIP

We do not normally use subject + verb + *it* + infinitive/ clause if there is no adjective.
I cannot bear it to hear a baby crying.
We can use introductory *it* with *like, love, hate,* etc. in sentences like:
I hate it when you keep changing the channel like that.
I can't stand it when the person next to me on a plane occupies both armrests.

---

4 Rewrite the sentences using the introductory *it*.

1 That we have become so disconnected from the natural environment is sad.

2 To learn basic first aid skills is vital for schoolchildren.

3 How dependent people have become on mobile phones worries me.

4 You should get the credit for the work done on the project, not me.

5 To make new friends was difficult for me.

6 For people to contact a member of staff first is vital.

7 Not to throw away letters with your name and address on them makes good sense.

8 Telling Charles how I felt was embarrassing.

5 Look at the list you wrote in Activity 1 and choose four items that you consider important or would like to learn. Rewrite the items using the introductory *it*. Compare your choices with a partner.

Collaborative task and discussion (Parts 3 and 4)

responding to and expanding on your partner's ideas

▶ **EXAM** FOCUS p.183

1 ▶ 10 **Listen to two candidates, Daniela and Martin, doing both parts of the Part 3 task. Which candidate responds to and expands on what the other candidate says?**

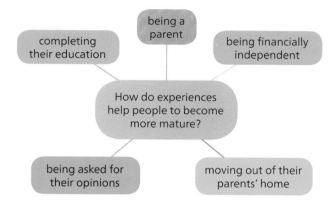

EXAM TIP

In Parts 3 and 4 your ability to interact with the other candidate is assessed. Express your opinion and make sure you pick up on what the other candidate says.

2 **Listen again and look at some of the exchanges. Underline the phrases that Daniela uses to respond to what Martin says. Then circle the phrases she uses to expand on what he says.**

1 **M:** If you are still reliant on your parents for money, you are never entirely free to make your own decisions, so, in some senses, you remain in the position that you were in when you were a child.

   D: You mean, because you're having to ask your parents for money and possibly also having to justify what you spend it on?

   M: Yes.

   D: There's a lot to be said for that argument. In many cases, I think it does make people less able to take responsibility for their own decisions and it often creates tensions in a family.

2 **M:** Apart from earning your own living, I think the thing that really gives you adult status is having your own family. With children of your own, you grow up fast.

   D: Yes, you're forced to mature by having to make sacrifices and by being responsible for other people, aren't you?

3 **Work in pairs. Take turns responding to and expanding on Daniela's ideas. Use the suggestions in brackets to help you.**

1

> It's more and more common for people to return to study throughout their lives.

(Agree and give an example of someone who has returned to study.)

2

> I don't think moving into your own flat or house necessarily makes you an adult either. A lot of people move out when they start university – I did – but, although I probably thought of myself as very grown up, I wasn't, really.

(Express interest in Daniela's comment about not being grown up and then comment on your own experience.)

3

> That's why the real transition from childhood to adulthood is being treated as an adult. Do you see what I mean?

(Say that you do and give an example of being treated like an adult to check that this is what Daniela means.)

4 ▶ 11 **Work in pairs. Listen to the candidates doing the Part 4 task and answer the questions.**

1 Which of the candidates has ideas that are closest to your point of view?

2 How would each of you respond to and expand on these ideas?

3 Is there anything either of the students says that either of you disagree with?

5 **Work in groups of three. Turn to page 135 and do the activity.**

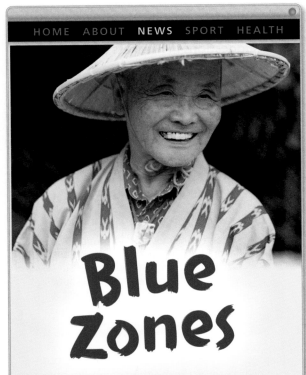

HOME ABOUT **NEWS** SPORT HEALTH

Blue Zones

Although the aging **(0)** *A. process* isn't fully understood, scientists have come to the conclusion that environmental factors play a particularly important **(1)** .... Researcher Dan Buettner has spent years visiting areas of the world where people tend to **(2)** .... longer, healthier lives in a bid to **(3)** .... at a definitive list of these factors. He identified areas he calls 'Blue Zones', where longevity and good health are common. Sardinia, for example, has the highest **(4)** .... of male centenarians in the world, Okinawa the longest disability-free life **(5)** .... and Costa Rica's Nicoya Peninsula middle-aged residents are four times more likely to **(6)** .... to their ninetieth birthdays than their peers in the USA. As diverse as the people in the Blue Zones may be, what they have in common are homes with stairs, a simple diet, purposeful lives and being **(7)** .... by others who value and appreciate them. As Buettner observes, these patterns not only **(8)** .... in lives that are longer but in lives well led.

Multiple-choice cloze (Part 1)

▶ **EXAM** FOCUS p.178

1 Work in pairs. What's the average life expectancy for people in your country? What environmental factors do you think contribute to a longer life?

2 Read the article about parts of the world where longevity is particularly common. Are any of the places or factors you talked about mentioned?

3 Which option would you choose to complete these two sentences? Compare your answers with a partner.

1 Many people nowadays .... on satellite navigation to find their way around unfamiliar cities.

   A trust   **C** believe

   B rely   **D** confide

2 He had taken a large .... of money out of the bank earlier that morning.

   A amount   **C** collection

   B proportion **D** accumulation

EXAM TIP

Sometimes the choice between the options depends on a preposition which follows one verb and not another.

4 Work in pairs. Which item in Activity 3 depends on a preposition that follows the verb?

5 Read the article again. For questions 1–8, decide which answer (A, B, C or D) best fits each gap.

0	**A** process	**B** system	**C** progression	**D** manner
1	**A** function	**B** responsibility	**C** task	**D** role
2	**A** live	**B** survive	**C** exist	**D** maintain
3	**A** create	**B** compile	**C** arrive	**D** determine
4	**A** amount	**B** instance	**C** concentration	**D** figure
5	**A** anticipation	**B** prognosis	**C** probability	**D** expectancy
6	**A** celebrate	**B** get	**C** reach	**D** have
7	**A** involved	**B** connected	**C** surrounded	**D** related
8	**A** result	**B** produce	**C** lead	**D** make

6 Answer the questions. Then compare your answers with other students.

1 If you could live anywhere when you retire, would you choose one of these places or somewhere else? Why?

2 If it became possible to live to be 150, would you want to?

1 Work in pairs and discuss the questions.

1 Do you think life gets easier as you grow older?

2 How would you divide a person's lifespan into periods, e.g. babyhood = from birth to eighteen months.

3 Which periods do you think are the happiest?

Multiple choice (Part 3)

▶ **EXAM** FOCUS p.182

2 ▶ 12 **You will hear an interview with Dan Johnson, who does research into longevity. For questions 1–6, choose the answer (A, B, C or D) which fits best according to what you hear.**

EXAM TIP

The questions in Part 3 are usually concerned with the speaker's opinions. Listen out for phrases that indicate the speaker is about to express an opinion (e.g. *It strikes me that … , As I see it, … , In my view, …*).

1 Dan thinks people who attribute longevity to genetic factors

  A are right to be proud of having relatives who lived long lives.

  B are not well informed about the scientific evidence.

  C are unwilling to take responsibility for their health.

  D are sceptical about predicting the future.

2 Dan believes that old photographs

  A help to redress a common misconception.

  B accurately reflect our ideas about the past.

  C misrepresent how many children died young.

  D are frequently ignored as a source of accurate information.

3 How does Dan feel about the effects of stress in the modern age?

  A He thinks they are no greater than they were in the past.

  B He agrees that they are much worse than they were in the past.

  C He is unsure about whether they are worse than they were in the past.

  D He is convinced they are less severe than they were in the past.

4 How does Dan explain the relationship between attitudes to work and longevity?

  A People who are successful want to live longer.

  B People who behave in certain ways at work behave similarly in relation to health.

  C People who have interesting jobs often tend to be concerned about eating healthily.

  D People who are unemployed often develop unhealthy habits.

5 How have the results of Dan's research into marriage and longevity affected him?

  A They have acted as a trigger for personal reflection.

  B They have confirmed his beliefs about marriage.

  C They have made him feel glad to be a man.

  D They have made him feel guilty about his own behaviour.

6 What is Dan's attitude to the theory about widows?

  A He thinks there isn't much evidence to support it.

  B He believes more research needs to be carried out.

  C He acknowledges the possible existence of alternatives.

  D He dismisses it as mere speculation.

3 Work in pairs. What surprises you most about the longevity factors mentioned in the interview?

Vocabulary
working out meaning from context

4 Work in pairs. Look at the sentences from the interview and discuss the meaning of the underlined words and phrases.

1 I'd be hoping science would tell me … but in fact that's just <u>wishful thinking</u>.

2 <u>Granted</u>, a miserable job you dislike causes the wrong kind of stress.

3 <u>I'd take</u> the boring office job <u>any day</u>.

4 There's a common belief … that <u>laid-back</u> people live longer.

5 You'll probably avoid eating a lot of junk food … but you won't <u>veer to the other extreme</u> of starving yourself either.

6 <u>When the boot is on the other foot</u> … it won't have such a positive impact.

Report (Part 2)
dos and don'ts

▶ **WRITING** REFERENCE p.174

1 **Work in pairs and discuss the questions.**

1 How much contact do you have with people of different generations in your family or neighbourhood?

2 What might younger people enjoy or find difficult about talking to older people?

3 What might older people enjoy or find difficult about talking to younger people?

2 **Look at the exam task and some advice on writing reports. Which piece of advice (1–8) should start with 'Don't'?**

An international development agency has been looking into attitudes to aging around the world. The research director has asked you to conduct a survey and write a report. Your report should discuss how young people where you live feel about older people in the community and the prospect of growing old themselves. You have also been asked to make recommendations about how attitudes could be changed.

Write your report in **220–260** words in an appropriate style.

1 Begin by stating the purpose of your report.

2 Use statistics to provide a succinct summary of your results (you can invent these if necessary).

3 Use lists of points where appropriate.

4 Divide your report into sections according to the input.

5 Develop the ideas in the task input.

6 Use a clear layout with headings.

7 Make your report look the same as an essay.

8 Use an impersonal, formal style.

3 **Look at three students' plans for the task. Which two plans are missing an important element from the task input? Which element is it?**

> *A*
> 1 *questions I asked*
> 2 *descriptions of people I asked*
> 3 *problems with survey*
> 4 *analysis of survey results*

> *B*
> 1 *description of problem*
> 2 *survey results*
> 3 *reasons why young people feel positive towards older people*
> 4 *reasons why young people are not looking forward to growing old themselves*

> *C*
> 1 *introduction*
> 2 *attitudes to older people*
> 3 *attitudes to growing old*
> 4 *recommendations*

4 **Look at the model report on page 174. Tick (✓) the elements in the report mentioned in Activity 2. Which of the plans in Activity 3 is most similar to the structure of the model report?**

5 **Look at the useful language for report writing on page 175. Choose expressions to use for the task in Activity 2.**

6 **Write a draft of your report and show it to another student. Then work in pairs and use the advice in the model report on page 174 to check each other's work. Can you make any suggestions about how your reports could be improved?**

REVIEW

1 **Match 1–6 to A–F to make sentences.**

1 Ten years from now most of my friends
2 By the time I'm twenty-five
3 Within the next six months
4 It's only a matter of time
5 For the time being
6 It's about time

A I'll have started my own business.
B you faced reality and got a job.
C before scientists work out a way of extending the human life span.
D I'm not planning to move anywhere.
E I anticipate that I'll finish a big project that I've been working on.
F expect to be happily married.

2 **Complete the second sentence so that it has a similar meaning to the first sentence, using the word given. Do not change the word given. You must use between three and six words, including the word given.**

1 We really must learn to use less water.
VITAL
It is .... to use less water.

2 We may have moved by this time next year.
STILL
I am not sure if we .... here this time next year.

3 The council are the ones that should do something about graffiti.
THAT
It's .... something about graffiti.

4 Very few people make an effort to recycle their rubbish, which I find astonishing.
HOW
It's .... make an effort to recycle their rubbish.

5 Adults behaving like teenagers really embarrass me.
FIND
I .... when adults behave like teenagers.

6 I should have got some more up-to-date qualifications by now.
TIME
It's about .... some more up-to-date qualifications.

3 **Read the article and decide which answer (A, B, C or D) best fits each gap.**

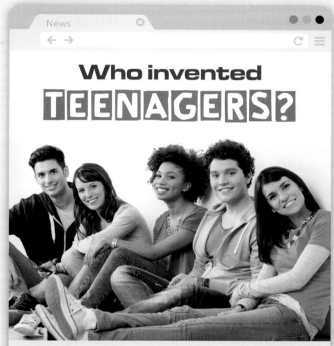

Who invented TEENAGERS?

There is some debate about who coined the **(1)** .... or when it was first used but teenagers have, of course, always **(2)** .... Even so, until the 1930s no one paid them much **(3)** .... It was then that we began to see teenage actors, many of whom were **(4)** .... child stars, on cinema screens. Initially the films were comedies, but later teenage actors starred in dramas depicting the conflicts **(5)** .... from the so-called 'generation gap'. The clothing and food industries quickly jumped on the bandwagon and began to produce goods **(6)** .... this newly discovered social group. These same fashions and foods still **(7)** .... their own today. How many people, after all, can claim they have never owned a pair of jeans or eaten a hamburger, both of which were originally products **(8)** .... at the teenage market? Teenagers rule but it seems strange to think that their reign began less than a century ago.

1 **A** name **B** idea **C** term **D** idiom
2 **A** been **B** existed **C** subsisted **D** endured
3 **A** notice **B** thought **C** mind **D** attention
4 **A** former **B** earlier **C** prior **D** past
5 **A** causing **B** happening **C** arising **D** occurring
6 **A** aiming **B** seeking **C** focusing **D** targeting
7 **A** hold **B** maintain **C** stand **D** occupy
8 **A** offered **B** pitched **C** delivered **D** proposed

PROGRESS TEST 1

Multiple-choice cloze (Part 1)

1 For questions 1–8, read the text below and decide which answer (A, B, C or D) best fits each gap. There is an example at the beginning (0).

Be a better listener

Listening is the most important of all skills for successful conversations at work, college or in social **(0)** A, situations . Generally, people are very **(1)** .... listeners. The reason for this is that when talking to a colleague or a friend, they are often already preparing their **(2)** .... while the colleague or friend is still speaking. But effective listening requires that you listen as though there were nothing else in the world more fascinating to you than what that person is saying.

Even in the **(3)** .... of an extremely noisy party, the very best listeners seem to have **(4)** .... the gift of making the person who is speaking feel as if he or she were the only person in the room. They do this by paying **(5)** .... attention and asking lots of questions.

One very useful technique to **(6)** .... the conversation going is to ask, 'What do you mean, exactly?' It's impossible for the other person not to **(7)** .... more detail. You can then follow **(8)** .... with other open-ended questions and keep the conversation rolling along.

Open cloze (Part 2)

2 For questions 1–8, read the text below and think of the word which best fits each gap. Use only one word in each gap. There is an example at the beginning (0).

Planning ahead

Sally Keating, **(0)** who. runs an online recruitment service, admits **(1)** .... often worries about the future. 'My biggest concern for my future is that my company may not turn **(2)** .... to be the success that I hope it will be as I'm depending **(3)** .... that to make all my dreams come true.' But when Sally starts worrying about the future, she isn't just thinking about the immediate needs of her business. By the **(4)** .... her online business becomes successful, she also wants to **(5)** .... bought a flat and got married. At the same time, she wants to save for her retirement.

This is the advice life coach Paddy Carson had to offer Sally: 'It's a good idea to think about your goals in life but Sally's problem is that she's identified far **(6)** .... many. Instead, Sally needs to focus on her priorities. First, she needs to focus on making her business a success. She should get **(7)** .... decent advice from someone who understands the recruitment business and set some realistic targets. She should not delay doing this. Rather than allowing herself to wonder whether her business will be successful, she should only picture **(8)** .... it will be like when she's achieved her goals.'

0	A situations	B locations	C places	D settings
1	A faint	B poor	C frail	D hopeless
2	A speech	B response	C reaction	D expression
3	A heart	B depth	C middle	D peak
4	A possessed	B achieved	C received	D acquired
5	A strong	B close	C hard	D deep
6	A give	B put	C get	D make
7	A provide	B participate	C contribute	D attach
8	A along	B in	C up	D after

Word formation (Part 3)

3 For questions 1–8, read the text below. Use the word given in capitals at the end of some of the lines to form a word that fits in the gap in the same line. There is an example at the beginning (0).

Message in a bottle

News that a bottle **(0)** _containing_ a message sent by two twelve-year-old French–Canadian girls has been found on a beach in Ireland, eight years after it had first set sail from Canada, has been met with **(1)** .... The story has captured the **(2)** .... of people all over the world. **CONTAIN**

AMAZE
IMAGINE

The girls threw the bottle into the St Lawrence River in Quebec while on holiday. But the chances of it being picked up by ten-year-old Oisin Millea eight years later on the other side of the world were **(3)** .... The message, which was placed in a two-litre Sprite bottle, was written in French and is still **(4)** .... legible.

LIKE

EXPECT

Oisin made the **(5)** .... while walking on the beach near his home in County Waterford. His mother said Oisin was an **(6)** .... treasure-hunter but this was by far the most incredible find he'd yet made. She added that one of the most **(7)** .... things about this story was the amount of media attention it has attracted from news **(8)** .... all over the world. **DISCOVER**

ENTHUSIASM

REMARK

AGENT

Key word transformation (Part 4)

4 For questions 1–6, complete the second sentence so that it has a similar meaning to the first sentence, using the word given. Do not change the word given. You must use between three and six words, including the word given.

Example:
We're going to camp whether or not it's raining.
EVEN
We're going to camp even if it's raining.

1 Tim isn't worried about not having made any plans for the future.
NOR
Tim hasn't made any plans for the future .... worried about it.

2 I've made an official complaint but haven't had an answer.
AS
Despite having made an official complaint, ... received an answer.

3 I can't think of a logical explanation for his behaviour.
MYSTERY
It .... why he should have behaved like that.

4 Someone found my stolen wallet and returned it to me by post.
FOUND
The person .... returned it to me by post.

5 I can't understand why she doesn't respond to my emails anymore.
IDEA
I've .... have stopped responding to my emails.

6 I caught the bus before they got to the airport to collect me.
ALREADY
By the time they got to the airport to collect me .... caught the bus.

4 No pain without gain

1 Work in pairs and add three more statements to the questionnaire. Then ask and answer questions to find out whether anyone in your class is a perfectionist.

ARE YOU A PERFECTIONIST?	Yes	No
1 I get upset if I get less than 99 percent in a test.		

Sentence completion (Part 2)

▶ **EXAM** FOCUS p.181

2 You will hear part of a talk by a sports psychologist called Jon Hayes about the work he does with top footballers. Read the sentences carefully. Can you predict what kind of information is missing?

Psychology for top footballers

Jon thinks that players experience much more **(1)** .... than in the past.

Jon says that helping players to avoid feelings of **(2)** .... during a game is an important part of his job.

Jon thinks young players need help dealing with negative comments about **(3)** .... made during a match.

A useful technique Jon uses is training players to leave behind **(4)** .... emotions using certain rituals.

All the techniques Jon uses focus on the part of the brain which is responsible for **(5)** ....

Jon says the techniques are designed to release certain chemicals in the brain which have a positive impact on **(6)** .... levels.

When selecting players for **(7)** ...., Jon recommends that managers study their body language.

To control negative emotions, Jon trains players to use keywords such as **(8)** '..............'.

EXAM TIP

Read the sentences very carefully before you listen to make sure you choose the right word/phrase to fit the gap.

3 ▶ **13 Listen to the first part of the talk and look at Question 1 in Activity 2.**

1 What things are mentioned that players can 'experience'?

2 What does Jon say has increased for players?

4 ▶ **14 Listen to the whole talk. For questions 2–8, complete the sentences.**

5 Work in pairs and answer the questions. Give reasons for your answers.

1 Do you agree that these techniques could be useful in everyday life?

2 Do you think perfectionism can be dangerous?

Verb patterns: -ing/infinitive

▶ **GRAMMAR** REFERENCE p.153

6 Write at least one more verb from the box which follows each verb pattern.

---

attempted   avoided   continued   encouraged
failed   intended   let   noticed   persuaded
pretended   recommended   stopped   suggested
tried

---

1 I avoided/............. working hard. (verb + -ing)

2 I attempted/............. to work hard. (verb + to infinitive)

3 I encouraged/............. him to work hard. (verb + object + to infinitive)

4 I noticed/............. him working hard. (verb + object + -ing)

5 I recommended/............. he work hard. (verb + object + infinitive without to)

LANGUAGE TIP

Some verbs such as *start, love, hate, prefer* can be followed by either *-ing* or an infinitive with very little difference in meaning.

*I started **to watch/watching** the film at 9p.m.*

---

7 Work in pairs and answer the questions.

1 Which sentence means Frank no longer buys a newspaper?

   A Frank stopped to buy a newspaper.

   B Frank stopped buying a newspaper.

2 Which sentence expresses regret for something that was said in the past?

   A I regret saying you were wrong.

   B I regret to say you were wrong.

3 In which sentence does booking the appointment happen before Alice remembered something?

   A Alice remembered to book an appointment at the dentist.

   B Alice remembered booking an appointment at the dentist.

8 Work in pairs and discuss the questions. Give reasons for your answers.

1 Do you worry about how you're going to turn your dreams into reality?

2 Do you think it's important to try to fulfil your ambitions?

3 How do you feel about leaving your comfort zone?

4 Do you think it's important to make a contribution to society?

9 Read the text. Which of the verb patterns in Activity 6 do the verbs in brackets follow? Complete the text with the correct form of the verbs in brackets.

Too afraid to fail

Very few people can claim that they have achieved all that they'd ever hoped **(1)** .... (*achieve*). So what is stopping you right now from making a much greater contribution to society? What is preventing you from **(2)** .... (*fulfil*) your potential? You don't want to look back in twenty years' time and regret not **(3)** .... (*have*) tried hard enough. Here are some possible reasons:

You do not have enough belief in yourself. All successful people have enormous self-belief. They know that they have something special to contribute and they expect **(4)** .... (*make*) their mark.

You are too comfortable where you are. Why try something new when you are already doing what you are good at? High achievers go further. They grab every opportunity and are prepared **(5)** .... (*take on*) difficult challenges. This means that they risk **(6)** .... (*fail*) again and again. Do you dare **(7)** .... (*leave*) your comfort zone or do you avoid **(8)** .... (*take*) risks?

You're not forcing yourself **(9)** .... (*work*) hard enough. Either that or you keep **(10)** .... (*do*) unproductive tasks. If you have clear goals but are not making progress towards them, consider **(11)** .... (*increase*) your activity level. Picasso painted over 20,000 pictures. Persistence pays dividends.

You are not mixing with high achievers. Let's face it – your friends and family are really nice people but they are not challenging you enough. Spend more time with high flyers and positive thinkers who understand what it takes to succeed. They will help **(12)** .... (*turn*) your dreams into reality.

10 Work in pairs and discuss the questions.

1 Do you think the advice in the text is useful? Why/Why not?

2 What kind of person do you think the writer is?

1 **Work in pairs and discuss the questions.**

1 Why do you think many people find successful entrepreneurs so inspiring?

2 Do you think you've got what it takes to be a successful entrepreneur? Why/Why not?

2 **Read the article and say what is unusual about the success of Levi Roots.**

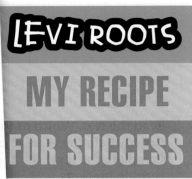

LEVI ROOTS

MY RECIPE FOR SUCCESS

When I was making Reggae Reggae Sauce in my kitchen, I knew it was going to be popular because I had sold the sauce at the Notting Hill Carnival and to local businesses. But I did not imagine I would get to where I am now. I don't think I could have become so big without the exposure of *Dragons' Den* on the BBC. That TV programme had about 4.5 million viewers. Until this, the banks weren't interested in a forty-nine-year-old Rastafarian who produced a sauce in his kitchen and called it *Reggae Reggae*.

No one could have envisaged then the level of success that my business has had in the past five years. Sales reached more than £1 million within the first year. My first order from a large supermarket of 250,000 bottles sold out within a week, outselling Heinz tomato ketchup.

My basic business philosophy is a quote from Shakespeare's *Julius Caesar*: *We must take the current when it serves or lose our ventures*. I always say this is an entrepreneur's mantra. You must grab an opportunity when it comes.

I don't think I want to work until I drop – not at all. I want to enjoy the success I have been granted. I have been going to Jamaica recently and I would like to retire there. I have just started distributing Reggae Reggae Sauce in Jamaica but it is not made there. It is my dream to set up a factory in Clarendon, the sugar cane community where I grew up with my grandmother.

3 **Match words 1–6 with meanings A–F.**

1	exposure	**A**	a project or enterprise
2	envisage	**B**	be given or rewarded with
3	mantra	**C**	imagine or visualise
4	granted	**D**	a repeated phrase, e.g. in meditation
5	venture	**E**	take hold of something
6	grab	**F**	publicity or attention

Verb/Noun collocations

4 **Answer the questions about the verbs *grasp*, *grab*, *take* and *seize*.**

1 Which is the most formal word?

2 Which words suggest doing something suddenly?

3 Can all of the verbs be used in sentences A and B?

A Entrepreneurs .... every opportunity.

B The military .... power in 1927.

5 **Look at the underlined verbs in the collocations. Add verbs from the box which also collocate with the nouns.**

doubt exceed face find follow fulfil gain realise receive rely on suffer reach win

1 <u>encounter</u> a setback/difficulties (x2)

2 <u>trust</u> your intuition (x3)

3 <u>get</u> exposure (x3)

4 <u>get</u> inspiration (x3)

5 <u>have</u> expectations (x2)

6 <u>achieve</u> an ambition/a target (x4)

7 <u>give</u> praise (x2)

8 <u>develop</u> your potential (x5)

EXAM TIP

Many words that you are familiar with may have additional collocations that you don't yet know. You need to keep extending your knowledge of collocations of both familiar words and new words. This will be particularly useful for Use of English Part 1.

6 **Write six sentences using some of the collocations in Activity 5.**

7 **Work in pairs and discuss the questions.**

1 Why do you think Reggae Reggae Sauce has been such a success?

2 Would you like to start your own business? Why/Why not?

Key word transformation (Part 4)

▶ **EXAM** FOCUS p.179

1 **Look at the exam question and answer the questions.**

No one could have envisaged the success the business would have.

POSSIBLE

It .... to envisage the success the business would have.

1 Do you need to use an active or passive form?

2 Do you need to use a negative or a positive form?

3 Which of these options fits best?

A wouldn't have been possible

B couldn't be possible

C could have been possible

2 **Choose the correct option to complete the second sentence so that it has a similar meaning to the first sentence.**

1 Unfortunately, they failed to achieve their ambitious goals.

SUCCESSFUL

They .... their ambitious goals.

A were not successful in

B weren't successful in achieving

C are not successful to achieve

2 I wish I had started my own business sooner.

REGRET

I .... my own business sooner.

A have the regret not to have started

B regret I hadn't started

C regret not having started

3 Jack is completely trustworthy as a business partner.

RELIED

Jack .... as a business partner.

A is relied completely

B can be relied on completely

C relied on completely

3 **For questions 1–6, complete the second sentence so that it has a similar meaning to the first sentence, using the word given. Do not change the word given. You must use between three and six words, including the word given.**

1 Some people doubt whether Martin's new business venture will do well.

EXPECTED

Martin's new business venture .... well by everyone.

2 Unfortunately, I couldn't visit my brother in Australia as I didn't have enough money.

ABLE

If I'd had more money, I .... to visit my brother in Australia.

3 It's possible that he will fail in his ambition to be a doctor if he doesn't work hard.

REALISED

His ambition to be a doctor .... if he doesn't work hard.

4 Learning to drive is a waste of time unless you already have a car.

POINT

There .... to drive unless you already have a car.

5 The sales director is unsure about taking on new sales staff.

WHETHER

The sales director is unsure .... new sales staff or not.

6 My parents wouldn't allow me to go to the party.

PREVENTED

My parents .... to the party.

EXAM TIP

Make sure you don't write more than six words. Contractions (e.g. *won't*) count as two words.

Multiple choice (Part 5)

▶ **EXAM** FOCUS p.179

1 **Read the title and the article quickly. What kind of products does the museum contain?**

2 **Look at question 1 in Activity 3 and the first paragraph of the article.**

1 Are options A–D all mentioned in the text?

2 Underline the sentences which refer to the writer's reaction to the products on display. Which of the options answers the question?

3 **For questions 2–6, choose the answer (A, B, C or D) which you think fits best according to the text.**

1 What is the writer's initial reaction to the products on display in The Storehouse?

  A He is impressed by the huge range.

  B He can't identify any of them.

  C He dislikes the way they are arranged on the shelves.

  D He doesn't immediately understand why they look strange.

2 In the second paragraph, the writer refers to some of the products in order to

  A question whether their failure was the result of bad luck.

  B highlight possible problems which led to their failure.

  C explain the logic behind the way they are organised.

  D compare some of the worst examples.

3 What is Carol Sherry's attitude to the products on display?

  A She feels particularly attached to some of them.

  B She has sympathy for the people who invented them.

  C She thinks most of them were based on good ideas.

  D She is interested in finding out more about them.

4 The writer suggests that Robert McMath

  A should have been more selective when buying products.

  B failed to organise his collection appropriately.

  C excluded some important new products from his collection.

  D was unaware that very few products would be a commercial success.

5 What does the writer think is remarkable about some of The Storehouse's visitors?

  A their ignorance of their own company's products in the collection

  B their repetition of their competitors' mistakes

  C their lack of appreciation for the service provided by the museum

  D their confidence in the future success of their new brands

6 In the final paragraph, the writer refers to the 'positive-thinking culture' in order to

  A speculate about how companies allow products to fail.

  B criticise companies for making very basic mistakes.

  C identify who is to blame in a company when products fail.

  D express doubt about whether things have improved.

EXAM TIP

You will need to read the text containing the answer for each question very carefully to check that there is evidence for each option you choose. Also check that it actually answers the question.

4 **Work in pairs and discuss the questions.**

1 Why do you think there is such a constant demand for new products?

2 Why do you think most products fail?

Vocabulary

Working out meaning from context

5 **Look at the underlined words in the article and use the context to help you choose the correct meaning.**

1 poignant

  A sad   **B** significant

2 haphazardly

  A logically   **B** randomly

3 fleeting

  A passing quickly   **B** durable

4 indiscriminately

  A in a planned way   **B** in an unplanned way

5 aversion

  A willingness   **B** unwillingness

6 doomed

  A bound to fail   **B** might fail

The Museum of Failed Products

Our business editor, **Liam Ellis**, pays a visit to The Storehouse; a huge collection of failed supermarket products.

In an unremarkable business park outside the city of Ann Arbor in Michigan stands a <u>poignant</u> memorial to humanity's shattered dreams. It doesn't look like that from the outside, though. Even when you get inside The Storehouse, it takes a few moments for your eyes to adjust to what you're seeing. It appears to be a vast and <u>haphazardly</u> organised supermarket; along every aisle, grey metal shelves are crammed with thousands of packages of food and household products. There is, however, something not quite right about the displays and soon enough you work out the reason: unlike in a real supermarket, there is only one example of each product.

The Storehouse, operated by a company called GfK Custom Research North America, has acquired a nickname: the Museum of Failed Products. This is consumer capitalism's graveyard or, to put it less grandly, it's almost certainly the only place on the planet where you'll find A Touch of Yogurt shampoo alongside the equally unappealing For Oily Hair Only. These products may well have been perfectly adequate shampoos let down only by their off-putting names. Whereas some of the other products obviously had more serious flaws, such as the self-heating soup cans that had a regrettable tendency to explode in customers' faces.

There is a Japanese term, *mono no aware*, that translates roughly as 'the pathos of things'. It captures a kind of bittersweet melancholy at life's impermanence – that additional beauty imparted to cherry blossoms, for their <u>fleeting</u> nature. It's only stretching the concept slightly to suggest that this is how the museum's manager, an understatedly stylish GfK employee named Carol Sherry, feels about the cartons of Morning Banana Juice in her care or about Fortune Snookies, a short-lived line of fortune cookies for dogs. Every failure, the way she sees it, embodies its own sad story on the part of designers, marketers and salespeople. It is never far from her mind that real people had their mortgages, their car payments and their family holidays riding on the success of products such as Fortune Snookies.

The Museum of Failed Products was itself a kind of accident, albeit a happier one. Its creator, a now retired marketing man named Robert McMath, merely intended to accumulate a 'reference library' of consumer products, not failures per se. And so, starting in the 1960s, he began purchasing and preserving a sample of every new item he could find. Soon, the collection outgrew his office in upstate New York and he was forced to move into a converted granary to accommodate it. Later, GfK bought him out, moving the whole lot to its current home at The Storehouse in Michigan. What McMath hadn't taken into account was the three-word truth that was to prove the making of his career: *most products fail*. According to some estimates, the failure rate is as high as ninety percent. Simply by collecting new products <u>indiscriminately</u>, McMath had ensured that his hoard would come to consist overwhelmingly of unsuccessful ones.

By far the most striking thing about the museum, though, is that it should exist as a viable, profit-making business in the first place. You might have assumed that any consumer product manufacturer worthy of the name would have its own such collection – a carefully stewarded resource to help it avoid making errors its competitors had already made. Yet the executives who arrive every week at Sherry's door are evidence of how rarely this happens. Product developers are so focused on their next hoped-for success, so unwilling to invest time or energy thinking about their industry's past failures that they only belatedly realise how much they need to access GfK's collection. Most surprising of all is that many of the designers who have found their way to the museum have come there to examine – or been surprised to discover – brands that their own companies had created, then abandoned.

It isn't hard to imagine how one downside of the positive-thinking culture, an <u>aversion</u> to confronting failure, might have been responsible for the very existence of many of the products lining its shelves. Each one must have made it through a series of meetings at which nobody realised that the product was <u>doomed</u>. Perhaps nobody wanted to contemplate the prospect of failure; perhaps someone did but didn't want to bring it up for discussion. By the time the truth became obvious, the original developers would have moved to other products or other firms. Little energy would have been invested in discovering what went wrong. Everyone involved would have conspired, perhaps without realising what they're doing, never to speak of it again. Failure is everywhere. It's just that most of the time we'd rather avoid confronting that fact. ●

1 **Read the article about Dina Jones and decide if the statements are true (T) or false (F).**

1 A terrible misfortune had a positive outcome.

2 She never achieved her dream of playing for her country.

3 She is having problems coming to terms with what has happened.

an INSPIRATIONAL athlete

It's true what they say; every cloud really does have a silver lining. I learnt that when I was seventeen. What **(1)** *should/must* seem a complete disaster to everyone else, I'm actually OK with. My dream of playing professional basketball was about to come true. I'd been scouted for the national youth team, but soon after I was involved in a cycling accident and ended up in a wheelchair. I **(2)** *had to/must* accept that the dream was over and I would never be able to play for my country. Understandably, I was pretty depressed at first and everyone **(3)** *must have been/should be* really worried about me. I didn't realise I was lucky because I **(4)** *could/should* still use my arms.

But I **(5)** *should have listened/must have listened* to my granddad when he told me that as one door closes, another one opens. I felt totally demotivated and didn't want to think about doing anything else. After a few months though, my family persuaded me to join the wheelchair basketball team. On the first day the coach said 'OK, so things haven't exactly gone to plan but you **(6)** *need/can* to make the best of your misfortune. You **(7)** *must/could* have a great career as a wheelchair player.' He was right. The best thing was that I **(8)** *mustn't/didn't have to* give up the sport I loved. And to cut a long story short, I ended up playing for my country at the Paralympic games – something I never thought was possible. My family were so proud.

There's no point saying I **(9)** *should be/could have been* a world-famous basketball star. That just wasn't meant to be. And the way I look at it now, I **(10)** *shouldn't make/might not have made* it as a professional basketball player and **(11)** *needn't have had/might not have had* the chance to play for my country. This whole experience has also taught me that you **(12)** *should/could* never give up on your dreams.

2 **Read the article again and choose the correct alternatives.**

3 **Work in pairs and answer the questions.**

1 In what way is this story an inspiration to young people?

2 What do you think is the best way to encourage someone who feels demotivated?

Modal verbs

▶ **GRAMMAR** REFERENCE p.154

4 **Find one or more examples in the article of modals used to:**

1 describe past ability.

(4) I could still use my arms

2 criticise past behaviour.

3 express certainty about the present.

4 express certainty about the past.

5 talk about a future possibility.

6 talk about a possibility in the past.

7 talk about a present obligation/necessity.

8 describe a past lack of obligation/necessity.

LANGUAGE TIP

Need has two past forms with slightly different meanings.

*She **didn't need to catch** the early flight.* (It wasn't necessary to do this. It's not clear if she did or not.)

*She **needn't have caught** the early flight.* (She did this but it wasn't necessary.)

5 **Complete the questions with the correct form of the verbs in brackets. Then ask and answer them with a partner.**

1 Is there anything you feel you .... (*should/achieve*) by now that you haven't?

2 What .... (*have to*) do that you hated doing at school?

3 Which of your dreams do you think .... (*might/come*) true?

4 Is there anything that you .... (*not need/do*) that you have done recently?

5 What do you think your parents .... (*could/do*) differently when you were a child?

6 How do you think your teachers .... (*must/see*) you when you were in primary school?

Collaborative task and discussion (Parts 3 and 4)

justifying an opinion

▶ **EXAM** FOCUS p.183

1 Have you ever given up a sport or a hobby? If so, why did you give it up?

2 ▶ 15 Look at the exam task and listen to two candidates, Jan and Marisol, doing both parts of the task. What do they think makes people give up a sport or hobby? Do you agree?

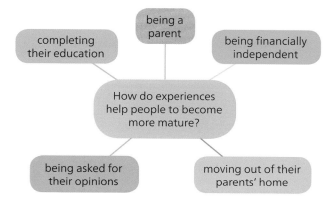

being a parent

completing their education

being financially independent

How do experiences help people to become more mature?

being asked for their opinions

moving out of their parents' home

3 Complete the phrases the speakers use when justifying an opinion. Then listen again and check.

1 In my opinion, ... many people give up a sport or hobby is because of the costs involved.

2 I believe that .... to explaining why people have to give up.

3 I .... but I imagine many people get demotivated because they realise they're never going to be an amazing pianist or guitar player.

4 I know from .... that that's quite common.

4 Which of the phrases in Activity 3 is used by the candidates to

A introduce a point?

B emphasise a point?

C give personal evidence?

D speculate without evidence?

5 ▶ 16 Listen to Marisol and Jan answering these questions. Which candidate answers the question well?

1 What do you think is the value of having a hobby?

2 Do you believe playing computer games is a good hobby?

6 Work in pairs. Turn to page 135 and do the activities.

EXAM TIP

Discuss each of the options on the task sheet in some detail with your partner. Don't dismiss any as being insignificant or unimportant too early in the discussion or you may run out of things to say. Also, don't be afraid to state the obvious.

7 How would you evaluate your own performance? Use the General marking guidelines on page 185 to help you. Can you suggest any ways in which the other students you worked with could improve?

1 **How useful are these tips for helping people to achieve more in their lives?**

- Smile more.
- Never use negative words such as *fail* or *lose*.
- Expect only positive outcomes.
- Use visualisation techniques to imagine yourself succeeding.

Essay (Part 1)
effective introductory and concluding paragraphs

▶ **WRITING** REFERENCE p.168

2 **Look at the exam task below and the introductions on the right. Which one is better? Think about appropriate academic style and inclusion of specific examples.**

Your class has attended a seminar on the benefits of training students to think positively. You have made the notes below.

The benefits of training students to think positively

- reduces stress
- improves productivity
- increases creativity

Some opinions expressed during the seminar

- 'The training is empowering. I feel I can achieve so much more.'
- 'Having a positive outlook helps people to put their problems into perspective.'
- 'It gives people the tools they need to find alternative solutions to their problems.'

Write an essay for your tutor, discussing **two** of the benefits in your notes. You should **explain which benefit you think is more important, giving reasons** to support your opinion.

You may, if you wish, make use of the opinions expressed during the seminar but you should use your own words as far as possible.

Write your **essay** in **220–260** words in an appropriate style.

A It is undoubtedly true that there are many benefits to training students to think positively. Many students struggle with problems such as time management or feeling demotivated when they get a lower mark than they were hoping for. These types of problems can have a very negative impact on their performance and may sometimes lead to them dropping out of college.

B Training students to think positively is a very good idea, in my opinion. It's very easy to become negative when things aren't going well and you're not enjoying the course for whatever reason. I know from my own experience that students can find this very hard, especially if they have no one to help them deal with their problems.

EXAM TIP

In the introduction, give a brief outline of the issue, saying why it is important or why people have different opinions about it.

3 **Work in pairs and write a plan setting out your ideas for the main body of the essay in Activity 2. Make sure you include some evidence to support your ideas.**

4 **Decide if the statements about writing a conclusion are true (T) or false (F).**

1 You should give your opinion.
2 You should add some more examples to support your opinion.
3 You should briefly explain which benefit is more important.
4 You should summarise your main point(s).

5 **Complete the phrases that are often used in concluding paragraphs.**

1 To .... up, I would argue that reducing stress is of the greatest benefit.
2 It .... to me that everyone could benefit from this type of training.
3 Above .... , I think that positive thinking creates a better attitude.
4 The main point I would like to .... can be summarised as …

6 **Work in pairs. Turn to page 144 and do the activity.**

7 **Write your essay and check your work using the checklist on page 166.**

1 Choose the correct alternative in each sentence.

1 Nobody *might/could* have predicted how successful the company would be.

2 You *shouldn't/mustn't* have given up so easily when you had a chance of winning.

3 Dan *didn't need to be/shouldn't have* told what his mistake was.

4 The company *should know/must have known* that there would be serious losses.

5 We *would/will* never have expected that things would turn out so well.

6 That *can't/mustn't be* Sophie. She's supposed to be in Australia.

2 Complete the second sentence so that it has a similar meaning to the first sentence, using the word given. Do not change the word given. You must use between three and six words, including the word given.

1 It wasn't necessary for Emma to book her train ticket so far in advance because there were plenty of seats available.

BOOKED

Emma .... her train ticket so far in advance because there were plenty of seats available.

2 Unfortunately, I didn't have enough money to go travelling with my friends.

WOULD

If I'd had more money, I .... travelling with my friends.

3 Lucy was sorry she hadn't applied for the course in time.

REGRETTED

Lucy .... for the course in time.

4 I realised I hadn't booked an appointment when I got to the hair salon.

FORGOTTEN

I realised I .... an appointment when I got to the hair salon.

5 As children, we were forbidden from watching TV until all our homework was done.

ALLOWED

As children, we .... TV until all our homework was done.

6 Kevin thinks it might be a good idea to sell the house.

CONSIDERING

Kevin .... the house.

3 Choose the correct option to complete the sentences.

1 Great business leaders always .... adversity.

 A suffer **B** overcome **C** exceed

2 Don't expect to .... any thanks for speaking the truth.

 A win **B** receive **C** earn

3 We were able to .... an advantage over the competition.

 A gain **B** exceed **C** beat

4 We were so lucky to be able to .... our ambition of travelling the world.

 A recognise **B** find **C** realise

5 I was really happy when I .... my target of running ten kilometres in fifty minutes.

 A followed **B** overcame **C** reached

6 The book .... a lot of praise from critics.

 A achieved **B** received **C** gained

7 Sometimes it's hard to .... the lecturer's main argument.

 A receive **B** find **C** follow

8 The idea is beginning to .... popularity, although it was unpopular at first.

 A gain **B** follow **C** reach

4 Read the text below. Use the word given in capitals at the end of some of the lines to form a word that fits in the gap in the same line.

Advice for budding entrepreneurs	
It's nearly impossible to succeed without people to help you. Nobody can do everything on their own and being friendly and **(1)** .... is one of the most important **(2)** .... for a young entrepreneur to have. Without the ability to network and work with people, you won't be able to develop the **(3)** .... that you need to provide the support you'll need.	**HELP** **CHARACTER** **RELATION**
Many young entrepreneurs get **(4)** .... when things do not live up to their **(5)** .... It's a mistake to believe you can instantly start making millions of dollars. Most ideas will end in **(6)** .... Don't take this to heart, treat it as a **(7)** .... from which you will recover. Remember that luck plays a major part in the success of any project. You may think you have the perfect idea but luck may not be on your side and you may not always get the **(8)** .... that you deserve.	**MOTIVATE** **EXPECT** **FAIL** **FORTUNE** **RECOGNISE**

Open cloze (Part 2)

▶ **EXAM** FOCUS p.178

▶ **EXAM** FOCUS p.178

EXAM TIP

Try reading the text 'aloud' in your head. That may help you to work out what some of the missing words are.

1 Work in pairs and discuss the questions.

1 Is there a particular activity that makes you feel happy?
2 What one change to your current lifestyle would make you happier?
3 What has been the happiest period of your life so far?

2 Read an article about a new way to investigate happiness. How does the writer feel about using technology in this way?

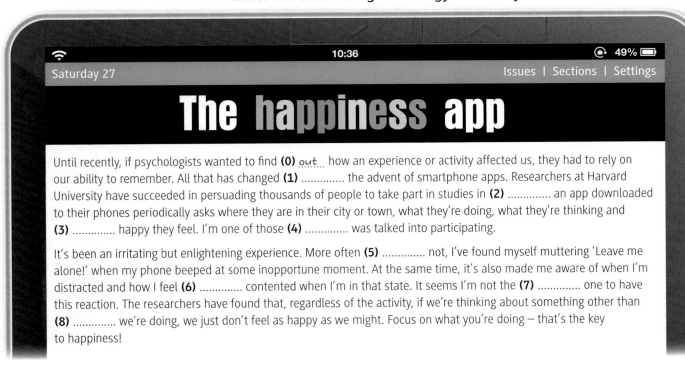

10:36   49%

Saturday 27   Issues | Sections | Settings

The happiness app

Until recently, if psychologists wanted to find **(0)** out how an experience or activity affected us, they had to rely on our ability to remember. All that has changed **(1)** .... the advent of smartphone apps. Researchers at Harvard University have succeeded in persuading thousands of people to take part in studies in **(2)** .... an app downloaded to their phones periodically asks where they are in their city or town, what they're doing, what they're thinking and **(3)** .... happy they feel. I'm one of those **(4)** .... was talked into participating.

It's been an irritating but enlightening experience. More often **(5)** .... not, I've found myself muttering 'Leave me alone!' when my phone beeped at some inopportune moment. At the same time, it's also made me aware of when I'm distracted and how I feel **(6)** .... contented when I'm in that state. It seems I'm not the **(7)** .... one to have this reaction. The researchers have found that, regardless of the activity, if we're thinking about something other than **(8)** .... we're doing, we just don't feel as happy as we might. Focus on what you're doing – that's the key to happiness!

3 Read the article again. For questions 1–8, think of the word which best fits each gap. Use only one word for each gap.

Long turn (Part 2)
Speculating (1)
▶ **EXAM** FOCUS p.183

4 **Work in pairs and look at the pictures. Discuss the questions using the expressions in the box.**

I can't be completely sure
I don't know why
I may be wrong about this
I suppose it/he/she/they could
One possible explanation might be
This is just a guess, but

1 What do the pictures have in common?

2 In what ways are they different from one another?

3 Is there anything in the pictures that is difficult for you to identify or explain?

EXAM TIP

Don't worry if there are things in the pictures that you cannot identify or explain. The Speaking exam is not intended to test your general knowledge. You're expected to speculate in answer to the examiner's question about things like why the people are there, how they might be feeling or what might happen next.

5 ▶ **17** **Listen to the instructions an examiner gives a candidate. Which things does he NOT ask them to do?**

1 talk about all three pictures

2 choose two of the pictures

3 describe each of the pictures

4 compare the pictures

5 decide where the pictures were taken

6 talk generally about people in situations similar to those in the pictures

6 **Work in pairs.**

Student A: compare two of the pictures according to the examiner's instructions.

Student B: listen and make a note of the phrases Student A uses to speculate.

7 ▶ **18** **Listen to the next part of the examiner's instructions. What does the other candidate have to do? Discuss the question with a partner.**

8 **Work in pairs. Turn to page 136 and do Task 1. Then turn to page 140 and do Task 2.**

1   **Work in pairs and discuss the questions.**

1   Is there such a thing as having too much money?

2   If someone has more money than they need to live comfortably, what should they do with the rest?

Multiple choice (Part 3)

▶ **EXAM** FOCUS p.182

2   **You will hear an interview with two psychologists called Donna Marchant and Graham Donovan, who are discussing the topic of happiness. Look at question 1 in Activity 4 and underline the key words in the question and options.**

3   ▶ 19   **Listen to the first part of the interview and look at question 1 in Activity 4. Answer the questions.**

1   Which key words or words with a similar meaning did you hear?

2   Which option is correct?

4   ▶ 20   **Read through questions 2–6 and underline the key words. Then listen to the interview and choose the answer (A, B, C or D) which fits best according to what you hear.**

1   What is Donna's attitude towards research into the relationship between money and happiness?

   A   It has given her a good understanding of the issue.

   B   It raises more questions than it answers.

   C   It is not relevant to the questions she wants to address.

   D   It falls outside her area of expertise.

2   What does Graham suggest about the way Donna defines excess income?

   A   She misunderstands the key issues.

   B   She knows more than he does.

   C   She needs information he can provide.

   D   She has no research experience in this area.

3   Graham believes that Maslow's hierarchy

   A   has not received enough attention from researchers.

   B   helps to answer questions about money and happiness.

   C   is only relevant to discussions of human development.

   D   takes into account important factors that contribute to happiness.

4   Donna thinks the way people spend their excess income

   A   should be a matter of personal choice.

   B   is based on a worrying misconception.

   C   should not be a cause of unnecessary anxiety.

   D   appears to be the result of their inherent selfishness.

5   Graham's opinion of the research into spending and happiness is that

   A   it proves an important point.

   B   it has been the target of unreasonable attack.

   C   it is fraught with design problems.

   D   it does not merit the attention it has received.

6   Graham says that the recent study Donna and her team conducted

   A   was a great success.

   B   failed to take certain factors into account.

   C   improved upon earlier research.

   D   provides important information for society.

EXAM TIP

The interviewer's questions will help you to follow the discussion so you know which question you should be listening for.

5   **Look at the underlined words and phrases in the extracts from the discussion 1–6 and match them to meanings A–F.**

1   If you have more than you need to <u>make ends meet</u>, you won't necessarily be any happier.

2   People often <u>squander</u> their wealth on the very things that are least likely to make them feel good.

3   The more they indulge in consumer goods, the more <u>inclined</u> they are to obsess about money.

4   It's not quite that <u>straightforward</u>.

5   There's a research study that tried to establish a link between <u>altruistic</u> spending and happiness.

6   I don't want to <u>quibble</u> but how do you know there were no other factors?

A   have just enough money to buy the things you need

B   argue about small unimportant details

C   carelessly waste

D   simple and easy to understand

E   caring about and willing to help others

F   likely

6   **Work in pairs and discuss the questions.**

1   If someone gave you €20, what would you spend it on?

2   Describe the happiest person you know.

1 Read an extract from a book review. What is the reviewer's overall impression of the book?

HEALTHY YOU

Naturally High

A friend had been telling me to read Jean Rossner's *Naturally High* but it took me ages to actually get round to doing **(1)** <u>it</u> and **(2)** ↑ even longer to try to put some of the book's excellent advice into practice.

Despite my inherent cynicism, I found *Naturally High* extraordinarily helpful in many ways – so many **(3)** ↑, in fact, that I'm emulating my friend and **(4)** ↑ recommending **(5)** <u>it</u> to almost everyone I meet. All the usual suggestions are there; you know the **(6)** <u>ones</u> I mean: meditation, eating foods that boost the feel-good hormone serotonin and training for the marathon to get those endorphins pumping.

But if you're not much of an athlete, you might prefer to just get your taste buds used to really hot chillies. Rossner explains that we get a similar endorphin boost after the agony of eating **(7)** <u>them</u> fades. **(8)** ↑ Misgivings about eating chillies? Try chocolate instead. It will do the endorphin trick too and **(9)** ↑ painlessly into the bargain.

For those **(10)** ↑ who live in colder parts of the world, Rossner explains how to banish 'Seasonal Affective Disorder' or SAD. Giving yourself a blast with a special sunlamp first thing on those dark winter mornings apparently turns SAD into happy. Even

hardened misanthropes need the occasional natural high. If you're one of **(11)** <u>them</u>, then why not try curling up on the sofa with a pet dog or cat? Rossner tells us that pet patting reduces stress and **(12)** ↑ will make both pet and person purr with contentment. Well, maybe **(13)** <u>not</u> if it's a dog but **(14)** <u>they</u> keep you warm too!

2 Would you be interested in reading this book? Why/Why not?

Substitution and ellipsis

▶ **GRAMMAR** REFERENCE p.155

3 Look at the underlined words and phrases in the review. What do they refer to?

4 Look at the review again. Where you see the symbol ↑, decide which word or words have been left out by the writer.

LANGUAGE TIP

Ellipsis is used a lot in informal spoken English. For example, we often omit the auxiliary verb and even the subject pronoun in questions about future plans and our responses.

A: *(Are you) Going on holiday this year?*
B: *(I'm) Not sure – (it) depends how much money I save.*

---

5 Work in pairs. Read the sentence aloud and discuss how to replace the underlined words.

My friend Susan wanted me to buy <u>my friend Susan</u> a book for <u>my friend Susan's</u> birthday but I couldn't find the <u>book</u> that <u>my friend Susan</u> wanted in our local bookshop, so I got <u>my friend Susan</u> another <u>book</u> that I found <u>in our local bookshop</u> instead of the <u>book</u> <u>my friend Susan</u> had asked for.

6 Complete the sentences with the words in the box.

do either it not one so that there

1 **A:** Are you and Janna going to come to that meditation course with us?
  B: I'm not sure. We might ....

2 **A:** We'll probably have something quick to eat in that new café on the corner.
  B: Great! I'll meet you ....

3 **A:** Will someone meet you at the airport in Zurich?
  B: I hope .... I've never been there before.

4 I'm not sure whether to get a black jacket or a red ....

5 I finally read the book last month. .... was far better than I had expected.

6 She wanted to know whether we were coming to the party or ....

7 Simon and Clare say they can't manage next weekend and I can't ....

8 He won quite a big prize in the lottery. .... meant he could finally give up work and write a novel.

Multiple matching (Part 8)

▶ **EXAM** FOCUS p.180

1 Work in pairs and discuss the questions.

1 Are there any circumstances in which you would consider working without being paid?

2 Do students or graduates in your country take up unpaid internships? What do you think of this way of getting work experience?

2 You are going to read a magazine article in which five young women talk about doing unpaid internships. Read the article quickly. In which section does each of the young women talk about

1 an important upcoming event?

2 a fortunate change in her employment conditions?

3 a quick decision she made?

4 how long it takes her to get to work?

5 information she didn't have when she began the internship?

3 Look at question 1 below. The correct answer is E. Find words or phrases in section E that correspond to the underlined words in question 1.

Which intern says that:

getting <u>clear information</u> about <u>work practices</u> is <u>crucial</u>? `1`

direct contact with people gives her a sense of the value of her work? `2`

she expected to be able to stay on and earn some money? `3`

other interns may find challenging conditions unacceptable? `4`

it's unwise to work too hard? `5`

the demands of the job will increase? `6`

the rewarding work makes up for not having much money? `7`

not everyone can take up an offer such as the one she had? `8`

she was not optimistic about her future? `9`

working as an intern would be less tolerable in other circumstances? `10`

4 Read the article again. For questions 2–10, choose from the interns (A–E). The interns may be chosen more than once.

5 Match the underlined words and phrases in the article to meanings 1–7.

1 journey to work every day

2 accept a challenging situation

3 was useful

4 increase over a period of time

5 use all or most of your time and effort in order to do something

6 agreed to do

7 prepare what will be needed for an activity

6 Complete the sentences with the correct form of the words and phrases in Activity 5.

1 People have had to .... earning less money over the last few years.

2 One of those new vacuum cleaners would certainly .... around here.

3 She .... a lot of her time to caring for her elderly grandmother.

4 .... from Cambridge to London every day can be very tiring.

5 The amount of study we have to do is .... as the course progresses.

6 .... the stands for the trade fair took all morning.

7 I wouldn't .... any more projects if I were you. You're too busy already.

7 Answer the questions. Then tell a partner about your answers.

1 Do you find it difficult to <u>keep your nose to the grindstone</u>?

2 Have you ever had a teacher or boss who was <u>a real slave driver</u>?

3 How can people <u>get a foot on the career ladder</u> in your country?

Happy to be an intern ... for the time being

Sarah Barnes meets five young women who are getting a foot on the career ladder.

Intern A

I've been a script-development intern since March. Working on scripts that you know are going to become films one day is really exciting. We get a broad variety of genres sent to us. Personally, I love anything that's been adapted from a book, especially if I've read the book. I read scripts, sometimes I attend meetings with writers, and I've also researched potential writers and directors online. Although I'm only paid expenses, I haven't <u>taken on</u> any more paid work. To avoid burn-out, interns need time off and a bit of work–life balance. My placement was due to come to an end this month but I've been asked to stay on and be paid for it! Had I not been, I would have been a bit surprised as I knew they were really happy with me.

Intern B

I left Lithuania two years ago to study fashion and won an internship with a famous fashion designer after entering a competition. The designer can be a bit of a slave driver but she treats everyone equally, whether they're paid staff or interns. When I started, in June, I was working on the archive, so I had the opportunity to see past collections up close, which was really fascinating. I work 10a.m. to 6p.m., but the <u>build-up</u> to Fashion Week will mean we'll really have our noses to the grindstone and will be expected to work much longer hours. It might seem exploitative but, in fashion, if you want to establish yourself over the competition, you have to show your willingness to work hard and for free. If you don't, others will be only too happy to take your place.

Intern C

I've been interning at an emergency relief charity since March. Over the past few years I've been doing volunteer work for NGOs in Calcutta, Bogotá and Tehran, so it's quite hard to <u>come to terms with</u> being back in the UK. Most of my friends are buying houses and have cars and go on holidays. But I never feel I missed out, because I'm making a real contribution. I'm really fortunate that I can live with my mum, although it does mean my <u>commute</u> can take up to two hours. Without my family I don't think I could be doing this. Next month I am starting a six-month placement abroad. After that I might actually be in a position to earn a salary. If I was thirty-five and still working unpaid I would think, 'What am I doing?' but I'm still young and the sacrifice is more than worth it.

Intern D

I've just finished secondary school and will be <u>devoting</u> my summer to interning at the parliamentary office of a local politician. About two years ago some people from the same political party came canvassing at my door, asking if I'd like to help out. About five seconds later I was out canvassing with them! I wouldn't say there is an average day, but there are always emails from constituents to deal with. To be able to reply to these people individually gives you the sense that you are actually making a difference. I am lucky enough to be staying with my aunt and uncle who live nearby. A lot of incredibly able people are closed off from the opportunity of an internship in parliament because they can't afford to travel or live in London.

Intern E

I came to London in February with no plans and I didn't know how long it would take to get a job. I'd resigned myself to staying on a friend's sofa and relying on her generosity. Contrary to my expectations, luck was on my side and I found a job as a seamstress. My placement at the gallery came along a week later. I've helped <u>set up</u> exhibitions and create gallery publications. One of the most exciting tasks was helping an artist create an installation. Because some of the piece is sewn, my seamstress skills <u>came in handy</u>. The main advice I would give any intern is that you have to be very proactive. Find out how things are done. Otherwise you'll be putting yourself under a lot of unnecessary stress. That's what happened to me so I learnt to ask questions – the hard way.

1 Work in pairs and discuss which three things would most affect your level of job satisfaction.

working hours   commute
being in control of your destiny   job security
moving home to get a job
making an important contribution

2 Match the underlined forms in the comments 1–7 to the functions A–G.

1 I <u>wish</u> my boss <u>wouldn't</u> keep criticising me in front of everyone else.

2 I <u>wish</u> I <u>could</u> stop sleeping through my alarm!

3 <u>If only</u> they <u>would give</u> me a chance to show them what I can do at work.

4 I<u>'d rather</u> James <u>didn't</u> always make the decisions.

5 I <u>wish</u> I <u>had chosen</u> to study something scientific or technical.

6 <u>It's high time</u> the government <u>did</u> more to promote student exchange programmes.

7 I <u>wish</u> I <u>didn't</u> have to get up so early in the morning.

A complaint about someone else's irritating behaviour
B comment about a past situation that can't be changed
C a wish for an ability we don't have or a change in our own behaviour
D saying we think something should have been done before now
E talking about our preferences for the present or the future
F a very strong wish for something to change or a strong regret
G the desire for circumstances to change in the present

Hypothetical meaning

▶ **GRAMMAR** REFERENCE p.156

3 Complete the rules about hypothetical meaning with the terms in the box.

past simple (x2)   past perfect
if only + noun/pronoun + past simple
rather + noun/pronoun + past simple
noun/pronoun + *would* + infinitive
could + infinitive

1 We use *wish* + ... to express the desire for circumstances to change in the present.

2 We use *wish* + ... to talk about other people's irritating habits. This form is only rarely used with *I* or *we*.

3 We use .... with the same verb forms as *wish* but to express stronger feelings.

4 We use *wish* + ... to refer to things we are sorry about in the past or to express regret.

5 We use *wish* + ... to talk about an ability we would like to have or habit we would like to change.

6 We use *it's* (*high/about*) *time* + ... to talk about the present or the future. We mean that the action should have been done before.

7 We use *would* .... to talk about our preferences in the present.

4 Complete the second sentence so that it has a similar meaning to the first sentence, using the word in brackets.

1 I regret having quit my job.
I .... quit my job. (*wish*)

2 It really gets on my nerves when my classmate borrows my stapler.
I wish my classmate .... my stapler. (*stop*)

3 I don't want to hear every detail about your date with Charlie.
I'd rather .... me every detail about your date with Charlie. (*you*)

4 Things would be so much better if people learnt to be a bit kinder.
If .... to be a bit kinder, things would be so much better. (*only*)

5 I have to spend so long answering emails and I hate it!
I .... to spend so long answering emails. (*wish*)

6 I should have written long before this and told you about my new internship.
It's .... and told you about my new internship. (*high*)

LANGUAGE TIP

When we use *wish* + *be* to say how we would change a present or future situation, we often use *were* instead of *was*, especially in more formal styles.
*I **wish** I **were** a bit taller.*

---

5 Complete the sentences so they are true for you. Then tell a partner your answers and answer any questions they may have.

1 I know my friend wishes that ....

2 If I had the choice, I'd rather that my life ....

3 I really wish I wasn't ....

Prefix *mis-* and false opposites

1 **What does the prefix *mis-* mean? Complete the sentences with the correct form of the word in brackets. Use the prefix *mis-*.**

1 I think there must have been some kind of .... (*understand*). That's not what I meant.

2 Some of their decisions have been .... (*guide*), to say the least.

3 There are some important .... (*concept*) about what an unpaid intern's responsibilities should be.

4 Some of the promises interns are made before they start work are particularly .... (*lead*).

5 I had serious .... (*give*) about doing voluntary work but I really enjoyed it in the end.

6 The predictions were based on a serious .... (*interpret*) of the results of the survey.

7 My only other criticism of the book is that there is at least one .... (*print*) in every chapter.

8 Some people are very .... (*trust*) of conventional medicine but are happy to try the strangest natural remedies.

LANGUAGE TIP

Not all negative prefixes added to words make them the opposite of a base word. In some cases they mean something quite different, e.g. *disease*. In others, no base form exists, e.g. *misanthrope*.

2 **Work in pairs. Look at the underlined words in the sentences and discuss their meaning.**

1 He's quite <u>unassuming</u> and never seems to want any credit for all the wonderful work he does.

2 I <u>inadvertently</u> picked up someone else's suitcase in baggage reclaim and I don't have any of my own clothes.

3 I've never really liked watermelon juice – it's rather <u>insipid</u> if you ask me.

4 He was such a <u>nondescript</u> little man that no one would ever have imagined him capable of painting surrealist masterpieces.

5 'Does Joe have a girlfriend?' she asked, trying to look as <u>nonchalant</u> as she could.

6 A group of <u>disgruntled</u> students had occupied the main administration block.

3 **Match the underlined words in Activity 2 to meanings A–F.**

A without realising what you are doing

B without much taste

C behaving calmly and not seeming interested in anything or worried about anything

D annoyed or disappointed, especially because things have not happened in the way that you wanted

E very ordinary and not interesting or unusual

F showing no desire to be noticed or given special treatment

4 **Answer the questions. Then tell a partner about your answers.**

1 Have you ever felt disgruntled about conditions at your school or college or in your workplace?

2 What would you do if you inadvertently took something that belonged to someone else?

3 Are there any foods or drinks that you find insipid?

4 Can you think of any famous people who are actually rather nondescript?

5 Have you ever tried to appear nonchalant even though you were actually very curious about something?

6 Do you know anyone that you would describe as unassuming?

7 Have you ever misunderstood something someone said to you? What happened?

8 Would you agree that there is a lot of misleading information about health care on the internet? Can you think of any specific examples?

Review (Part 2)
covering key features
▶ **WRITING** REFERENCE p.176

1 Work in pairs and discuss the questions.

1 Do you normally read film reviews before you see a film? Do you ever read them afterwards?

2 Have you ever seen a film that the critics hated but you really loved or vice versa?

3 What information do you look for in a film review?

2 Look at these extracts from film reviews. Which extracts provide factual information? Which ones express negative opinions?

1 '.............., this was to be the last time the two friends would meet.'

2 '.............., the authors pride themselves on their exhaustive research while only mentioning one or two studies by other scholars.'

3 '.............., the lead, Tyler Swan, is from the south of the United States, though he doesn't have any trace of an accent.'

4 '.............., they were able to replace him with the absolutely stunning new talent, Kieran O'Halloran.'

5 '.............., the next time she directs, she will not have to deal with the bunch of miscast has-beens she was stuck with in this case.'

6 '.............., the script writer has not been able to reflect the detailed information about the invasion of Singapore we find in the novel.'

7 '.............., the disastrous performance finally came to an end and we were all able to head for nearby restaurants.'

8 '.............., a director of his calibre wanted to work with a more experienced cast.'

3 Match extracts 1–8 in Activity 2 to key features of reviews A–D.

A information about the writer, actors, director, etc.

B comments on the plot or contents

C critical comment on what the reviewer liked or disliked

D final evaluation

Vocabulary
sentence adverbs

4 Choose a sentence adverb from the box to add to each of the extracts in Activity 2.

Curiously   Happily   Hopefully   Ironically
Thankfully   Tragically   Understandably   Unfortunately

LANGUAGE TIP

Sentence adverbs are placed at the beginning to make a comment on the whole sentence. We use a comma after the adverb.
Clearly, she had difficulty remembering her lines.

---

5 Work in pairs. Look at the exam task and discuss which two films you would review.

You see this announcement in an international magazine called *Cinefilia*.

The most **uplifting** and the biggest **downer**

It's sometimes hard to choose a film that fits your mood purely on the basis of the poster or the description on the cover of the DVD. That's why we want to publish reviews of the most uplifting and the most depressing films our readers have seen, so that others know what to watch and what to avoid.

Send in a review which describes the most uplifting film you've ever seen and the one you found the biggest downer. Make sure you give reasons for your choices.

Write your **review** in **220–260** words in an appropriate style.

EXAM TIP

When you plan your review, think about what you are trying to achieve. You need to inform your readers so they can decide whether to see the film, read the book, etc. Don't tell them the whole plot.

---

6 Make notes about each of the films you chose using the features in Activity 3.

7 Write a draft of your review. Use sentence adverbs, substitution and ellipsis.

8 Show your draft to a partner to see what they like most about your review. Suggest any improvements, particularly to sentences where it would be better to use sentence adverbs, substitution and ellipsis.

1 Complete the sentences with the correct form of the verb in brackets.

1 I wish the papers .... (*stop*) reporting nothing but bad news. It's really depressing me.

2 It's high time you .... (*start*) taking more responsibility for your own well-being.

3 If only I .... (*realise*) the job was going to be so difficult! I would never have accepted it – I'd have kept my old job.

4 I love it here but I sometimes wish it .... (*not rain*) so much.

5 If only I .... (*get*) out of the habit of going to bed so late. I'm always so tired in the mornings.

6 I'd rather we .... (*not go*) out tonight. Let's stay in and watch a movie.

2 Choose the correct option to complete the sentences.

1 He was a genius in many ways but somewhat .... when it came to his very poor choice of friends.

   A misinterpreted   C misguided

   B misunderstood   D mistrusted

2 Much as I liked the first candidate, I do have some .... about offering her the job.

   A misgivings   C misinterpretations

   B misunderstandings   D misspellings

3 They live in a rather .... little grey house on the outskirts of town.

   A unassuming   C insipid

   B nondescript   D nonchalant

4 Some of the participants' names had been .... in the conference programme.

   A misspelt   C misled

   B misunderstood   D misinterpreted

5 The student representatives were more than a little .... about the school director's refusal to see them.

   A disturbed   C disillusioned

   B disgruntled   D disinclined

6 The idea that bread is fattening is a common .... that many people have.

   A misconception   C misprint

   B misinterpretation   D misgiving

3 Read the article below and think of the word which best fits each gap. Use only one word for each gap. There is an example at the beginning (0).

HOME	NEWS	SPORT	HEALTH	NATURE
FEATURES				#HAPPINES

Getting the measure of the happiest man on earth

Matthieu Ricard, 'the happiest man on earth', abandoned a successful scientific career **(0)** ~~to~~ become a Buddhist monk. Since **(1)** .... , this unassuming man has taken a host of stunning photographs of the Himalayas, acted **(2)** .... the Dalai Lama's interpreter and meditated for many thousands of hours.

According to Ricard, there are a number of misconceptions about meditation, the most common **(3)** .... being the idea that it's all about making the mind go blank. Instead, he explains, what we should be doing is learning to let our thoughts pass without holding on to **(4)** .... If Ricard himself is anything to go by, **(5)** .... is an approach which produces some fairly extraordinary results. When scientists recently measured the activity of the French monk's brain, they found that the parts known to generate positive emotions were far **(6)** .... active and highly developed in Ricard than they were in others, so much **(7)** .... that the scientists thought their equipment might be faulty. **(8)** .... wasn't. When it comes to measuring happiness, Matthieu Ricard is simply right off the scale.

4 Read the questions and choose the option that is not possible in each response.

1 Do you think Tina will come to the party?

   A She might.   B She might do.   C She might do it.

2 Are you and Max going to have a holiday this year?

   A We hope.   B We hope we are.   C We hope so.

3 Would your daughter like a drink?

   A No, thank you. She's just had it.

   B No, thank you. She's just had one.

   C No, thank you. She doesn't want one.

4 Were you thinking of coming into the office tomorrow?

   A No, but I can.   B No, but I can do.   C No, but I can be.

5 Which of your brothers is it who works as a scriptwriter?

   A The eldest.   B The eldest one is.   C The eldest one.

6 How many times have you been to Formentera?

   A Three.   B Three times.   C They are three.

6 Living with the past

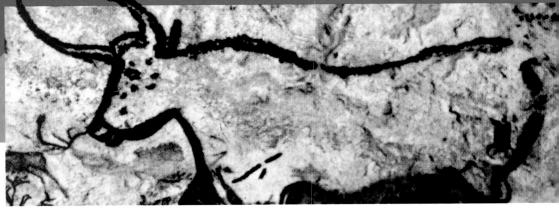

Word formation (Part 3)

▶ **EXAM** FOCUS p.179

1 **Work in pairs and discuss the questions.**

1 What do you think life was like 10,000 years ago?

2 Do you think people in the Stone Age were happier and less stressed? Why/Why not?

2 **Work in pairs. Read the article quickly and see how many facts about the mammoth you can remember.**

A MAMMOTH FIND

ZOOLOGISTS now believe that mammoths, which died out around 4,000 years ago, were driven to **(0)** _extinction_ by humans as well as by climate change.

EXTINCT

A mammoth, named Jenya after the eleven-year-old boy who made the astonishing find, is thought to be the most **(1)** .... preserved animal of its kind. A mammoth has not been found since 1901, so this finding has been extremely **(2)** .... for zoologists. Jenya's remains were excavated from the Siberian permafrost and taken to St Petersburg for **(3)** .... Tests show that Jenya was fifteen years old, two metres tall and weighed 500 kilograms, which makes it **(4)** .... smaller than other mammoths previously found. He also had a missing left tusk and it was this **(5)** .... that probably led to his death. He would have been **(6)** .... in fights with other mammoths or human **(7)** .... who were settling the Siberian marshes and swamps 20,000–30,000 years ago. So Jenya's death might have been the result of a **(8)** .... with an Ice Age man.

PERFECT
EXCITE
ANALYSE
CONSIDER
ABLE
POWER
HUNT
CONFRONT

3 **Which of the words in capitals in Activity 2:**

1 form a noun ending in the suffix *-tion*?

2 form an adjective with the suffix *-less*?

3 form the negative with the prefix *im-*?

4 **Read the article again. For questions 1–8, use the word given in capitals at the end of some of the lines to form a word that fits in the gap in the same line.**

5 **Work in pairs and discuss the questions.**

1 Why do you think many people are so fascinated by dinosaurs?

2 Do you think scientists should try to bring animals like mammoths back from extinction? Why/Why not?

EXAM TIP

Get into the habit of keeping an organised record of your vocabulary learning. Remember not just to record the meaning but also information about word formation (e.g. noun/adjective forms).

Multiple choice (Part 1)

▶ **EXAM** FOCUS p.181

6 ▶ 21 **You will hear three different extracts. For questions 1–6, choose the answer (A, B or C) which fits best according to what you hear. There are two questions for each extract.**

Extract 1

You hear two friends discussing an archaeological site in their town.

1 The woman finds it surprising that

A there are so few people working on it.

B residents were previously unaware of its existence.

C the excavation is making very slow progress.

2 How has the project changed their attitude to the town?

A It's given them a special connection with the past.

B It's made them curious about local history.

C It's given them a sense of pride in its unique character.

Extract 2

You hear two friends discussing a visit to a dinosaur exhibition at a natural history museum.

3 The man compares the exhibition with a video game in order to

A emphasise its failure as a piece of entertainment.

B explain its lack of appeal for young children.

C highlight its limited educational value.

4 They agree that the problem with the exhibition is that

A it only covered a limited period in history.

B the model dinosaurs were unconvincing.

C the information wasn't presented clearly.

Extract 3

You hear a brother and sister discussing the house they stayed in on holiday as children.

5 How did the woman feel when staying at the house?

A curious about previous inhabitants

B frustrated by the lack of modern comforts

C scared by stories she heard about it

6 They are hopeful that the new owner of the house will

A respect its character.

B hold a sale of its contents.

C convert it into holiday apartments.

7 **Which of the adjectives in the box can be used with the prefix _in-_? Which can be used with _un-_?**

accurate believable changed convincing covered discovered favourable informative modernised significant

1 **Work in pairs and discuss which of the quotes about history you agree with.**

1 'The distinction between the past, present and future is only a stubbornly persistent illusion.'
Albert Einstein

2 'We learn from history that we never learn anything from history.' *Georg Wilhelm Friedrich Hegel*

3 'Happy people have no history.' *Leo Tolstoy*

2 **Tick the comparative statements which are true for you and compare your opinions with a partner.**

1 Older generations are more interested in the past than our generation.

2 When I'm on holiday I'm as likely to visit a museum as a shopping mall.

3 I find it's less fun going to a museum by yourself.

4 I think the best way to learn about the past is by watching period dramas on TV.

Comparing

▶ **GRAMMAR** REFERENCE p.157

3 **Which of the phrases in the box can be used to modify the comparative statements in Activity 2?**

a bit   a great deal   a little   a lot   almost   (by) far
just   much   very much

LANGUAGE TIP

Like is used with nouns or gerunds to make comparisons. It means *similar to*.

*He's tall **like** his father.*
*Watching cricket is **like** watching paint dry.*

As is only used in comparisons in the phrases *as … as* and *not so/as … as*.

4 **Is there any difference in meaning between the phrases in italics?**

1 Museums are *no more/a bit more* expensive than they used to be.

2 *More people than ever/So many more people* are visiting museums than in the past.

3 *By far/One of* the most frequently visited museum(s) in the world is the Louvre in Paris.

4 Disabled access to museums is *no better than it was/ getting worse and worse*.

5 When I was younger, museums were *nothing like/ nowhere near as* crowded as they are now.

5 **Read the article. Does the writer approve of museums as places for entertainment?**

Museums as entertainment

The past three decades have seen a huge museum building boom all over the world. Museums are popular as **(1)** *ever/never* before. Visitors are now **(2)** *far more/so much* willing to stand in queues for hours in order to have **(3)** *the briefest/the briefer* of encounters with an old master painting. Some museums have been obliged to stay open round the clock to meet the demand. **(4)** *More than ever/ By far*, museum attendance is seen as a routine part of a modern lifestyle. Overall, the number of people visiting museums gets **(5)** *higher and higher/ just as high* each year. But are museums in danger of becoming just another leisure activity ending in yet another consumer opportunity at the museum shop? Does **(6)** *a great deal/far wider* accessibility inevitably mean a decline in the quest for serious reflection and deeper understanding?

6 **Read the article again and choose the correct alternatives.**

7 **Work in pairs and follow the steps 1–3.**

1 If you were asked to choose something worthy of representing your generation for a museum, what would it be? Think of an object and say what it would tell future generations about life today.

2 Present your museum object to the class.

3 Decide which would be the worthiest of the attention of future generations.

8 **Work in pairs. Turn to page 145 and do the activity.**

Long turn (Part 2)

comparing

▶ **EXAM** FOCUS p.183

1 ▶ **22** Look at the pictures and listen to the examiner. What three things do you have to do?

2 ▶ **23** Listen to Alessandra doing the task. Which of the pictures does she compare?

3 Tick the information about the pictures that Alessandra includes.

weather	possible reasons for the visit
nationality	historical significance of the place
location	what might happen next
clothes	how the people are feeling

4 Work in pairs and discuss Alessandra's answer. Is there anything you both agree/disagree with her about?

5 Listen again. Which of the words/expressions for comparing and contrasting do you hear?

Although   Having said that   However
Nevertheless   On the other hand
One significant difference is   Similarly
What both these photos have in common is
Whereas   Whilst

6 Compare the picture that Alessandra didn't discuss with one of the other pictures. Use some of the expressions in Activity 5.

7 Work in pairs. Turn to page 136 and do Task 1. Then turn to page 141 and do Task 2. Check whether your partner uses a good range of expressions for comparing and contrasting.

EXAM TIP

To give yourself the best opportunity to show what you can do, don't worry about the timing – just keep speaking until the examiner says *thank you*.

Multiple choice (Part 5)

▶ **EXAM** FOCUS p.179

1 **Work in pairs and discuss the questions.**

1 How much do you know about your ancestors?

2 Are you interested in finding out more about them? Why/Why not?

2 **You are going to read an article about a journalist called Lucy Kellaway and her investigation into her family history. For questions 1–6, choose the answer (A, B, C or D) which you think fits best according to the text.**

EXAM TIP

Mark the part of the text which gives the answer for each question and double-check that the option you choose both answers the question and matches what the text says.

1 Why did the writer accept the invitation by Ancestral Footsteps?

A She was tempted by the idea of a free holiday.

B She felt it would be relevant for her work.

C She thought it might be a good business opportunity.

D She wanted to discover why ancestor research was so popular.

2 What is the writer's opinion of the TV programme *Who Do You Think You Are*?

A She feels it doesn't help people to understand their true identities.

B She admits to secretly enjoying it despite disapproving of it.

C She fears it is only providing good publicity for celebrities.

D She suggests that it only presents a sensational view of history.

3 What does the writer say about her father's attitude to ancestor research?

A He thought it would always reveal unwelcome truths.

B He believed there was little to discover about his family history.

C He had resisted attempts to persuade him to find out more about it.

D He felt people should focus on building their own achievements.

4 When the writer saw the people doing family research at the National Archives, she

A was full of admiration for their dedication.

B was envious of their absorption in their task.

C became aware of what motivated them.

D started to share their enjoyment.

5 What was the writer's initial reaction to the information in the census about her ancestor called Amos?

A She was disappointed that his story had a predictable end.

B She was upset by his misfortune.

C She was proud of his achievements.

D She was concerned for the welfare of his wife and child.

6 In the final paragraph, the writer admits that she

A feels embarrassed about her feelings for her ancestors.

B has changed her mind about the attraction of ancestor research.

C regrets knowing so little about her family history.

D was surprised by her family's reaction to the story of Amos.

3 **Work in pairs. What do you find interesting about genealogy?**

Vocabulary

adjective/noun collocations

4 **Work out the meanings of the underlined compound adjectives in the article from the context. Compare answers with a partner.**

5 **Underline the nouns that collocate with the adjectives in italics.**

1 *a tailor-made*
trip   house   course   suit   service

2 *consumer-driven*
fashion   technology   money   design

3 *a high-minded*
person   school   ambition   reason   principle

6 **Match the adjectives in the box with the nouns to make collocations. Some adjectives can be used with more than one noun.**

close   common   direct   distant   early   extended   immediate   nuclear

1 a/an .... relative   2 a/an .... ancestor
3 .... family

7 **Use some of the collocations in Activity 6 to describe your family tree.**

DEAD interesting

Lucy Kellaway investigates her family history

Ancestral Footsteps, a travel company that organises exclusive tailor-made holidays to help people to investigate their family history, had offered to take me on a personal heritage tour. I'd accepted the invitation gladly, not because I had any particular interest in my forebears but because, as a journalist, I thought a story on genealogy would appeal to my readers. Genealogy, it seems, is big business. Genealogy tourism, combining holidays with ancestor hunts, is a rapidly growing sector in the travel market. A recent study by the University of Illinois argued that the trend is a response to our consumer-driven lifestyle – a search for connection and authenticity in an inauthentic world.

Maybe. But I think there's a more obvious cause at work: the runaway success of the BBC reality TV programme *Who Do You Think You Are?* The format, which has been copied in twelve countries, involves following famous people in search of their roots and watching their emotional reaction as they discover glorious and not so glorious facts about their ancestors. The show is good celebrity TV, with a nice bit of colourful social history thrown in, if you like that sort of thing. But the name of the programme is a bit of a sham. If we're being honest, we'll admit that who we actually are has nothing to do with our ancestors; it's down to our own personality, luck, circumstances, education and that of our parents.

I inherited my ancestor scepticism from my father who, unlike many Australians, couldn't care less about how his family had ended up in

Australia. When I told my dad I was going on a genealogical holiday, he quoted something his father used to say to him: 'It's more important to be an ancestor than to have them.' And he's right. Any bragging that begins with 'my great-great-uncle' is never going to go anywhere worthwhile. He brought my sister and I up to think that we should try to make something of ourselves and not dwell on the past.

As I awaited the results of my own ancestor research, I decided to research other people doing theirs. In the crowded upstairs room at the National Archives at Kew in south-west London, every desk was occupied by someone staring at a screen in a sort of rapture. I soon realised I'd got it all wrong. They were poring over microfiches with a focus more intense than any I've ever seen in any other library or anywhere else at all. For them, the fun isn't in the facts, it's in the hunting. With obvious delight, the woman nearest me explained that she'd just discovered an ancestor who'd been convicted of stealing.

Ancestral Footsteps arranged for me to meet my personal researcher, Jo Foster, in Dorset. Jo showed me a series of documents explaining how the Kellaways arrived in Australia: my great-grandfather's death certificate says that Alfred Charles Kellaway, son of Amos and Jane, was born in Dorset, England, and died in Australia. But the 1861 census reveals that while Alfred and Jane Kellaway were living

in Dorset, of Amos there was no trace at all. I tried instantly to resist the modern urge to apply psychobabble to explain Amos's disappearance. Would I have been able to forgive him for abandoning his family? But then I discovered that what actually happened was rather different. Ships' records recounted that my great-great-grandfather deserted ship in Sydney in 1857 to go in search of gold. He didn't find any. But he found New World riches of another sort. After six years in Australia, he had made enough money as a farmer for Jane and Alfred to sail out to join him. Their story ended happily ever after. The boy received an education and became a clergyman. His son, my grandfather, became a doctor, discovered a treatment for snakebite and lost all interest in his roots.

My father and sister predictably swallowed the story hungrily, forgetting all about their high-minded scruples. And although I still don't think of them as my family, I was more interested than I'd expected to be in the fate of Amos, Jane and Alfred and I'm only sorry I ignored them for so long. So who do I think I am now? The truth is that I'm not who I thought I was six months ago. I still maintain that who I am does not include deserting sailors and failed gold diggers. Time has washed them away. But it does include something less expected. Who I am now is a born-again ancestor bore.

1 Read the article. How does the writer feel about her national identity now?

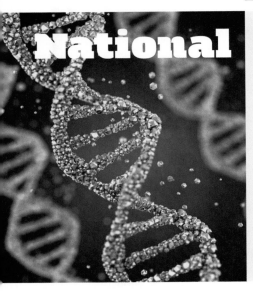

National IDENTITY

Discovering that you're not who you thought you were can be quite **(1)** .... (*settle*). I'd always assumed I was 100 percent British as all my grandparents came from the south of England and all had common British surnames. But the results of my DNA ethnicity test have revealed that I'm not as British as I thought I was. I'm actually 40 percent Irish, 20 percent Scandinavian, 11 percent Iberian and only 29 percent British. Although I was quite **(2)** .... (*amaze*) by this information, the results should have been fairly **(3)** .... (*predict*). I have blond hair and blue eyes, which explains the Scandinavian connection. And where I come from, there have been waves of migration from different parts of Europe over the centuries.

My **(4)** .... (*initiate*) reaction was to feel that it made absolutely no difference whatsoever, which is perfectly **(5)** .... (*understand*). Legally, I am a British national and that's all that matters. But gradually, my sense of cultural and national identity began to shift and I found myself gaining a more international perspective. I have also found it both extremely moving and quite **(6)** .... (*believe*) to discover distant cousins in places as far away as Canada and Australia who not only share my genes, but in a couple of cases, bear a striking resemblance to me.

2 Work in pairs. Would you consider doing a DNA test to discover more about your ancestry? What do you think people might be hoping to prove from the results of DNA tests?

Prefixes and suffixes

3 Complete the article with the correct adjective form of the words in brackets. Two of the adjectives require a negative prefix.

4 Which of the nouns in the box form an adjective ending in the suffix *-able*? Which form an adjective ending in *-ible*?

access belief change comfort comparison comprehension consideration denial excitement identity imagination movement notice profit resistance reverse variety vision

5 Which of the words in Activity 4 form a word with the opposite meaning with the prefix *un-*, *in-* or *ir-*?

6 Some words have two adjective forms. Choose the correct alternative in each sentence and say what the difference in meaning is.

1 Realising I have cousins in Australia is the weirdest feeling *imaginable/imaginative*.
2 This is an original and *imaginative/imaginable* idea.
3 The weather can be very *changing/changeable* at this time of year.
4 The quality of old black and white films is often *variable/varying*.
5 His grandfather's *exciting/excitable* moods were hard to deal with.
6 It's *comforting/comfortable* to be able to look at photographs of your childhood.
7 Consumers' *changing/changeable* attitudes are difficult to predict.
8 The film guide is selective – it's not intended to be *comprehensive/comprehensible*.

7 Work in pairs.

Student A: turn to page 145.
Student B: turn to page 147.

LANGUAGE TIP

Words beginning with *r-*, *m-* or *l-* take the prefixes *ir-*, *im-* or *il-* (not *in-* or *un-*).

irresponsible
immigration
illogical

Remember to double the initial consonant.

Modifying adverbs

▶ **GRAMMAR** REFERENCE p.157

1 Work in pairs. Look at the underlined examples of modifying adverbs. What is the purpose of the modifier? Does it make the adjective stronger or weaker?

I have found it both <u>extremely</u> moving and <u>quite</u> unbelievable to discover distant cousins in places as far away as Canada and Australia.

2 Which of the adjectives is ungradable (an 'extreme' adjective that can't be made stronger or weaker)?

awesome big disappointed enormous
furious good impossible perfect terrified

3 Which of the modifiers in the box cannot be used with the ungradable adjectives in Activity 2?

absolutely extremely practically pretty
quite really totally

LANGUAGE TIP

When *quite* is used with ungradable adjectives, it means 'completely', not 'fairly'.

*It's **quite** impossible.*

Some modifying adverbs collocate with certain adjectives.

bitterly/extremely NOT completely disappointed
perfectly/completely NOT seriously sure

4 Work in pairs. Tell your partner who or what makes you feel *absolutely awesome*, *extremely disappointed*, *quite furious*.

5 Read the article. How are false memories created?

6 Read the article again and choose the correct alternatives.

7 Answer the questions. Then compare your answers with a partner.
1 What is your earliest childhood memory?
2 How old were you at the time?
3 How reliable do you think this memory is?

8 With a partner, compare your early memories of
1 a trip to the dentist.
2 a holiday.
3 a birthday party.
4 your first day at school.

FALSE MEMORIES

Psychologists asked 127 people to recall four of their earliest childhood memories about which they were (1) *absolutely/seriously* sure. They were asked questions about specific details.

When the results were analysed, the researchers found that participants were much more likely to remember some sorts of details than others. It also turned out that many of these memories were found to be (2) *pretty/perfectly* unreliable.

Details such as what the participants were thinking at the time, the weather and their age were less likely to be recalled. The participants found it (3) *practically/seriously* impossible to remember certain information such as the time of day of an event or what they were wearing. However, what was (4) *extremely/totally* interesting was that the researchers discovered that in some cases (5) *completely/deeply* believable details had been added to a memory at a later stage. Possibly these may have been from accurate sources, for example, conversations with parents, family photographs and so forth. Or these details may have been inferred from other sources such as TV programmes or books and added in over a period of years, helping to create (6) *entirely/really* false details of the memory.

Essay (Part 1)
structuring an argument
▶ **WRITING** REFERENCE p.168

1 Work in pairs and decide on the three most important aspects of your country's cultural heritage. Think about buildings, archaeological sites, food, music, celebrations and books.

2 Look at the exam task and underline the key words.

> Your class has attended a lecture on the action governments can take to make sure cultural heritage is preserved for future generations. You have made the notes below.
>
> **Priorities for governments aiming to preserve cultural heritage**
> • increase funding for museums
> • protect old buildings
> • teach the importance of cultural heritage in schools
>
> **Some opinions expressed in the discussion**
> 'Cultural heritage isn't just about buildings – it's about a way of life.'
>
> 'It's the responsibility of the older generation to pass on cultural heritage to the next generation.'
>
> 'Museums are the best places to keep shared memories of a community.'
>
> Write an essay for your tutor discussing **two** of the priorities in your notes. You should **explain which priority you think is more important**, **giving reasons** to support your opinion.
>
> You may, if you wish, make use of the opinions expressed in the discussion but you should use your own words as far as possible.
>
> Write your **essay** in **220–260** words in an appropriate style.

EXAM TIP

It's important to provide specific examples to support your arguments.

3 Read the statements. Which ones do you agree with?

1 I would argue that it's unreasonable to expect governments to give more money to museums when they've got more important things to spend people's taxes on.

2 The problem is that because the government can no longer afford to maintain ancient monuments, it's become necessary to get support from corporate sponsors.

3 Perhaps retired people could offer to go into schools to share their memories and pass their knowledge on to younger generations.

4 I'm sure there are many voluntary organisations which would be prepared to work on conservation projects.

5 An urgent priority is for the government to provide training for teachers on teaching children about the importance of their cultural heritage.

6 For example, it may be that many people will choose not to speak to their children in the local dialect.

4 Decide whether the ideas in Activity 3 are main points (P) or supporting evidence (E).

5 Underline useful phrases in Activity 3 for giving main points and supporting evidence.

6 Choose which two priorities you will discuss in your essay. Plan your main points and supporting evidence.

7 Write your essay, including some of the phrases in Activity 3. Check for spelling and punctuation errors. Use the checklist on page 166 to help you.

1 Choose the correct alternative in each sentence.

1 The talk was *so/far* much more informative than I'd expected.

2 Most people would *much/more* rather go online than read a book.

3 It was *nowhere/nothing* like as impressive as I had imagined.

4 English is a *great/considerable* deal easier than Chinese.

5 It's by *far/much* the best film I've seen this year.

6 He's not interested in money *like/as* his father.

7 He's working harder than *ever/never* before.

8 Reality TV shows are getting *worst and worst/worse and worse*.

9 People are *just as/more* likely to visit a museum as go shopping.

10 It's easily the *simpler/simplest* of the suggestions I've heard so far.

2 Choose the correct option to complete the sentences.

1 He was .... serious when he suggested buying the castle.
   A bitterly   B deeply   C practically

2 I found the story .... believable.
   A totally   B considerably   C highly

3 It's .... incredible to think this building has been here for 800 years.
   A very   B absolutely   C virtually

4 Older people find it .... comforting to be able to talk about the past.
   A entirely   B totally   C extremely

5 The information is .... confusing – there are all sorts of contradictions.
   A rather   B perfectly   C practically

6 I'm not .... sure if the story is true.
   A extremely   B perfectly   C entirely

7 It's .... impossible to find anyone who remembers my great-grandfather.
   A extremely   B practically   C seriously

8 We found it .... unbelievable when we heard the good news.
   A quite   B practically   C seriously

9 She's been working so hard she's .... exhausted.
   A practically   B extremely   C completely

10 Luke's .... content to stay at home and look after the children.
   A perfectly   B seriously   C deeply

3 Complete the sentences with the correct form of the word in brackets.

1 Now is not the most .... (*favour*) climate for starting a new business.

2 He puts forward the most .... (*convince*) arguments I've ever heard – complete rubbish!

3 I think you have been .... (*inform*). All the tickets sold out months ago.

4 Peter should be a writer when he grows up – he's so .... (*imagine*).

5 Unfortunately, the fire caused .... (*reverse*) damage to the oldest part of the castle.

6 The only way to get to the site is on a footpath – it's .... (*access*) by road.

7 The news about the job losses was met with total .... (*believe*).

8 The story was reported .... (*accuracy*) by the press, who got all the basic facts wrong.

9 There are some accents I find .... (*comprehension*), especially when people speak too fast.

10 I hate it when people ignore you at parties and treat you as if you were .... (*vision*).

4 Complete the sentences with the words in the box. There are some words you do not need to use.

ambition course design person principles
reason school service suit technology trip

1 If I could afford it, I would take a tailor-made safari ....

2 It's rare to meet a politician who is acting out of high-minded ....

3 The most innovative products are not usually the result of consumer-driven ....

4 Wanting to help put an end to hunger in the world is a very high-minded ....

5 It would be interesting to see if you make more progress doing a tailor-made ....

6 The most high-minded .... I know doesn't care what people think.

7 The best advertising companies provide a tailor-made .... for each client.

8 The campaign group had a high-minded .... for objecting to the proposal.

Multiple-choice cloze (Part 1)

1 For questions 1–8, read the text below and decide which answer (A, B, C or D) best fits each gap. There is an example at the beginning (0).

Why Dutch children are so happy

The reason that Dutch children are regularly **(0)** *A, found* to be the happiest in the world is no surprise. Dutch parents have a healthy attitude towards their kids, treating them as individuals **(1)** .... of respect. They understand that achievement doesn't necessarily **(2)** .... to happiness. The Dutch have reined in the anxiety and stress of modern lifestyles and have redefined the meaning of success and well-being.

Sitting down to eat breakfast as a family is an **(3)** .... important part of Dutch family life. In **(4)** .... to American and British families, where breakfast is a meal that's often skipped in the rush to get out of the house on time, the Dutch are champions of breakfast time and seem to be happier and healthier because of it.

In the Netherlands, children also like going to school. Dutch children are among the least likely to **(5)** .... pressured by schoolwork and score **(6)** .... in terms of finding their classmates friendly and helpful. Parents **(7)** .... realistic expectations of their children and are not competitive about their achievements. Countries such as Britain, where children are less happy, should **(8)** .... inspiration from the Dutch example.

0	**A** found	**B** described	**C** viewed	**D** concluded
1	**A** suitable	**B** worthy	**C** justified	**D** rightful
2	**A** deliver	**B** fulfil	**C** realise	**D** lead
3	**A** absolutely	**B** entirely	**C** extremely	**D** utterly
4	**A** contrast	**B** opposition	**C** denial	**D** rejection
5	**A** experience	**B** feel	**C** admit	**D** act
6	**A** highly	**B** successfully	**C** hugely	**D** immensely
7	**A** make	**B** take	**C** have	**D** get
8	**A** follow	**B** grasp	**C** win	**D** gain

Open cloze (Part 2)

2 For questions 1–8, read the text below and think of the word which best fits each gap. Use only one word in each gap. There is an example at the beginning (0).

Failure leads to success

Success takes time, patience and commitment. **(0)** *In* the digital age of 'overnight' success stories, this hard graft is easily overlooked. **(1)** .... often than not, success is the result of months and years of consecutive all-nighters, involving trial and error and setback after setback. There is often nothing quite **(2)** .... failure to make people strive harder for success.

A worrying trend in some schools is the pretence that there are **(3)** .... winners or losers in school sports. It may be hard for children to accept failure but, equally, it's unfair not to encourage and reward talent. This applies **(4)** .... all subjects, including sport. Removing the competitive spirit from schools crushes the incentive to improve and does not prepare young people **(5)** .... the trials ahead. Instead, it would be so **(6)** .... more beneficial for children to be rewarded for their achievements and encouraged to try to improve **(7)** .... they fail to do their best. **(8)** .... must never be forgotten is that the sharp sting of failure can often be the motivation for children to strive for success.

Word formation (Part 3)

3 For questions 1–8, read the text below. Use the word given in capitals at the end of some of the lines to form a word that fits in the gap in the same line. There is an example at the beginning (0).

Stonehenge

Stonehenge is not only the most **(0)** <u>significant</u> prehistoric monument in the UK, it is also the most **(1)** .... It was built between 5,000 and 4,000 years ago and is formed of enormous stones in the shape of a circle.

SIGNIFY

IMPRESS

The biggest of the stones are 9 metres tall and weigh up to 40 tons. It is believed that these were brought from 32km away, a **(2)** .... distance in those days. The smaller 'bluestones' came from several sites in Wales and had to be transported even **(3)** ...., from a location 225km away. For centuries people have found it scarcely **(4)** .... that such an ambitious project could have been undertaken before the **(5)** .... of the wheel. One recent theory, which has generated a great deal of **(6)** ...., is that the stones were transported by the movements of glaciers. Others maintain that the stones were pulled by oxen over wooden tracks. Whatever the method used, one thing is **(7)** ....; such an undertaking would have required a great deal of determination and vision and the ability to come up with **(8)** .... ways of solving huge technical challenges.

CONSIDER

FAR

BELIEVE

INVENT

CURIOUS

DENY

IMAGINE

Key word transformation (Part 4)

4 For questions 1–6, complete the second sentence so that it has a similar meaning to the first sentence, using the word given. Do not change the word given. You must use between three and six words, including the word given.

Example:

We're going to camp whether or not it's raining.

EVEN

We're going to camp <u>even if it's</u> raining.

1 Many people resent having to pay so much tax.

WISH

Many people .... to pay so much tax.

2 Museums are far more interactive than they used to be.

NOTHING

In the past, museums .... interactive as they are now.

3 They should have told you by now whether your job application was successful.

HIGH

It's .... whether your job application was successful.

4 No-one could have imagined back then that Jake and Emma would get married.

IMPOSSIBLE

Back then, it .... to imagine Jake and Emma getting married.

5 Dan felt he should have worked harder at school.

REGRETTED

Dan .... harder at school.

6 The police wouldn't allow anyone into the street.

PREVENTED

The police .... the street.

7 The hard sell

Review of conditionals

▶ **GRAMMAR** REFERENCE p.158

1 Work in pairs. Have you ever been persuaded to buy something by a clever salesperson? What sales techniques do the following kinds of salespeople use?

- people selling mobile phones and computers
- people selling fashion clothing in boutiques
- people selling traditional handicrafts in a street market or bazaar

2 ▶ 24 Listen to the first part of a radio programme about sales techniques and answer the questions.

1 In what way is Majid different from the other rug sellers in the Tangiers kasbah?
2 What three different modes of selling does Majid use with his customers?
3 Would you buy something from a seller like this? Why/Why not? Discuss your answers with a partner.

3 Listen to the recording again and complete these sentences from the programme.

1 If you .... people to describe the archetypal salesperson, chances are the rug seller will come near the top of many lists.
2 If you .... upset, you lose the customer.
3 If I were a customer in someone else's shop, I .... friendly and polite.
4 If I hadn't treated him so well, he .... never .... bought a carpet.

4 Which sentence in Activity 3 refers to something that

A was not true in the past? C is true in the present or future?
B is not true in the present? D is always true?

5 Complete these sentences so that they are true for you and then compare answers with other students.

1 If I have a bit of free time this week, I …
2 If I could start my own business, I …
3 If I had the chance to live anywhere in the world for a year, I …
4 If I had been born fifty years earlier, I would probably …
5 If I were already able to speak another language completely fluently, I …

6 ▶ 25 **Listen to the second part of the programme. Why does the programme presenter think Apple's store design has been so successful?**

7 **Look at two sentences from the recording in Activity 6. Which parts of the conditional sentences refer to the present?**

1 If they could get them into the store, they had a chance of converting them.

2 If the other companies had moved on from their aggressive shark-like approach …, they would probably represent much stronger competition for Apple today.

LANGUAGE TIP

The most common type of mixed conditional is mixed third and second conditional.

*If I **hadn't bought** that expensive phone, I **would** still have some money left.*

A third conditional sentence can often convey the same idea.

*If I **hadn't bought** that expensive phone, I **would** still have had some money left.*

Conditionals of this type are often used to talk about things we regret.

There is a second type of mixed conditional which refers to an ongoing present state and an occurrence in the past.

*If you **weren't** so gullible, you **wouldn't have paid** so much for that carpet.*

Conditionals of this type are used when we want to stress the present circumstances.

8 **Complete the mixed conditional sentences. Then decide if it would be possible to express them using a normal third conditional sentence. Is there any change in meaning?**

1 If they .... (*do*) some more market research, they .... (*understand*) their customers better.

2 I .... (*be*) a better salesperson today if I .... (*have*) the benefit of better training in sales techniques.

3 If she .... (*be*) a more skilled salesperson, she .... (*made*) enough sales to keep her job.

4 If I .... (*not open*) the door to that nice salesman, I .... (*not be*) the happy owner of a brand new Whirlymix today!

5 The customer .... (*get*) in touch with you by now if she .... (*be*) seriously considering your offer.

6 If it .... (*be*) possible to try clothes on virtually, people .... (*stop*) bothering to go out to shop years ago.

9 **Tell another student about something you regret and what happened as a result. Talk about things you regret buying, saying or doing.**

Collocations: sales and marketing

10 **Work in pairs. What stereotypes do we have of people who sell used cars?**

11 **Read the article below about one of the world's most successful car salespeople. Why was his approach so successful?**

A very likeable super-salesperson

A man called Joe Girard held the title 'the World's Greatest Salesperson' for more than three decades after he retired. Girard was the number-one car and truck salesperson in the USA for twelve years running. Between 1963 and 1978 he sold a staggering total of 13,001 vehicles, all of them direct **(1)** .... sales to individual customers. In one year alone, he managed to sell 1,425 vehicles; that means he made four and a half sales every working day.

So how did he do it? Not with a highly sophisticated **(2)** .... strategy or advertising **(3)** .... as you might imagine. He simply believed wholeheartedly that he was selling the world's best **(4)** ...., namely, himself. Girard knew that customers buy from people they know, like and trust, so he focused most of his energy on establishing a **(5)** .... with potential customers and becoming likeable.

Of course, he used a variety of **(6)** .... techniques, one of which was to make sure people who had bought a car from him would never forget him. Once a month he sent them a letter. These arrived in plain envelopes, always a different size or colour so that they didn't look like junk **(7)** .... and get thrown away. All the letters said was 'I like you. Happy Fourth of July!' or whatever special day it happened to be. They were signed simply 'From Joe Girard.' Sending out 13,000 cards a month in the 1970s must have involved an enormous effort, but the payoffs came in repeat sales from **(8)** .... customers.

12 **Complete the article with the words in the box.**

campaign loyal mail marketing product
rapport retail sales

13 **Find two words in Activity 12 with silent letters.**

14 **How many collocations can you make with *sales*, *product*, *mail*, *business* and *customer*?**

1 Work in pairs and discuss the questions.

1 Which of the senses is most likely to evoke memories for you: sight, sound, smell, taste or touch?

2 Which of the senses are more frequently used in marketing?

3 How are they used?

Multiple choice (Part 3)

▶ **EXAM** FOCUS p.182

2 You will hear two marketing executives called Elena Vincent and Adam Carlisle talking about the use of the senses in marketing. Look at the questions in Activity 3 and underline the key words.

3 ▶ 26 Listen to the conversation. For questions 1–6, choose the answer (A, B, C or D) which fits best according to what you hear.

EXAM TIP

Look for words or phrases in the questions and options that summarise what is said in the interview.

1 Elena considers that her first job in the marketing industry was

A frustrating because she didn't have any marketing skills.

B satisfying because she was able to make a contribution.

C challenging because she had not done work like this before.

D boring because she didn't get to design any advertisements.

2 Elena says celebrities used in a campaign

A reacted in an unreasonable manner to the use of their photos.

B were too old to take part.

C shouldn't have allowed their photos to be taken.

D disliked being made to adopt particular poses.

3 Elena found a marketing course she took

A too demanding for someone with limited experience.

B potentially useful for someone working in sense marketing.

C of limited relevance to her current work.

D of lasting benefit for herself and her clients.

4 What does Adam say about his research into the psychological effects of scents?

A He lost interest in it after meeting his girlfriend.

B He worried that it would be used inappropriately.

C He felt discouraged that it was not being applied.

D He saw it as justified given the interest it was expected to generate.

5 Elena and Adam agree that scent marketing does not attract criticism if the scent used

A is directly connected to the product.

B is not overpowering.

C does not accentuate a naturally occurring smell.

D is associated with something people find attractive.

6 Elena believes that people who object to scent marketing on medical grounds

A aren't justified in complaining if the scent is undetectable.

B don't respond quickly enough to the dangers scents represent.

C have solid arguments against the use of scent marketing.

D are easily manipulated by scent marketing campaigns.

4 Listen again and match the words and expressions 1–6 to the meanings A–F.

1 coincidentally
2 put my heart and soul into
3 to great effect
4 was into
5 entice
6 fair enough

A successfully
B by chance
C liked and was interested in
D reasonable
E tried and made an effort
F persuade someone to do something by offering them something they want

5 Work in pairs and discuss the questions.

1 Do you think scent marketing should be more strictly controlled?

2 Do you have any favourite smells? What do they remind you of?

3 Would you choose the scent of cinnamon, lavender or vanilla to

• cheer you up if you were feeling lonely?

• wake you up if you were feeling drowsy?

• help you get to sleep?

Multiple-choice cloze (Part 1)

▶ **EXAM** FOCUS p.178

1 Work in pairs. What are the four tastes?

2 Read the article about a fifth taste quickly to find out what the taste is. Why didn't people see its potential until recently?

Life STYLE SELLING THE FIFTH TASTE

Until recently, if you had **(0)** _D. asked_ most people how many tastes existed, their answer would almost **(1)** .... have been four: sweet, salty, sour and bitter. Nowadays, however, more and more people **(2)** .... the existence of a fifth taste: umami. Umami has always been there, but it wasn't until 1907 that a Japanese chemist called Kikunae Ikeda **(3)** .... it a name. He had noticed there was a quality shared by foods as **(4)** .... from one another as asparagus and parmesan cheese, a quality he named umami, the Japanese word for 'delicious'. For many years, it was believed that human taste buds were **(5)** .... of detecting this fifth taste but it turns out that we can not only detect it, we go for it in a **(6)** .... way. Today, from the kitchens of the top avant-garde chefs to humble hamburger joints, umami-consciousness is making its **(7)** .... And it sells! You can now buy umami-flavoured paste in a tube at your local supermarket and if the advertising is to be **(8)** .... , try it once and you'll be back for more.

0	A questioned	B enquired	C quizzed	D asked
1	A absolutely	B certainly	C completely	D clearly
2	A acknowledge	B understand	C allow	D grant
3	A found	B put	C gave	D chose
4	A contrasting	B unalike	C different	D diverse
5	A incompetent	B incapable	C inefficient	D inexpert
6	A whole	B grand	C great	D big
7	A point	B mark	C claim	D grade
8	A believed	B considered	C credited	D assumed

3 Work in pairs. Look at the example (0) in the article and the answer, *asked*. Discuss why the other alternatives are not possible.

EXAM TIP

Try to work out what the options have in common and in what ways they might differ in terms of complementation patterns. For example, *question*, *quiz* and *enquire* are similar in meaning and are all followed by *about* but only *question* and *quiz* take a direct object.

4 Read the article again. For questions 1–8, decide which answer (A, B, C or D) best fits each gap.

5 Work in pairs. What kinds of foods do you find most tempting? What do you like about these foods: their texture or their taste?

Vocabulary

collocations with *go*

6 Look at the adjectives in the box and answer the questions.

bad bald bankrupt deaf
downhill grey hysterical mad
mouldy off salty sour tired

1 Which adjectives collocate with *go*?
2 What is the meaning of *go* in the collocations: *be*, *become* or *get*?

7 Replace the underlined words with the correct form of collocations from Activity 6.

1 Things have really <u>deteriorated</u> around here since you left – the sales figures have plummeted.

2 If you keep listening to such loud music, you'll <u>impair your hearing</u>.

3 Ugh, look at this bread! It's <u>grown a fungus</u>.

4 The company <u>didn't have enough money to pay its debts</u> and their shareholders lost a lot of money.

5 My friend's hair started <u>losing its original colour</u> when he was only twenty. It makes him look rather distinguished.

6 I think this mayonnaise might have <u>become too bad to eat</u> – it smells a bit strange.

7 My grandfather had <u>lost his hair</u> by the time he was fifty.

8 Our dog <u>gets very agitated</u> every time the postman comes.

1 Work in pairs. Think of brand names for products you use. Why do you think these names were chosen?

2 Read the article about brand names and how we perceive them. Were any of the reasons that you discussed in Activity 1 mentioned?

Gapped text (Part 7)

▶ **EXAM** FOCUS p.180

3 Read the first two paragraphs of the article and the paragraphs A–G that were removed. Look at the reasons a student gave for correctly choosing one of the missing paragraphs. Which of the missing paragraphs is the student referring to?

> 'The first paragraph ends with a question about what to call a car and the missing paragraph gives advice about choosing a name. The following paragraph also mentions things to consider when choosing a name. All three paragraphs address the reader directly using the second person.'

4 Read the article again and choose from the paragraphs A–G the one which fits each gap (1–6). There is one extra paragraph which you do not need to use.

EXAM TIP

Look for words and phrases in the options with connections to ideas and language in the sentences before and after each gap. For example, determiners such as *this* and *these*, near synonyms and antonyms.

5 Work in pairs and compare your answers. Give reasons for your choices similar to those the student gave in Activity 3.

6 Do words in your language fit this theory? Can you think of any examples?

A

The ancient Greek philosopher Plato observed that the 'r' sound seemed to him to represent rapid motion. Many others have commented on the correspondence between words meaning shiny or luminous and the combination of letters 'gl'. *Glitter, glow, glimmer* are examples.

B

The name needs to be memorable. Bear in mind that it will also need to be sufficiently different from any existing brand names to get through the trademark registration process.

C

Consonants signal certain meanings too. The sounds /**p**/, /**t**/ and /**k**/ all occur as the first letters of the world's most successful brand names. Just look at the most popular soft drink brands and you will see that this is true.

D

Juggling all these competing <u>concerns</u> is the challenge that marketers face when choosing a brand name for a new product. Failing to tick all the boxes can have disastrous consequences, in the most notorious cases even bringing about the brand's eventual demise.

E

In one study, subjects were asked to decide if two tables, one big and one small, should be labelled with the nonsense words 'mal' or 'mel'. Eighty percent of them identified the large table as 'mal' and the small one as 'mel'.

F

These successful brand names convince us that the ice-cream is creamier, the sports car zippier, the soft drink more refreshing or the mattress more comfortable than any others we might be considering.

G

Anthropologists have shown how we too use our voices and bodies to signal dominance and powerlessness. Sounds we produce at the front of the mouth make us extend our lips outwards. This is why photographers ask us to say 'cheese' rather than simply telling us to smile. A smile is friendly but also a sign of submissiveness.

Vocabulary
working out meaning from context

7 Look at the underlined words and phrases in the article and choose the correct meaning, A or B. Which clues did you use to help you?

1	concerns	**A** interests	**B** worries
2	terrains	**A** clients	**B** surfaces
3	sheer	**A** absolute	**B** translucent
4	host	**A** presenter	**B** multitude
5	intrinsic	**A** inherent	**B** hidden
6	hackles	**A** hair	**B** teeth

Sounds ...
speedy, creamy, refreshing and comfy

Think about a product. Let's say a car, in this case, one of those four-wheel-drive vehicles designed to cope with the roughest, rockiest, most challenging of <u>terrains</u>. What would you call a vehicle like this if you wanted to convey to your potential customers all the car's qualities: its resilience, <u>sheer</u> gutsiness and reliability?

1 You will have to steer clear of names that mean something potentially embarrassing or negative in another language. That said, your brand name should convey desirable qualities across language boundaries to people all over the world.

2 Presumably such a debacle would also put an end to the career of whichever marketing executive came up with a name that failed so dismally to appeal. When marketers get it right, however, they manage through a single word or a combination of two or three, to convey the presence of a <u>host</u> of desirable qualities and features.

3 But how can an invented word, often one that is apparently completely meaningless, transmit this kind of information? The short answer is that certain sounds have <u>intrinsic</u> meanings for us, meanings such as large or small, bright or dark, heavy or light. Contemporary linguists call this sound symbolism. The technical term may be new but awareness of these relationships is not.

4 Contemporary attempts to investigate these apparent connections scientifically have included research into the most frequent initial combinations of letters in successful brand names, and attempts to discover whether the same meanings are signalled across a range of languages and what a certain sound might symbolise.

5 This confirmed the hypothesis that the vowel sounds we make at the back of our mouth convey largeness while those we make at the front convey the opposite. We can find the same symbolic relationship between size and sound in the animal kingdom. Mammals and amphibians communicate an impression of size through their calls. Lower-frequency calls communicate large size and higher-frequency calls the opposite. Think of the low-frequency growl of an angry dog with his <u>hackles</u> raised, then think of the same dog frightened, submissive and whining or whimpering – both high-frequency sounds.

6 The work in linguistics, anthropology and animal biology shows that sounds in a brand inevitably signal certain qualities and these qualities should be those the product is supposed to possess. If we consumers pick up the signals, then we are more likely to choose that ice-cream, car, soft drink or mattress. Good news for the marketers, but if we want to resist their subtle powers we too can benefit from knowing how sound symbolism works.

Collaborative task and discussion (Parts 3 and 4)

agreeing and disagreeing

▶ **EXAM** FOCUS p.183

1 Work in pairs. Look at the pictures and discuss the questions.

1 What are they trying to say about advertising and its effects?

2 How useful do you think anti-advertising slogans like this are?

2 Look at the phrases in the box and find:

1 three ways of expressing complete agreement.
2 two ways of expressing complete disagreement.
3 one expression to use when you can't reach an agreement.
4 one expression for accepting someone else's point of view reluctantly.
5 one way of expressing partial disagreement.

Absolutely!   I can't argue with that, but …
I'm afraid I just don't see it like that at all.
Indeed it is.   I couldn't agree more.
Surely not!   That's not quite the way I see it.
We'll just have to agree to differ.

3 ▶ 27 Listen to two students doing the task in Activity 1. Tick (✓) the phrases in Activity 2 the students use. Note down their reasons for agreeing or disagreeing.

4 ▶ 28 Work in pairs. Look at the exam task and listen to the examiner. Discuss the advantages and disadvantages of each of the ways of promoting products and how effective you think each one would be.

using social networking sites

making a cool promotional video

How effective would these ways of promoting fashion products be?

sponsoring music festivals

giving free samples

using celebrities in print advertising

5 Now you have about a minute to decide which method would work best.

EXAM TIP

Try not to reach an agreement in the first part of your discussion. Wait until the examiner asks you to do this at the end of Part 3.

6 Work with another student and compare your answers. Give reasons for saying why a method would be effective or ineffective. Use some of the expressions in Activity 2 to express agreement and disagreement.

7 Work in groups of three. Turn to page 137 and do the activity.

Conditionals: advanced features

▶ **GRAMMAR** REFERENCE p.159

1 ▶ **29** Listen to part of a radio talk on 'stealth advertising'. What do you think of the techniques it describes?

2 Look at sentences A–D from the recording and find a word or phrase that

1 makes an event seem more hypothetical.
2 is an extremely polite form which is mainly used in writing.
3 makes a request less of an imposition.
4 makes a sentence sound more formal.

A If I were to learn that a friend was being paid to promote a product to me, I would be really angry.

B If you happen to be talking to your friends, can you just mention in passing that you use Lipluxe?

C Should you wish to make a complaint, we suggest you contact the Advertising Control Board.

D Had the company asked my friend's permission to use her blog to promote the product, she would never have agreed to it.

3 Change the meaning of the sentences following the instructions in brackets. Use the conditional forms in Activity 2.

1 If you inherited a lot of money, would you give up working? (more hypothetical)
2 If you require assistance, contact a member of staff. (extremely polite, formal and written)
3 If we had interviewed a larger number of people, we would have obtained more reliable results. (more formal)
4 If you see Joe, can you remind him to give me a call? (less of an imposition)
5 If your brother phones me in the next couple of days, I might be able to arrange an interview. (more hypothetical)

6 If I had known working as a journalist was so demanding, I would have done something else. (more formal)

4 Cross out the alternative that is NOT possible in each sentence.

1 *Unless the weather improves/If the weather doesn't improve/If the weather improves*, we won't be able to have the picnic.
2 I'd be really disappointed *if we didn't win/if we won/ unless we won* at least one gold medal.
3 You should try to get more sleep, *otherwise/if not/ unless* you'll exhaust yourself before the exams have even started.
4 *Provided/Supposing/What if* you don't manage to persuade anyone to sign up for the new phone service, what will you do then?
5 I have nothing against telemarketing, *provided that/ as long as/supposing* the people who phone you are willing to take no for an answer.
6 *In the event of/In case of/If* fire, do not use the lifts.

5 Think of a moral or ethical dilemma relating to advertising. Write your dilemma using one of the new conditional forms in Activity 2. Then exchange with another student and discuss your dilemmas.

Example: Supposing you were asked to promote a product on your blog, what would you do?

Report (Part 2)
formal language
▶ **WRITING** REFERENCE p.174

1 Look at the extract from a survey on attitudes to advertising. Respond to the questions and compare your responses with other students.

Advertising *survey*

For each statement, write **Agree**, **Disagree** or **Neither**

1 I like to look at most of the advertisements I am exposed to.

2 Most advertising insults my intelligence

3 In general, I feel I can trust advertising.

4 Products usually live up to the promises made in their advertisements

5 In general, I like advertising.

2 The survey in Activity 1 was conducted with a large group of people. Look at the results on page 145. Then read the report below. Does it give an accurate account of the results? How could you improve the answer?

Attitudes to advertising

The first question asked respondents about their experience of looking at advertisements. While a little more than a third expressed dislike, the rest gave either neutral or positive answers. Strange as it may seem, although there were many positive responses to the first question, nearly half the participants in the survey regard advertising as an insult to their intelligence. This apparent contradiction between positive and negative attitudes is reflected once more in the responses to the next two questions. On the one hand, many of those surveyed mistrusted the advertisements they saw. On the other hand, they considered that they provided an accurate picture of the qualities of the products they purchased.

Conclusion

Notwithstanding a lack of trust and a feeling of being patronised, many of those whose opinions we sought have a positive attitude to advertising overall.

3 Read the report again and underline

1 four formal ways of expressing contrast between two results or points of view.

2 four formal phrases referring to the people who answered the questionnaire.

3 two formal words for *think*.

EXAM TIP

Use headings to help you plan and structure your report.

4 Look at the task and some ideas a candidate wrote down while preparing her answer. What headings do you think the candidate used in her report?

An international market research company has asked you to write a report on advertising in your country. The company that has commissioned the report wants to know about the most common approaches used and how consumers respond to them. You are also asked to suggest changes to current approaches or alternative approaches which you believe would be more effective.

Write your **report** in **220–260** words in an appropriate style.

- telemarketing? advertising hoardings? junk mail? TV advertising? internet pop-ups? giveaways in magazines?

- contrast telemarketing with giveaways in magazines

- contradiction in responses to both: hate telemarketing but buy products/like giveaways (but suffer from giveaway overload)

- better training of telemarketers; fewer, better quality giveaways

5 Look at the model report on page 174. Use the ideas in Activity 4 or your own ideas to write your own report. Use headings, formal ways of expressing contrast and synonyms to refer to 'consumers'.

1 Complete the second sentence so that it has a similar meaning to the first sentence, using the word in brackets.

1 I don't have much money, so I probably won't go on holiday this year.

If .... , I would go on holiday this year. (*more*)

2 She didn't get very good marks in the exam, so she didn't get a scholarship.

She would have got a scholarship if .... marks in the exam. (*better*)

3 We'll have to save up if we want to be able to afford a new car.

We won't be able to afford a new car .... up. (*unless*)

4 I can't play the piano very well because I only studied it for a year.

Had .... than a year, I would be able to play better. (*longer*)

5 Buy one, get one free.

If .... get one free. (*can*)

6 I was born in Australia, so I have to apply for visas for some countries.

If I hadn't been born in Australia, it .... for me to apply for visas for some countries. (*necessary*)

7 Supposing you saw a friend shoplifting in a supermarket, what would you do?

If .... a friend shoplifting in a supermarket, what would you do? (*were*)

8 Please feel free to contact me if you require any further information.

Please feel free to contact me .... any further information. (*should*)

2 Choose the correct option to complete the sentences.

1 Smell this milk – I think it might have .... off.

A turned   **B** become   **C** changed   **D** gone

2 That restaurant has really gone .... – the food's terrible now.

A downturn   **B** downtown   **C** downhill   **D** downside

3 Olive oil is on special .... at the supermarket.

A bargain   **B** offer   **C** discount   **D** sale

4 She has a wonderful .... with all her students.

A rapport   **B** empathy   **C** sympathy   **D** identification

5 Have you seen the latest .... figures?

A selling   **B** sales   **C** sale   **D** sold

6 The company .... bankrupt in 2012.

A went   **B** turned   **C** got   **D** became

3 Read the article below and decide which answer (A, B, C or D) best fits each gap.

Therapy

TIME TO STOP SHOPPING?

Were you aware that clothes are the most rapidly **(1)** .... waste item in the UK? Our wardrobes are **(2)** .... of things we seldom wear either because they don't fit us anymore or because we've been **(3)** .... that they're no longer in fashion. Rather than having them **(4)** .... so they do fit or look more up-to-date, we simply go out and buy more. It's not surprising that this overindulgence is now being tackled **(5)** .... by people who suggest we should either stop shopping altogether or go on a temporary 'shopping fast'. For example, you might set yourself the **(6)** .... of not buying anything for six months or even a year. For those who really can't stand the **(7)** .... of having nothing new to wear, there's always the possibility of **(8)** .... your clothes with friends. Why buy two expensive outfits for two special occasions held on different dates when you could share?

1	**A** raising	**B** developing	**C** growing	**D** mounting
2	**A** full	**B** filled	**C** crowded	**D** occupied
3	**A** induced	**B** influenced	**C** persuaded	**D** swayed
4	**A** changed	**B** fixed	**C** mended	**D** altered
5	**A** front-on	**B** head-on	**C** face-on	**D** right-on
6	**A** aim	**B** focus	**C** promise	**D** target
7	**A** concept	**B** plan	**C** notion	**D** thought
8	**A** getting	**B** taking	**C** swapping	**D** giving

8 Passing through

Sentence completion (Part 2)

▶ **EXAM** FOCUS p.181

1 Work in pairs. Think of three reasons for and against using a guidebook during a trip.

2 Look at the exam task in Activity 3. Try to think of some possible answers for questions 2 and 4.

3 ▶ 30 You will hear a travel writer called Tim Cole talking about travel guidebooks. For questions 1–8, complete the sentences with a word or short phrase.

TRAVEL GUIDEBOOKS

Tim describes a time when he ended up at a **(1)** .... instead of a hotel.

Tim recommends checking the **(2)** .... of a guidebook before buying it.

Tim believes that the advice on **(3)** .... can be particularly unreliable.

Tim dislikes guidebooks which contain an excessive amount of **(4)** .... because he thinks these aren't useful.

Tim says he prefers not to use digital travel guides because he finds **(5)** .... difficult.

Tim would only like to have the kind of digital guidebook that he calls **(6)** '...' for each trip.

The app Tim used in Hawaii gave him access to information from someone who works as a **(7)** ....

The most memorable experience Tim had in Hawaii was swimming in a **(8)** .... at night.

4 Work in pairs. What places have you been to that haven't lived up to your expectations?

Reported speech

▶ **GRAMMAR** REFERENCE p.160

5 Choose the correct alternative in each sentence to report what Tim said about guidebooks.

1 Tim told people *not to believe/he didn't believe* everything they read in guidebooks.

2 He said that people *don't check/didn't use to check* the date of publication.

3 He said he *wouldn't buy/hadn't bought* a guidebook which had lots of pictures.

4 He said he *couldn't/wouldn't* use a digital guidebook.

5 He was told by a local that he *should visit/had visited* the Ukulele Festival.

6 He says that without local recommendations he *might have missed/might miss* swimming with manta rays.

6 ▶ 31 Work in pairs. Listen and summarise what the speakers say.

7 Choose the correct alternative in each sentence. In which sentences are both alternatives possible?

1 Mia told Matt that her trip to Thailand *had been/was* amazing.

2 Matt asked if Mia *could/can* recommend a guidebook.

3 Mia says *she'll/she'd* never use a guidebook again.

4 Mia said she's considering relying on Twitter recommendations next time she *was travelling/is travelling*.

5 Mia offered to show Matt her photos of Thailand *this/that* evening.

8 Match comments A–E to sentences 1–5 in Activity 7.

A No tense change should be made because the information is still true.

B You only need to make tense changes when referring to a past event if it happened a long time ago or the information is out of date.

C Some modal verbs always change in reported speech.

D You need to make changes to time references if the information is being reported at a later date.

E It isn't necessary to make tense changes if the reporting verb is in the present tense.

LANGUAGE TIP

That is often omitted when it is followed by a subject pronoun.

She said (that) she was hungry.

9 Read the travel tips and complete the reported statements 1–6.

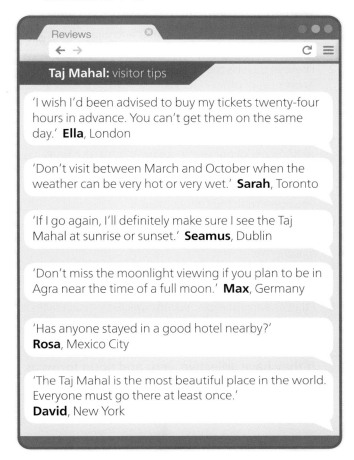

Reviews

Taj Mahal: visitor tips

'I wish I'd been advised to buy my tickets twenty-four hours in advance. You can't get them on the same day.' **Ella**, London

'Don't visit between March and October when the weather can be very hot or very wet.' **Sarah**, Toronto

'If I go again, I'll definitely make sure I see the Taj Mahal at sunrise or sunset.' **Seamus**, Dublin

'Don't miss the moonlight viewing if you plan to be in Agra near the time of a full moon.' **Max**, Germany

'Has anyone stayed in a good hotel nearby?' **Rosa**, Mexico City

'The Taj Mahal is the most beautiful place in the world. Everyone must go there at least once.' **David**, New York

1 Ella said she .... to buy her tickets 24 hours in advance.

2 Sarah told people .... between March and October when the weather can be very hot or very wet.

3 Seamus said if he .... the Taj Mahal at sunrise or sunset.

4 Max said that if you .... in Agra near the time of the full moon, you .... the moonlight viewing.

5 Rosa asked .... in a good hotel nearby.

6 David said the Taj Mahal .... and that everyone ....

10 Work in pairs and plan an itinerary for a visitor to your city or region. Then swap partners and give your recommendations to another student, who should then report what you said to his/her partner. Give recommendations on

- what to visit.
- when to travel.
- tourist traps to avoid.
- managing on a tight budget.
- getting off the beaten track.

1 **Choose the correct alternative in each sentence. Then tick (✓) the ideas you agree with and compare answers with a partner.**

1 I think visiting famous landmarks encourages a *respectful/respected* attitude to the past.

2 I believe travel is the best way to develop an *aware/awareness* of other cultures.

3 I don't find the idea of luxury holidays in remote locations at all *resistant/irresistible* – I'd rather camp.

4 Taking a selfie in a famous location is *symbolic/symbolically* of our search for meaning in our lives.

5 It's always *worthless/worthwhile* making an effort to understand local customs and traditions – that way you appreciate the culture more.

6 I prefer not to eat in touristy places. I prefer restaurants where locals eat because they are more *authentic/inauthentic*.

7 I always buy postcards of places I visit as a *remind/reminder* of where I've been.

8 I think having *unexpected/unexpectedly* experiences is the best thing about travelling.

2 **Look at the words in italics in Activity 1. Check if they have adjective, verb and noun forms as well as any negative prefixes that can be used with them.**

Word formation (Part 3)

▶ **EXAM** FOCUS p.179

3 **Read the article. Do you agree with the writer's attitude towards souvenirs?**

SOUVENIR HUNTING

The idea of souvenirs comes from *memento mori*: religious objects which were supposed to heighten people's **(0)** *awareness* of the spiritual world. *Memento mori* is actually a Latin phrase meaning 'Remember you will die'. Like *memento mori*, souvenirs also act as **(1)** .... but of happy events such as holidays and celebrations.   **AWARE**   **REMIND**

It's the **(2)** .... nature of souvenirs, such as fridge magnets and plastic miniature statues, which make them so **(3)** .... for tourists, who are looking for things which are cheap and easily **(4)** ....   **SYMBOL**   **RESIST**   **TRANSPORT**

Because they're often mass-produced in a far-off land, they can lack **(5)** .... For this reason, many people consider them to be **(6)** .... but for the people who buy them, their artistic or monetary value is **(7)** ....   **AUTHENTIC**   **WORTH**   **RELEVANCE**

However, unique souvenirs which you may come across **(8)** .... are always precious. My mother's favourite souvenir, for example, is a seahorse which my father found on the beach on their honeymoon.   **EXPECT**

4 **Read the article again. For questions 1–8, use the word given in capitals at the end of some of the lines to form a word that fits in the gap in the same line.**

EXAM TIP

Make sure you read the text all the way through to get a general understanding before trying to do the task.

5 **Work in pairs and discuss the questions.**

1 What kind of souvenirs do you like buying for yourself or your friends?

2 Describe the last souvenir you bought or were given.

3 What souvenirs are typical of your country/city/region?

Long turn (Part 2)

speculating (2)

▶ **EXAM** FOCUS p.183

1 Work in pairs. Look at the pictures and decide what they have in common and in what way they are different.

2 What do you think the instruction for this task might be?

3 ▶ 32 Listen to the examiner's instructions and see if you were right.

4 Add to the list of things that you can talk about for these photos.

> • what is being sold
> • where the pictures were taken
> •
> •
> •

EXAM TIP

In this part of the test you are being invited to speculate. Try to use a variety of phrases for doing this – don't keep repeating the same ones.

5 ▶ 33 Listen to a candidate doing the task. Does she include all your ideas in Activity 4?

6 Choose the correct expression for speculating and then complete the sentences with your own ideas.

1 I *would/must* imagine that most people who travel to a new country …

2 I doubt *whether/for* most tourists …

3 It's not certain in either picture *whether/which* the people are …

4 I *wouldn't/couldn't* say if they're buying …

5 In *all/any* likelihood, they …

7 Work in pairs. Turn to page 137 and do Task 1. Then turn to page 141 and do Task 2.

8 Work in pairs. Turn to page 147 and do the activity.

Cross-text multiple matching (Part 6)
identifying attitude and opinion
▶ **EXAM** FOCUS p.180

1 **Work in pairs and answer the questions.**

1 What do you think the difference is between an expatriate (expat) and an immigrant?

2 How much of a problem are these things for people working abroad temporarily? Which would be the most difficult thing to cope with?
 • being cut off from your roots
 • maintaining a sense of cultural identity
 • experiencing culture shock
 • finding a sense of belonging
 • overcoming the language barrier
 • maintaining relationships at home

2 **Work in pairs and read extracts from articles about expats in New York. Which of the issues in Activity 1 are mentioned by writers A–D?**

3 **Look at the underlined words and phrases in Text A (1–4). Match them to descriptions A–D below.**

A an opinion about something stated as fact
B an adverb of attitude
C an expression for giving opinions
D an impersonal phrase for making a recommendation

4 **Find four examples of adverbs of attitude and two impersonal phrases for making recommendations in extracts B–D.**

5 **Read the extracts again. For questions 1–4, choose from extracts A–D. The extracts may be chosen more than once. Which writer**

1 regards the attitude of New Yorkers to newly arrived expats in a different way to writer A? `1 [ ]`

2 holds a different view to the others about the way to deal with language differences? `2 [ ]`

3 feels differently about returning to their country of origin to writer D? `3 [ ]`

4 expresses a similar view to writer C about how some expats underestimate the challenges they will face? `4 [ ]`

6 **Work in pairs. Find the highlighted words and phrases in the extracts and answer the questions.**

1 Do you think relationships with friends need to be *nurtured*? (Text A)
2 What other changes in life may seem like a *daunting prospect*? (Text B)
3 What kind of experiences do you find *liberating*? (Text B)
4 How important is it to try and *blend in* when you're in a new situation? (Text C)

7 **Work in pairs. How far do you agree with the statements from the extracts?**

1 Technology has made it possible to maintain ties with friends and family across oceans and time zones.

2 The best thing about leaving your old life behind is that you are free to reinvent yourself.

EXAM TIP

You need to identify different ways in which writers express their attitude and opinions. Opinions are not only expressed through expressions such as *to my mind* or *in my experience*. To discover the writer's attitude, you also need to look for opinions stated as facts, adverbs of attitude and impersonal phrases for making recommendations.

EXPATS IN NEW YORK

Four journalists reflect on the experience of being an expat in New York.

A Adjusting to life in New York can seem overwhelming for newly arrived expats. Any hopes of fitting in seamlessly are misplaced. The language barrier is **(1)** unquestionably the easiest part to deal with, as long as you manage to dispense with your accent as soon as possible. Far worse are the initial culture shock, the homesickness and the realisation that the average New Yorker is entirely indifferent to the challenges recent arrivals face. But really all this should not be an issue. The polite detachment of New Yorkers **(2)** should be of no consequence because technology has made it possible to maintain ties with friends and family across oceans and time zones. **(3)** It's worth making the effort to do this because then it will be possible to slip effortlessly back into your old life when the time comes. Unlike immigrants, expats do not expect to make New York their home long term. **(4)** To my mind, there isn't the same need to nurture new relationships.

B Adapting to life in a new city, country and culture needn't be such a daunting prospect. Many expats find the experience liberating and may even come to dread the moment they have to leave. The best thing about leaving your old life behind is that you are free to reinvent yourself because New Yorkers won't judge you. Refreshingly, they probably won't take any notice of you at all. They'll merely treat you as an object of curiosity for the way you speak, regardless of what you have to say. So one thing you will have to put up with is your new identity as a foreigner. It can't be avoided, so it's best to embrace and even celebrate your 'charming' or 'cute' manner of speaking.

C Many expats from English-speaking countries arriving to work in New York mistakenly assume that blending in will be easy. After all, they speak the language and they're already familiar with the culture (even if that's only through a diet of American TV series such as *Friends*). This over-confidence can prompt something of an identity crisis and precipitate an inevitable yearning for familiar faces and places, once it becomes clear that many New Yorkers regard native English speakers in the same cold light as any other expat. But perversely, this is to be welcomed. Otherwise, you might find yourself, in your desperation for friendship, tagging on to people that you would have nothing to do with back home. Most people end up picking up an American accent, vocabulary and expressions but those who resolutely refuse to change will find their accent becomes a topic of conversation wherever they go.

D Most expats in New York lose the sense of being a stranger quite quickly, but try as they might to act and even speak like a native New Yorker, they'll never be taken for one. Life becomes routine, yet there's always the comforting thought at the back of their minds that this existence is transient and that one day they'll be able to return home. New Yorkers sense this and, understandably, aren't interested in forming a friendship that is ultimately going nowhere. This distance can be hurtful at first. Far from forming lifelong bonds, socialising for most expats is reduced to a series of disappointing casual encounters, compounding a sense of loneliness and isolation. It takes people a little while before it eventually dawns on them that true acceptance by New Yorkers will have to be earned over a minimum of five years – way too long for someone on a two-year contract, already dreaming of the warm welcome awaiting them at home.

Describing trends

1 Work in pairs and check you understand the meaning of the underlined words/phrases.

1 The population of New York City <u>reached a peak</u> in the year 2000.

2 The number of people living in New York <u>remained relatively stable</u> from 1900 to 1950.

3 The number of people moving out of New York <u>overtook</u> those moving to the city during the 1950s.

4 New York experienced a <u>brief dip</u> in its population after 1950.

5 The <u>decrease</u> in the number of people leaving New York for the suburbs continued until 1980.

6 There is expected to be a <u>steep fall</u> in the population of New York between 2020 and 2030.

2 ▶ 34 Listen to part of a radio programme with an economist and decide if the statements in Activity 1 are true (T) or false (F).

3 Which words in the recording match meanings 1–4?

1 a lot (two words)

2 a little (one word)

3 go up (four words)

4 go down (two words)

4 Work in pairs. How do you think the population trends in New York City compare to where you live? What do you think it would be like to emigrate? What would you miss about home?

5 Complete the text with the words in the box.

decline dropping overtaken peak risen sudden

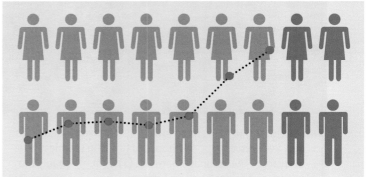

POPULATION SURVEY

A recent survey has revealed that the city's population has **(1)** .... unexpectedly. After a period of slow population **(2)** ...., with increasingly larger numbers of young people leaving to find jobs in the bigger metropolitan areas, the number of people settling in the city has **(3)** .... those leaving for the first time in six years. Over 7,000 more people arrived in the city last year than left, which brings the total population to just under 319,000. This **(4)** .... rise is welcome news for some local schools where pupil numbers had been **(5)** .... The trend is likely to continue but researchers don't expect the population to reach its former **(6)** .... of 350,000.

6 Work in pairs. Make some predictions about future trends where you live. Then compare your predictions with another pair. Think about

- population growth.
- immigration.
- emigration.

7 How do you think the predicted trends for your country compare with worldwide trends?

Verb patterns with reporting verbs

▶ **GRAMMAR** REFERENCE p.161

1 **Cross out the verb(s) which CANNOT be used to complete each reported statement.**

1 The government *admitted/reminded/denied/accepted* that immigration was rising.

2 The president *insisted/persuaded/warned/urged* people not to emigrate.

3 The doctor *claimed/admitted/regretted/denied* having to leave his country to find work.

4 The student *claimed/denied/insisted/reminded* that he wanted to get work experience abroad.

5 The immigration officer *advised/encouraged/requested/denied* the man to renew his visa.

6 The lawyer *blamed/accused/claimed/denied* the witness of not being entirely truthful.

7 The unemployed man *blamed/accused/forgave/warned* the government for not providing enough jobs.

8 The politician *objected/regretted/consented/accepted* to being asked about the high unemployment rate.

2 **Look at the examples in Activity 1. Which of the verbs can be followed by**

1 *that* + clause?
2 *-ing*?
3 object + infinitive?
4 object + preposition + *-ing*?
5 *to + -ing*?

3 **Look at the statement. Then match the reporting verbs with one or more of the verb patterns.**

'There are lots of opportunities here; you should emigrate too,' Louis told his brother.

1 Louis suggested/recommended …
2 Louis advised/urged/encouraged/invited …
A his brother to emigrate.
B that his brother should emigrate.
C emigrating to his brother.
D that his brother emigrate.

4 ▶ 35 **What did the speakers actually say? Change the sentences into direct speech. Then listen and compare.**

1 Orla admitted that there was no alternative to her emigrating.

2 Una reassured her mother that she was fine.

3 Sean regretted leaving home to set up a business abroad.

4 Conor blamed the government for not creating enough employment.

5 Ryan's dad encouraged him to stay in Australia.

6 Keira claimed that emigrating was the best decision she'd ever made.

Impersonal reporting verbs

▶ **GRAMMAR** REFERENCE p.161

5 **Which of the sentences sounds more formal and official? In which types of text would you be likely to find it?**

1 Everyone believes that there aren't enough opportunities for young people.

2 It is believed that there aren't enough opportunities for young people.

6 **Tick (✓) the statements you agree with and discuss with a partner. Then rewrite the underlined words using an impersonal reporting form and the verb in brackets.**

1 Everyone is sure that the number of young people moving abroad to work will increase. (*accepted*)

2 Recent studies seem to show that young migrant workers find culture shock more difficult to deal with than the language barrier. (*suggested*)

3 People think that having access to social networking sites makes it easy to stay in touch with friends and family. (*claimed*)

4 Most people believe that young people with good qualifications will be able to find well-paid work abroad. (*expected*)

5 Most people used to think that young people would have the same standard of living as their parents. (*assumed*)

6 Some people have been saying that it's better to have qualifications from a university abroad. (*argued*)

7 **Work in pairs and think of some facts about language learning. Present them to the class using impersonal reporting verbs.**

Proposal (Part 2)
using an appropriate style

▶ **WRITING** REFERENCE p.174

1 **Look at the exam task and think about what information you need to include in the proposal, why you are writing it and who it is for.**

> Your college has been invited to participate in an exchange programme with colleges in other countries. You see this notice in the library.
>
> *The college would like to find out whether students would be interested in participating in an exchange programme with colleges in other countries. Students are invited to send in a proposal outlining the possible benefits of the exchange programme and suggesting ways it could be promoted. The proposal will help the college to decide whether to accept the invitation to join the exchange programme.*
>
> Write your **proposal** in **220–260** words in an appropriate style.

2 **Organise your ideas under the headings.**

1 Introduction
2 Benefits of the exchange programme
3 Ways to promote the exchange programme
4 Recommendations

3 **Which of the recommendations are written in an appropriate style for a proposal?**

1 I think it would be a great idea if people who've already been on an exchange programme could give a talk to other students about it.

2 It is recommended that the college should hold an open day to give information about the exchange programme to students and their parents.

3 The college should certainly accept the invitation to join the exchange programme as it would provide a great opportunity for students to gain valuable skills and experience.

4 The college would be able to offer students a place on an exchange programme as early as next year.

5 You'd think students would grab this chance but a lot of them are too lazy.

6 It is doubtful whether there would be sufficient funding available to sponsor all students in the college interested in participating and it is suggested that the college would only be able to offer some funding to the most disadvantaged students.

4 **Which of the language features below would be suitable to use in a proposal?**

1 use of the pronouns *I* and *you*
2 impersonal reporting verbs
3 phrases for speculating
4 passive forms
5 reporting verbs
6 contractions

5 **Write your proposal for the exam task in Activity 1 OR for the task below.**

> Your college currently doesn't provide enough support for students planning to spend time studying in another country. You see this notice in the library.
>
> *The college is planning to introduce a special course for students planning to spend time studying in another country. The college principal invites students to send a proposal outlining any problems students may face when studying abroad and suggesting ways in which the course could address these problems. A decision can then be made about what to include on the course.*
>
> Write your **proposal** in **220–260** words in an appropriate style.

6 **Work in pairs. Read your partner's proposal and make suggestions for ways it could be improved.**

1 Choose the correct option to complete the sentences.

1 My boss .... me to apply for a promotion.
   A recommended   **B** advised   **C** suggested

2 The applicants were .... to arrive early.
   A warned   **B** recommended   **C** encouraged

3 The tourist .... to missing out the museum.
   A claimed   **B** objected   **C** insisted

4 The student .... that he hadn't finished his essay on time.
   A admitted   **B** blamed   **C** accused

5 The teacher .... the student not to be late.
   A warned   **B** objected   **C** recommended

6 The journalist .... the politician of not being honest.
   A blamed   **B** regretted   **C** accused

7 The hotel manager .... that there would be more jobs available in the summer.
   A urged   **B** doubted   **C** encouraged

8 My aunt .... on paying for our trip to Paris.
   A admitted   **B** announced   **C** insisted

2 Complete the second sentence so that it has a similar meaning to the first sentence, using the word in brackets.

1 'I think it would be best for Sam to travel by bus,' said Mia.

   Mia .... by bus. (*recommended*)

2 It is predicted that the population will not fluctuate in the short term.

   It is predicted that the population .... in the short term. (*stable*)

3 The number of visitors to the museum was at its highest point in June.

   The number of visitors to the museum .... June. (*peak*)

4 The demand for luxury travel fell last year.

   There .... for luxury travel last year. (*drop*)

5 People claim that the government hasn't built enough new homes for migrant workers.

   The government .... enough new homes for migrant workers. (*accused*)

6 You have to have such a good knowledge of the city to be a tour guide.

   You .... the city to be a tour guide. (*knowledgeable*)

3 Complete the article with the words in the box.

drop expected growth increasing lower
overtaken rise steadily

One **(1)** .... trend in tourism is the 'digital detox': hotel packages which offer gadget-free holidays. This trend has been rising **(2)** .... in popularity over the last few years. It indicates a significant **(3)** .... in demand for quality family time. Another expected area of **(4)** .... is the luxury shopping package, which has seen large numbers of Asian tourists flock to Europe to take advantage of the **(5)** .... taxes and favourable exchange rates. Demand for luxury shopping trips has **(6)** .... demand for cultural tourism in the large European cities, with tourists citing shopping as their main purpose for travelling. It is **(7)** .... that the luxury shopping market will continue to grow as there is no sign of a(n) **(8)** .... in demand for these products.

4 Choose the correct alternative in each sentence.

1 Many people whose grandparents emigrated from the countryside to the city are cut *off/out* from their roots.

2 It can be very hard for immigrant communities to *manipulate/maintain* a sense of cultural identity.

3 I experienced culture *stress/shock* when I moved from a small village in Scotland to Hong Kong.

4 It's important for everyone to find a sense of *belonging/background* in the community where they live.

5 Once you overcome the language *bridge/barrier*, it's so much easier to make friends.

6 Some people don't want to *assimilate/accept* into the host culture.

9 Reading the mind

Open cloze (Part 2)

▶ **EXAM** FOCUS p.178

1 **Answer the questions. Then discuss your answers with other students.**

1 Which do you think has more impact on intelligence: nature or nurture?
2 Do you think babies are born knowing certain things (e.g. about language) or are their brains more like the hard drive of a new computer?

2 **Read the article about what babies know. Why did researchers in the 1980s think babies understood the laws of physics?**

3 **Read the article again. For questions 1–8, think of the word which best fits each gap. Use only one word in each gap.**

EXAM TIP

Before you decide on how to fill a gap, check that the word isn't being used in combination with other words in an unexpected way. For example, you might expect *look* to be followed by *at* but when you read on you might see that *into* or *through* are the required prepositions.

N E W S

Reading babies' minds

It used to **(0)** *be* thought that babies knew a lot more than they actually do.
In the 1980s, researchers conducted experiments where babies were shown images that appeared to defy the laws of physics. The babies stared **(1)** ....
apparent disbelief, as if they had just seen something completely mind-boggling.
But it turns **(2)** .... that this wasn't because the babies understood physics
(3) .... because they were learning something new.

Whether you show a baby an unusual occurrence involving an unfamiliar object,
a familiar object in an odd situation or an unfamiliar object in a normal setting,
the baby will do exactly the **(4)** .... thing.

It would seem that babies react by staring fixedly at absolutely **(5)** ....
they haven't seen before. They stare **(6)** .... a short time and then they
look away. Babies do this because they are learning and, having learnt what is new
for them, have **(7)** .... further reason to go on looking. So babies know
(8) .... whatsoever about physics – they just know how to learn.

Expressions with *brain* and *mind*

4 ▶ 36 **Work in pairs. Put the developmental milestones in the order that a child learns to do them. Then listen to the extract from a radio programme and check.**

- recognise familiar faces
- learn to put on her own clothes
- know her own name and respond to it
- enjoy hiding games
- try to be a help
- return a smile

5 **Listen again and note down the phrases the speaker uses for each of the milestones in Activity 4.**

Example: return a smile – smile back

6 **Look at the words in the box and answer the questions.**

boggling child damage drain reader scan storm teaser wash wave

1 Which words can be used in compound nouns, verbs or adjectives with *brain*?

2 Which words can be used with *mind* to complete sentences A and B?

A I always found maths completely .... when I was at school.

B You must be a .... ! How did you know I was going to say that?

7 **Complete the sentences with compound nouns or verbs from Activity 6. Change the form if necessary.**

1 The current lack of research funding is leading to a ...., with some of our country's best scientists being forced to go abroad to continue their work.

2 The design for the new centre was the .... of Stephanie Wilson but it was finally built several years after she retired.

3 Initially, the doctors feared she had suffered permanent .... but, if anything, she seemed more intelligent after the accident.

4 Why don't we try and .... some ideas for the new TV series?

5 I didn't think we would be able to go to the party but then I had a .... and realised I could invite everyone to our house.

6 I love doing .... like cryptic crosswords and Sudoku.

7 The group have been accused of .... members and persuading them to donate all their money.

8 She was having such terrible migraines that the doctor suggested she had a .... to find out what was wrong.

8 **Work in pairs and discuss the questions.**

1 What might have happened to you if a friend said, 'Never mind!'?

2 If you give a friend some advice and she says she will bear that in mind, has she accepted your advice?

3 If you offer someone a drink and they say, 'I wouldn't mind,' do they want one or not?

4 Why might someone say, 'Mind your language!'?

5 Why might you begin a sentence with, 'Mind you, ...'?

6 What kind of question might you begin with, 'If you don't mind my asking, ...?'

LANGUAGE TIP

Collocations are adjectives, verbs and nouns that frequently occur together to create phrases, e.g. *make an effort, tell the time, bear something in mind*. It's always worth looking at the examples in a dictionary so that you can see the way a word combines frequently with other words. Using collocations will make your English sound more natural.

On the crest of a brainwave

NEUROIMAGING TECHNOLOGY developed in the 1990s allowed researchers to monitor brain activity for the first time. Psychologists **(1)** were aiming to find out how acquiring new skills, such as speaking a foreign language, **(2)** could affect the structure of the brain. They assumed that these changes **(3)** would not take place at the same rate in older people and wanted to find out **(4)** if there was an optimal age for learning a language.

Back in the 1990s, the current developments in neuroimaging technology **(5)** would have been impossible to imagine but today scientists are teaching people to use brainwaves to actually control electronic devices. It will soon be possible to change the TV channel simply by thinking you would rather watch something more interesting and there are even efforts to create systems that will allow us to have our thoughts appear in a smartphone message without even having to type.

The benefits of developments like these might seem trivial, but for those who are unable to communicate through speech, they represent a major breakthrough. Rosemary Johnson, a young violinist who suffered brain damage in an accident three decades ago, thought **(6)** she was never going to be able to make music again. Now, thanks to the latest developments in neuroimaging technology, she is able to use her brainwaves to direct other musicians to play the sequences of notes she wants to hear. Rosemary can, once again, communicate through music as she did before.

1 Read the article and find two uses of brainwave technology.

2 Work in pairs. Can you envisage any possible unethical uses of neuroimaging technology? Do you think the benefits outweigh the potential dangers?

Future in the past

▶ **GRAMMAR** REFERENCE p.161

3 Look at the underlined verbs in the article. Are they referring to a future plan or a prediction about the future that was made in the past?

4 Rewrite the first paragraph of the article as if it were the 1990s. What changes do you need to make?

Example: Neuroimaging technology developed recently allows researchers to monitor brain activity for the first time. Psychologists …

LANGUAGE TIP

The future in the past is often used to talk about a change of plan or to make excuses for things you haven't done.

Scientists were planning to study/would have studied/ were going to study what happens to the brain when people are deprived of sleep for a week but they decided the experiment was/would be unethical.

5 Choose the correct alternative in each sentence.

1 The government *was considering/would consider* banning drones but has decided not to.

2 I was sure my mum *was going to be/would have been* angry when I lost my phone but she was OK about it.

3 I never dreamt that I *was winning/would win* the lottery. I still can't believe it.

4 We *would hope/were hoping* to get tickets but they've all just sold out.

5 The lesson *would have been/would be* cancelled but too many students had already arrived.

6 When I set off for work this morning, I had no idea it *was going to take/was taking* three hours to get there.

6 Work in pairs.

Student A: turn to page 147.
Student B: turn to page 145.

Long turn (Part 2)
paraphrasing
▶ **EXAM** FOCUS p.183

1 Work in pairs and look at the pictures. How often, if ever, do you play a game, go to the cinema or eat in a restaurant alone?

2 ▶ 37 Listen to an examiner giving candidates instructions about the pictures. What does he ask the first candidate to do?

3 Work in pairs. Take it in turns to choose two of the pictures and talk about them, following the examiner's instructions.

4 ▶ 38 Listen to a candidate talking about two of the pictures. Does she compare the same pictures as you did? Does she follow the examiner's instructions?

5 Listen again and complete the sentences with words and expressions which have a similar meaning to *on their own*.

1 There is a young boy ...., watching a film in a cinema.

2 … whatever it is he is watching and perfectly happy to be there ....

3 He's got a huge container of popcorn ....

4 In the second picture, a man is having a(n) .... meal in a restaurant.

5 … he's feeling a bit self-conscious about being a .... diner.

6 In a fast food restaurant people probably wouldn't even notice whether people dining were .... or with friends.

6 ▶ 39 Listen to the question the examiner asks the other candidate and the candidate's response. What does the examiner ask? Does the candidate respond effectively?

7 Work in pairs. Turn to page 138 and do Task 1. Then turn to page 142 and do Task 2.

EXAM TIP

Try to paraphrase any vocabulary the examiner uses in the instructions rather than repeating their actual words.

1 What can you remember about your first day at primary school and your first teacher? Compare your answers with a partner.

2 Here are some comments people made about things they found difficult in primary school. Did you find any of these things particularly easy or difficult?

- It took me ages to be able to tell the time on an analogue clock.
- We had to memorise loads of stuff. That was really hard.
- I couldn't tie my shoelaces properly myself.
- I don't know why but I sometimes couldn't understand what I read or what the teacher explained to us.
- I hated reading aloud. I used to hide behind my friend so the teacher wouldn't pick me.

Gapped text (Part 7)

▶ **EXAM** FOCUS p.180

3 You are going to read an article about a woman who had learning difficulties in primary school. Read the text and the missing paragraphs quickly. Which of the difficulties you discussed in Activity 2 are mentioned?

4 Read the article again. Six paragraphs have been removed from the article. Choose from the paragraphs A–G the one which fits each gap (1–6). There is one extra paragraph which you do not need to use.

EXAM TIP

Read the whole text so that you have an understanding of its meaning and structure before trying to fill the gap.

Vocabulary
working out meaning from context

5 Complete the sentences with the correct form of the underlined words and phrases in the article and missing paragraphs.

1 The government's attempts to deal with the problem of youth unemployment have been a .... failure.
2 Scientists have made a major .... in the treatment of cancer.
3 She has .... a method for quicker communication between the offices.
4 I don't think she .... that joke I told.
5 The legal system rests on the .... that a person is innocent until proven guilty.
6 The project was eventually .... as a non-starter after over six months' work.

6 Tell a partner about something you had difficulty learning. Why do you think you experienced this difficulty? Did you overcome it?

A

She started devising exercises for herself to develop the parts of her brain that weren't functioning. She drew 100 two-handed clock faces on cards and wrote the time each told on the back. Then she started trying to tell the time from each. She did this eight to ten hours a day, gradually becoming faster and more accurate.

B

On the one hand, she was brilliant, with near-total auditory and visual memory. 'I could memorise whole books.' On the other hand, she was a dolt. 'I didn't understand anything,' she says. 'Meaning just never crystallised. Everything was fragmented, disconnected.'

C

She occasionally came across a boy she knew during these study vigils but if he had any of the problems Arrowsmith-Young experienced, they certainly weren't of the same order. He, in fact, went on to get top marks in all his subjects.

D

Encouraged by the progress she had made, Arrowsmith-Young developed more exercises, for different parts of her brain, and found they worked too. Now almost thirty, she was finally beginning to function normally.

E

Faced with little receptivity for her ideas, Arrowsmith-Young decided to found her own school in Toronto in 1980; she now has thirty-five such schools. Thousands of children dismissed as impossible to teach have used Arrowsmith-Young's exercises and gone on to academic and professional success.

F

The breakthrough came when she was twenty-six. A fellow student gave her a book by a Russian neuropsychologist. The book contained his research on the writings of a highly intelligent Russian soldier, who had been shot in the brain during a battle and recorded in great detail his subsequent disabilities.

G

The bullet had lodged in a part of the Russian's brain where information from sight, sound, language and touch is synthesised, analysed and made sense of. Arrowsmith-Young began to realise that, in all probability, this was the region of her own brain that had been malfunctioning since she was born.

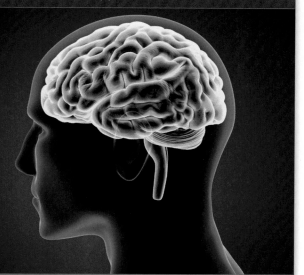

How to rebuild your own brain

It's not the kind of thing you would ever forget. When Barbara Arrowsmith-Young started school in Canada in the early 1950s, her teacher told her mother – in her presence – that she would never be able to learn. Having helped over 4,000 children overcome exactly the same diagnosis, now she can laugh at it. But she didn't at the time. Today Arrowsmith-Young holds a master's degree in psychology and has published a groundbreaking book called *The Woman Who Changed Her Brain*. But until she was in her mid-twenties, she was desperate, tormented and often depressed. She didn't know what was wrong.

1 In exams, she sometimes got 100 percent but whenever the task involved reasoning and interpretation, she would fail <u>dismally</u>. 'The teachers didn't understand,' she says. 'They thought I wasn't trying and I was often punished.' To help her, her mother <u>devised</u> a series of flashcards with numbers and letters and, after much hard work, she achieved literacy and numeracy of a sort, even getting into university, where she disguised her learning disabilities by working twenty hours a day. 'I used to hide when the security guards came to close the library at night, then come back out and carry on.'

2 For the first time, Arrowsmith-Young says, 'I recognised somebody describing exactly what I experienced. The injured man's expressions were the same: living life in a fog. His difficulties were the same: he couldn't tell the time from a clock, he couldn't tell the difference between the sentences *the boy chases the dog* and *the dog chases the boy*. I began to see that maybe an area of my brain wasn't working.'

3 The realisation led her to continue her reading, this time with the work of Mark Rosenzweig, an American researcher who found that laboratory rats given a rich and stimulating environment developed larger brains. Rosenzweig concluded that the brain continues developing rather than being fixed at birth – a concept known as 'neuroplasticity'. Arrowsmith-Young decided that if rats could grow bigger and better brains, so could she.

4 'I was experiencing mental exhaustion like I had never known,' she says, 'so I figured something was happening. After three or four months of this, it really felt like something had fundamentally changed in my brain. I watched an edition of a news programme and I <u>got</u> it. I read pages from ten books and understood every single one. It was like stepping from darkness into light.'

5 Her approach was revolutionary. 'At that time,' she says, 'all the work around learning disabilities involved compensating for what learners couldn't do. It all started from the <u>premise</u> that they were unchangeable.'

6 'So many wrong diagnoses get made,' says Arrowsmith-Young. 'So many children get <u>written off</u>, so many people make wrong decisions and end up in lives and careers they did not choose for themselves but were chosen for them by cognitive limitations that can be identified and strengthened. There is hope for these people.'

1 Work in pairs. Look at the comments about forgetfulness. Which ones apply to you?

Without reminders on my mobile, I think I'd forget half the things I have to do. I've got a memory like a sieve.

I never forget a face. Names? Well, that's another matter.

If I'm very busy, I can be quite absent-minded. I leave my keys at home and things like that.

I remember what I choose to remember and forget the rest.

Multiple matching (Part 4)

▶ **EXAM** FOCUS p.182

2 Work in pairs. Look at Task 1 below. Discuss how the consequences of being forgetful might arise and how the problem might be overcome.

3 Look at Task 2 and the strategies people use to overcome forgetfulness. Are they good strategies? Can you improve on them?

4 ▶ 40 You will hear five short extracts in which people are talking about being forgetful. While you listen you must complete both tasks.

Task 1

For questions 1–5, choose from the list (A–H) what each speaker's forgetfulness led to.

A causing disappointment
B having to pay a lot of money
C feeling embarrassed
D being misunderstood
E losing a friend
F failing to achieve something
G provoking an angry reaction
H experiencing anxiety

Speaker 1	1
Speaker 2	2
Speaker 3	3
Speaker 4	4
Speaker 5	5

Task 2

For questions 6–10, choose from the list (A–H) how each speaker intends to overcome their forgetfulness.

A keeping a record in a diary or notebook
B doing a memory improvement course
C trying a technique others recommend
D accepting the need to pay more attention
E recalling how the information was learnt
F translating into another language
G getting support from technology
H leaving reminders in unlikely places

Speaker 1	6
Speaker 2	7
Speaker 3	8
Speaker 4	9
Speaker 5	10

5 Work in pairs.

Student A turn to page 145.

Student B turn to page 147.

6 Work in pairs. Tell your partner about something you forgot, what happened as a result and how you would avoid forgetting something like that again.

Future in the past: advanced features

▶ **GRAMMAR** REFERENCE p.162

1 Which of the phrases in the box can be used to replace the underlined phrases in the sentences? Do you need to make any other changes?

was/were about to	was/were due to
was/were meant to	was/were thinking of

1 I <u>was going to</u> call you last night but then I realised I'd forgotten your number.

2 We <u>weren't supposed to</u> know what the scientists were trying to find out. It would have ruined the experiment.

3 I was told the train <u>would be leaving</u> at 10.30 but it was over half an hour late.

4 We <u>were going to</u> invite Clara to the cinema but she's already seen the film.

5 I had no idea that she <u>was going to</u> make such a terrible mistake.

6 He didn't know it at the time but he <u>would</u> become world-famous.

2 Look at the examples and answer the questions.

1 *Ella was to have got married last June.*
Did Ella get married last June?

2 *They were to have finished the report by Tuesday.*
Does this mean the same as 'They didn't manage to finish the report by Tuesday.'?

3 *The institute was to close within the year.*
Does this mean the same as 'The institute would close within the year.'?

4 *Three thousand language students were to take part in the study.*
Did people expect that 3,000 language students would take part in the study?

3 Complete the sentences using *was/were to* and the correct form of the verb in brackets.

1 They .... (*leave*) this morning but the flight's been cancelled.

2 No one had thought she was particularly intelligent but she .... (*go on*) to produce some of the greatest writing of her generation.

3 The study of babies' ability to recognise languages .... (*publish*) in a major scientific journal but the authors decided to make it available online instead.

4 Employees .... (*inform*) about the company's decision by letter but they've heard nothing yet.

5 We .... (*sign*) the contract this afternoon but there's been a delay.

6 The psychologist .... (*become*) a member of a major neuroimaging project in the USA but eventually she decided to continue to live and work in Europe.

4 Complete the second sentence so that it has a similar meaning to the first sentence, using the word given. Do not change the word given. You must use between three and six words, including the word given.

1 He was to finish the project by today.
SUPPOSED
The project .... by today.

2 The research paper was to be published this week.
DUE
The researchers .... their research paper this week.

3 They were to tell us today if we'd won the competition.
BEEN
We .... today if we'd won the competition.

4 I was going to ask you for some advice.
THINKING
I .... your advice.

5 It was almost closing time but the shop assistant let us into the shop.
ABOUT
The shop .... but the shop assistant let us in.

6 We were going to invite Sarah but we knew she'd be away.
WOULD
We .... but we knew she'd be away.

LANGUAGE TIP

Was/Were to is often used in formal writing instead of *would*.

He *was to* become famous for his work on neurophysiology.

Email (Part 2)
adopting the right tone

▶ **WRITING** REFERENCE p.172

1 Read the blog entry about a woman's experience of learning Spanish. What advice in the blog do you agree or disagree with?

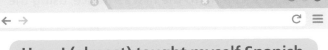

How I (almost) taught myself Spanish

I just can't live without books. It was hard to get hold of English books in Spain, so what I did was to teach myself to read. I used to listen to the news on the BBC in the morning and then buy *El País* and read the same news again in Spanish. I also started re-reading some novels I'd read years before in English. I resisted the temptation to look up every word I didn't recognise and tried to work out what the unfamiliar words meant in the context. I tried to remember them and to use them as soon as I could in a conversation to test out whether they really did mean what I thought they meant. Sometimes I got it wrong, though. I was reading a novel set in Peru and I kept using this very colloquial Peruvian vocabulary from the novel. People thought it was hilarious, especially with my very English accent. But my total immersion approach was only getting me so far. I decided to enrol in a language course. It was a great way of meeting people, though we did end up speaking English a lot of the time outside class.

2 Read the blog again. Do you think the style is formal or informal? Why?

3 Read the pieces of advice and decide if they are formal (F) or informal (I).

1 You would be well advised to invest in a good dictionary.

2 Get yourself a Spanish boyfriend!

3 If I were intending to learn another language, in all likelihood, I would enrol on a course.

4 I would suggest reading as widely as possible.

5 Spending a week living with a Spanish family is worth a try.

6 Something that I found really useful was joining a club where I had to speak to people.

7 I would not recommend trying to learn the language entirely on your own.

8 What seems to work for a lot of people is learning pop songs.

4 Do you agree with the advice in Activity 3? Rewrite the formal items in a less formal tone.

5 Look at the exam task and the points a student has written for her answer. The points are not in a logical order. Put them in the right order to make a coherent plan for a six-paragraph email message.

> Read part of an email from a friend who is planning to come and live in your country.
>
> > Of course, I'd really need to learn the language. I know you've been learning English for years, so you've had loads of experience. Are there any tricks of the trade that might help me pick up your language a bit more quickly?
>
> Reply to the email message offering your friend some advice. Write your **email** in **220–260** words in an appropriate style.

Points for inclusion:
- Express the hope of having been of some assistance.
- Make a series of suggestions about learning my language drawing on my own and others' experience.
- Express pleasure about friend's plans to relocate and reiterate the question in the email.
- Conclude with the wish to receive a reply and the usual salutation.
- Comment briefly on my experience of learning English.
- Acknowledge receipt of the message and apologise for not writing before.

6 The student has used very formal language in the list of points. Use the points to help you write a draft of your email message but make sure you use an informal tone.

7 Show your answer to other students and see if they can suggest any improvement.

1 Read the conversation and choose the correct alternatives.

A: Hi, Angie – have you managed to get tickets for the festival yet?

B: I **(1)** *was planning/would be planning* to but it completely slipped my mind

A: So who are you going with?

B: Well, Belinda **(2)** *was meant to be coming/was about to come* with me but she says she has to revise for an exam, so I **(3)** *was due ask to/was going to ask* around and see if anyone else **(4)** *would have been/would be* interested.

A: Well, I'd be interested.

B: Would you? I thought you **(5)** *were to work/were babysitting* this weekend.

A: I **(6)** *was supposed to/was about to* but then my sister changed her mind about going away so I'm free.

B: Great! Well, I'll try and get tickets again later. Can you send me a text to remind me? You know how forgetful I am.

A: I heard that Summer **(7)** *would have played/were due to play*.

B: No, I don't think so. That was just a rumour. There **(8)** *would have been/was going to be* something about it on the website by now.

2 Cross out the alternative that is not possible in each sentence.

1 Advertising seems to be *brainwashing/brainstorming* people into thinking they have to be thin.

2 None of the doctors could work out why he had lost his eyesight, so they sent him for a brain *scan/wave*.

3 I found the explanation of the new mathematical theory completely *mind/brain* boggling.

4 *Brainchild/Brainteaser* of legendary rock producer Eddie Bond, The Mitfords' new album is everything fans were hoping for.

5 You must be a *mind/brain* reader. Vegetarian lasagne was exactly what I was thinking of cooking for dinner and you've bought all the ingredients.

6 Now the former minister for science wants not only to keep local talent at home but to reverse the brain *drain/damage*.

3 Read the text below. Use the word given in capitals at the end of some of the lines to form a word that fits in the gap in the same line.

A team-building TASK

I recently signed up for a weekend course to develop **(1)** .... skills **LEADER**
and the ability to work in a team. I'd been **(2)** .... for a couple of **EMPLOY**
months when I heard about the course. Even though I knew it was a good
idea to do something like this, the night before I started to feel really
(3) .... about it and was actually thinking about cancelling my **EASY**
(4) .... I'm really glad I didn't. **REGISTER**

The course involved playing a series of problem-solving games in which the
only way we could find a **(5)** .... was by working as a team. In one of **SOLVE**
these games we had to work as two groups of four, each standing on a space
about a step apart. There were four people on one side and four people on
the other with an **(6)** .... space in the middle. Working **OCCUPY**
(7) .... , we had to organise ourselves so that all the people on the **COLLABORATE**
right-hand side of the extra space ended up on the left-hand side and vice
versa. There was quite a bit of **(8)** .... but we managed to carry out **CONFUSE**
the task quite successfully in the end.

Multiple-choice cloze (Part 1)

1 For questions 1–8, read the text below and decide which answer (A, B, C or D) best fits each gap. There is an example at the beginning (0).

Srinivasa Ramanujan

Srinivasa Ramanujan, possibly the **(0)** _A_ _greatest_ mathematical genius of the last century, was born in Tamil Nadu, India. He came from a poor family and did not go to university but he developed his own individual way of writing formulae and even **(1)** .... to publish some of his work in an Indian mathematics journal. Ramanujan believed that his results were **(2)** .... to him by a Hindu goddess and so he did not show how he had arrived at his conclusions. Because of this, his work **(3)** .... largely ignored until he sent letters to prominent international mathematicians, **(4)** .... them the British mathematician G. H. Hardy. As Hardy read Ramanujan's letter, his amazement steadily **(5)** .... He recognised that the young Indian had **(6)** .... at several results in pure mathematics that were already **(7)** .... but had used completely new techniques. Even more astounding was the fact that there were some entirely new results quoted without proofs. Hardy immediately invited Ramanujan to work with him. Ramanujan made the journey to Cambridge in April 1914 and began a very productive **(8)** .... with Hardy.

Open cloze (Part 2)

2 For questions 1–8, read the text below and think of the word which best fits each gap. Use only one word in each gap. There is an example at the beginning (0).

Language across borders

Sali Tagliamonte, a language researcher specialising **(0)** _in_ young people's speech, had noticed that Canadian young people telling stories and reporting their **(1)** .... and others' actual words had started to use _be like_ instead of _said_. As this trend had begun in the USA, Tagliamonte's assumption **(2)** .... that the Canadians had picked it **(3)** .... from Americans they had actually spoken to. Tagliamonte, **(4)** .... with other linguists, believed that people only change their speech if they interact with others who have already adopted the change. But she wanted to test her hypothesis by recording some British students as **(5)** .... She thought they would use _like_ to quote far **(6)** .... frequently than the Canadians since they had only limited and sporadic contact with Americans. When she analysed the recordings, she found, **(7)** .... her astonishment, that the British teens were using _like_ to quote even more than their Canadian counterparts. Her results showed that for the first time, a language change was spreading **(8)** .... means of movies and TV rather than interaction.

0	**A** greatest	**B** best	**C** highest	**D** strongest
1	**A** accepted	**B** achieved	**C** managed	**D** succeeded
2	**A** communicated	**B** provided	**C** distributed	**D** shared
3	**A** maintained	**B** remained	**C** kept	**D** continued
4	**A** among	**B** within	**C** inside	**D** between
5	**A** multiplied	**B** increased	**C** boosted	**D** expanded
6	**A** gained	**B** acquired	**C** landed	**D** arrived
7	**A** noticed	**B** discovered	**C** realised	**D** known
8	**A** teamwork	**B** collaboration	**C** cooperation	**D** participation

Word formation (Part 3)

3 For questions 1–8, read the text below. Use the word given in capitals at the end of some of the lines to form a word that fits in the gap in the same line. There is an example at the beginning (0).

Hospitable career opportunities	
Travel and **(0)** tourism provides more jobs than any other industry, accounting for 255 million jobs worldwide. Given the high levels of youth **(1)** .... in large parts of the developed world and a severe **(2)** .... of jobs in developing countries, you might think the industry should have no difficulty filling those vacancies. But the hospitality sector has to contend with negative **(3)** .... among **(4)** .... employees of low wages, unsociable hours and a lack of career opportunities. These **(5)** .... are false, according to Suzy Jackson of the Hospitality Guild, which was set up in 2011 to improve **(6)** .... She makes the point that there are many career **(7)** .... for young people in the industry at entry level, and that they can rise through the ranks to become chief executive or managing director. This may only happen in **(8)** .... circumstances but because the hospitality industry takes so many young people with minimal formal qualifications, it devotes time and money to training. This makes it a very good choice for young people considering a long-term career.	TOUR EMPLOY SHORT PERCEIVE PROSPECT ASSUME RECRUIT OPEN EXCEPT

Key word transformation (Part 4)

4 For questions 1–6, complete the second sentence so that it has a similar meaning to the first sentence, using the word given. Do not change the word given. You must use between three and six words, including the word given.

Example:

We're going to camp whether or not it's raining.

EVEN

We're going to camp even if it's *raining.*

1 Waiting another day to book my ticket would have meant paying a lot more.

IF

I would have had to pay a lot more .... another day to book my ticket.

2 If there's any chance of your passing the post office, could you get me some stamps?

HAPPEN

If .... the post office, could you get me some stamps?

3 There is no possibility whatsoever of my attending the meeting.

QUITE

It's .... the meeting.

4 'Have any of you stayed at the Hotel Belmondo?' asked Kim.

IF

Kim asked .... stayed at the Hotel Belmondo.

5 'I wish I hadn't told Angela about the row with Miriam,' said Carla.

REGRETTED

Carla .... about the row with Miriam.

6 I'll stay and look after my sister until I'm not needed anymore.

AS

I'll stay and look after my sister .... necessary.

10 A perfect match

Expressions for describing compatibility

1 Work in pairs. Is compatibility the most important thing for you in a friendship?

2 Complete the questions. Then ask and answer them with a partner.

1 What kinds of people are you usually *compatible* with?
2 Do you enjoy spending time with people whose opinions differ .... yours but are in some ways complementary?
3 Are all your friends .... exactly the same wavelength as you?
4 Do you have any friends who are .... different .... chalk and cheese, yet still get on like a house .... fire?
5 Do the ads that come up when you are online correspond .... your interests or are you offered products and services that have nothing to do with your needs at all?
6 Have you ever clicked .... someone instantly?

3 Complete the sentences with the correct form of *fit* or *match*.

1 He never .... in with the students in his new school.
2 They are a very ill-.............. couple.
3 Reality rarely .... up to her high expectations.
4 Their marriage was a .... end to the film.

4 Discuss the questions in pairs. Give reasons for your answers and examples where possible. Use some of the expressions in Activities 2 and 3.

1 Is it possible to tell immediately if someone is on a different wavelength to you?
2 Why do you think opposites sometimes attract?
3 Do you think people form the strongest bonds with those from similar backgrounds?
4 Have you ever been in a situation where you felt you fitted in perfectly?
5 Have you ever had a friend your parents considered unsuitable?

LANGUAGE TIP

Fit is an adjective, noun and verb.

*This building is not **fit** for purpose.*

*This dress is a very tight **fit**.*

*This course **fits** my needs perfectly.*

5 Answer the questions. Then compare your answers with a partner.

1 What information do you include in your profile on social networking sites? Is there anything you tend to leave out? Why?

2 What kind of photos do you post on social networking sites? Do you get upset if people don't like them?

6 Look at the advice about using social networking sites. Which advice do you agree with? Change the advice you disagree with.

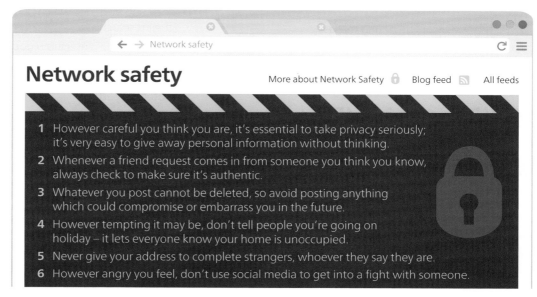

Network safety
More about Network Safety 🔒 Blog feed 📶 All feeds

1 However careful you think you are, it's essential to take privacy seriously; it's very easy to give away personal information without thinking.

2 Whenever a friend request comes in from someone you think you know, always check to make sure it's authentic.

3 Whatever you post cannot be deleted, so avoid posting anything which could compromise or embarrass you in the future.

4 However tempting it may be, don't tell people you're going on holiday – it lets everyone know your home is unoccupied.

5 Never give your address to complete strangers, whoever they say they are.

6 However angry you feel, don't use social media to get into a fight with someone.

whoever, whatever, etc.

▶ **GRAMMAR** REFERENCE p.162

7 Look at the sentences in Activity 6 and rewrite them without using -*ever* words. What does each -*ever* word mean?

8 Complete the sentences with *however, whoever, whatever, whichever, wherever* or *whenever*.

1 .... she wears, she always looks great.

2 .... hard I try, I always forget the number.

3 I don't have anything planned, so we can meet up .... it suits you.

4 I like both shirts – .... one you buy will look good on you.

5 He's willing to move .... he can find work.

6 You need to send the report to .... is in charge of international sales.

9 Rewrite the advice about social networking sites using -*ever* words.

1 It doesn't matter how well you know and trust the person – never share your log-in details.

2 Set your notifications to tell you every time someone tags you in a photo.

3 Regardless of how much you enjoy spending time on social media, try to limit yourself to two hours a day.

4 It doesn't matter where you're going on holiday – don't broadcast the fact. You might not want everyone to know you're away.

10 Work in pairs. Take turns to make suggestions about things to do at the weekend and respond using *whatever*.

LANGUAGE TIP

Whatever can be used as a short response meaning 'I don't mind'. It can sound impatient or rude.

A: Would you rather have tea or coffee?

B: Whatever.

To make it more polite, add *you like/prefer*.

---

1 Work in pairs and discuss the statement.

Online services that match people to compatible friends, romantic partners or professional contacts do a better job than real people who try to match-make their friends.

2 Read the article about online dating services and choose the best alternative title.

1 Reasons why online dating may not always work

2 A history of online dating services

3 Couple finds true love through online dating

Multiple choice (Part 5)

▶ **EXAM** FOCUS p.179

3 Look at the underlined word in the first paragraph of the article. What do you think it means? Use the information that comes later in the paragraph to help you.

EXAM TIP

Don't be put off by vocabulary you don't know. Keep reading and the meaning may become clear.

4 Read the article again. For questions 1–6, choose the answer (A, B, C or D) which you think fits best according to the text.

1 Why did Peter Lake feel the need to sign up to Operation Match?

A He believed the investment was worth the risk.

B He felt it was an efficient way of meeting a large number of women.

C He was tired of dating and wanted to settle down.

D He and the girls he met at university didn't seem to be compatible.

2 What is the writer's attitude to the modern versions of computer dating?

A He is impressed by the sophistication of their approach.

B He thinks the simpler methods of the past were just as effective.

C He is not entirely convinced that they always fulfil their claims.

D He dislikes the way they restrict access to their database.

3 Psychologists were concerned about the claims made by some dating services because

A they doubted whether it was possible to establish the qualities needed for successful relationships.

B they believed the method they used to match their clients should be reviewed by experts.

C they felt their criteria for finding suitable matches was too narrow.

D they had evidence which undermined the validity of their research.

4 According to the writer, how does what's called 'selection bias' account for the apparent success of the matching services?

A Subscribers are willing to consider a diverse range of potential partners.

B Unsuitable people are excluded from subscribing to particular sites.

C Many subscribers try to give what they think is the correct answer in the survey.

D Subscribers to services like these all share a number of characteristics.

5 According to Professor Eastwick, matching services are successfully able to

A connect subscribers with people they get on quite well with.

B convince subscribers that the methods used actually work.

C eliminate subscribers who are unlikely to find partners.

D make subscribers feel better about their chances of finding a partner.

6 Why does the writer return to Peter Lake's story in the last paragraph?

A to demonstrate that online matching services are declining in popularity

B to give an example of someone who has never given up hope of finding a partner

C to show that people expect more from a relationship as they get older

D to suggest that methods other than matching services may be preferable

5 Replace the underlined verbs with phrasal verbs from the article. You may need to change the form of the verbs.

1 I'm thinking of registering to do a yoga course.

2 He asked her out but she refused him.

3 Education spending cannot be reduced any further.

4 There's no evidence to support his claims.

5 Personality tests sometimes help human resources staff eliminate unsuitable candidates.

6 He spent the whole evening talking seductively to my best friend.

9:48 | 67%

| News | Voices | **Technology** | Politics | Travel | Finance |

Online dating: the way to find Mr or Mrs Right?

Staff Reporter

In Autumn 1965, Peter Lake filled out a survey that changed the course of his life. He signed up to Operation Match, a computer dating service. 'It was such a good deal you couldn't turn it down,' Lake says. 'For three dollars they would guarantee to match you with at least three compatible people or they would give you your money back.' But there was more to Lake's decision than the fact that it made good economic sense. Although he had met lots of girls during his first semester at college, he just hadn't clicked with any of them. He mailed the survey back and was matched with a <u>dozen</u> women. With the exception of one who lived too far away, he met all of them. 'The eleventh was a student at Wellesley College. She and I talked on the phone and then we met for coffee and I just fell in love with her right there and then. We started dating immediately and married a year later.' Computer dating was simple way back then.

Fast forward fifty years and the dating industry has graduated from paper-based surveys directed at lonely students to become a multi-billion-dollar global industry, generating income from both subscriptions and advertising. While many dating sites allow their subscribers to freely roam through lists of potential mates, niche services promise to match you with that special someone. The punch-card technology that united Peter Lake with his future wife has been replaced by patented online personality tests, devised by psychologists and anthropologists. One site, for example, uses a questionnaire with more than 400 items – cut back to 100 if you're using the mobile app – supposedly designed to match clients with the man or woman of their dreams. But can they?

Specialised matching services claim that their products are backed up by rigorous research into the characteristics of couples in committed, long-term relationships and that they have managed to identify the shared personality characteristics and values that best predict successful matches. Not everyone is sold on the science, however. In a recent issue of a major psychology journal, psychologists sought to pour cold water on the scientific claims made by these companies. They were especially critical of the fact that none of these matching services has ever subjected their secret algorithms – the calculations designed to match couples – to any kind of objective analysis or independent scrutiny.

In fact, a 'selection bias' – a statistical bias that occurs when a sample population is different from the norm – may be at work. People using matching sites are, after all, different from the average Joe or Jill. For starters, they're likely to have a higher disposable income and, given that they sit through a 400-question survey, more highly motivated than the average dater. The claimed success of matching services may have more to do with narrowing the pool of eligible daters than psychological tests or computer science.

Associate Professor of Psychology Paul Eastwick says that another problem is that the matching sites claim to do much more than weed out Mr or Ms Wrong. 'They promise to find you someone who is especially compatible with you – your soul mate. That's a very different promise that they cannot fulfil,' says Eastwick. He argues, for example, that there may be a placebo effect at work. Just as placebos work because of the aura of authority around the person prescribing the 'drug', rather than its inherent medicinal value, so online matching services may work because the couple believe their compatibility has been validated by relationship experts using complex computer science.

But how far can the digital Cupids guarantee that couples will live happily ever after? Peter Lake and his wife, two of computer matching's first success stories, divorced after eleven years of marriage. Lake has returned to computer dating but the barrier to finding true love has turned out to be more geographical than technological. 'I met a really nice dentist but she lived too far away,' says Lake. 'Eventually, I realised unless they live down the street, I'm really not interested.' He has abandoned algorithm-assisted online dating in favour of online chat rooms and forums. 'Now, if I want to meet somebody, I just go online, find them and chat them up.' Matching software, it seems, is no match for a good chat-up line.

Open cloze (Part 2)

▶ **EXAM** FOCUS p.178

1 **Work in pairs and discuss the questions.**

1 What makes it easy or difficult to meet people where you live?

2 What would be the best way for someone who is new in town to meet people and make friends?

3 Have you heard of speed dating? Do you think it would work best for students or professional people? Why?

2 **Read the title and the article quickly. How is speed networking different to speed dating?**

3 **Read the article again. For questions 1–8, think of the word which best fits each gap. Use only one word in each gap.**

EXAM TIP

Rather than focusing on individual phrases, make sure you have understood the meaning of the whole sentence, paragraph and text before you decide on your answer.

4 **Choose the correct alternative in each sentence. Why is the other alternative not possible?**

1 They married a *couple/few* weeks after they met.

2 I'd like to be someone who really *makes/does* something for other people.

3 He set *up/out* to make as many friends as he possibly could.

4 *Instead/Rather* than going home first, let's meet straight after work.

5 Someone offered me a job in the USA but I decided not to take them *up/out* on it.

6 They wasted *all/some* their time at the meeting arguing about something unimportant.

5 **Answer the questions. Then compare your answers with a partner.**

1 What advantages does speed dating have over other ways of meeting new people?

2 What are the disadvantages?

3 Would you be more (or less) interested in attending a speed-dating event if you knew it was an opportunity to network with people in your profession or with those who study similar things to you?

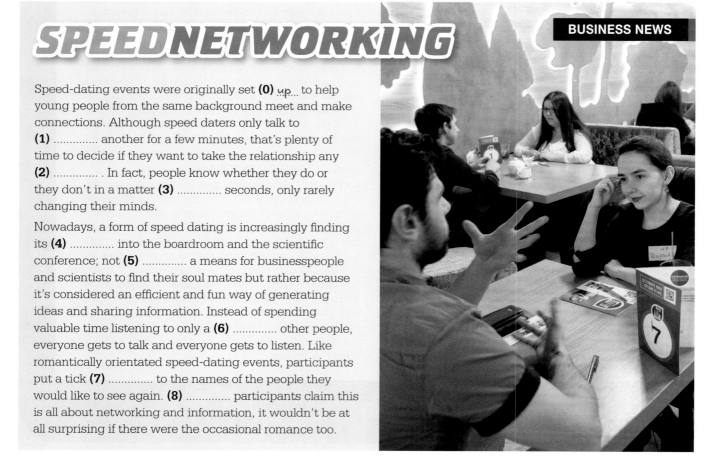

SPEEDNETWORKING

BUSINESS NEWS

Speed-dating events were originally set **(0)** up to help young people from the same background meet and make connections. Although speed daters only talk to **(1)** .... another for a few minutes, that's plenty of time to decide if they want to take the relationship any **(2)** .... In fact, people know whether they do or they don't in a matter **(3)** .... seconds, only rarely changing their minds.

Nowadays, a form of speed dating is increasingly finding its **(4)** .... into the boardroom and the scientific conference; not **(5)** .... a means for businesspeople and scientists to find their soul mates but rather because it's considered an efficient and fun way of generating ideas and sharing information. Instead of spending valuable time listening to only a **(6)** .... other people, everyone gets to talk and everyone gets to listen. Like romantically orientated speed-dating events, participants put a tick **(7)** .... to the names of the people they would like to see again. **(8)** .... participants claim this is all about networking and information, it wouldn't be at all surprising if there were the occasional romance too.

Multiple matching (Part 4)

▶ **EXAM** FOCUS p.182

1 Look at the two exam tasks in Activity 3. Have you ever done a personality test for any of the reasons listed in Task 1? Have you ever reacted to the results in any of the ways mentioned in Task 2?

2 ▶ 41 You will hear five short extracts in which people are talking about personality tests. Listen to the first extract. Does the information come in the same order as the two tasks?

3 ▶ 42 Listen to all five extracts. While you listen you must complete both tasks.

Task 1

For questions 1–5, choose from the list (A–H) the reason each speaker gives for doing the test

A to satisfy a curiosity
B to provide amusement
C to follow an instruction
D to solve a problem
E to improve a relationship
F to pass the time
G to get promotion
H to impress a friend

Speaker 1	**1**
Speaker 2	**2**
Speaker 3	**3**
Speaker 4	**4**
Speaker 5	**5**

Task 2

For questions 6–10, choose from the list (A–H) how each speaker felt about their own test results.

A motivated by their implications
B surprised because they were better than expected
C amazed at their accuracy
D indignant because of an unfair criticism
E pleased at the positive interpretation
F worried about what they revealed
G confused because they seemed inconsistent
H suspicious because they were similar to someone else's

Speaker 1	**6**
Speaker 2	**7**
Speaker 3	**8**
Speaker 4	**9**
Speaker 5	**10**

4 Discuss the questions with other students.

1 How would you feel if you were asked to do a personality test for a job?

2 When do you think personality testing can be helpful?

3 If you see a personality quiz in a magazine or online, are you tempted to do it? How much faith do you have in the results of tests like these?

4 Would you ever lie or bend the truth in a personality test?

1 Do you think it's possible to fall in love with an android?

2 Read the article. Do you think it will always be possible to tell the difference between an android and a human?

Almost human

A major goal in robotics and a key feature of science fiction is how to make androids look and behave like humans. Androids and humans <u>living side by side</u> is a future <u>envisaged by science fiction writers</u> and many robotics engineers. <u>Having reached a point</u> where this fantasy world may soon be a reality, many people are questioning what kind of relationships will develop between humans and androids.

Having developed relationships with inanimate objects, such as a doll or teddy bear, as children, many adults don't find it at all strange to give their cars names or form a special attachment to their musical instruments. People have also become used to talking to machines, as long as they are robot-like and 'mechanical'. But the idea of human-like androids looking and behaving like humans is something we find much harder to accept. Studies have shown we are more likely to feel threatened by them than develop a meaningful relationship with them.

Can we learn to feel affection for an android in the same way as we feel affection for a teddy bear or a car? Philip K. Dick, the science fiction writer, anticipated this problem in the 1968 novel *Do Androids Dream of Electric Sheep?* (adapted into the film *Blade Runner* in 1982). In the story, Rick Deckard's task is to decide if the woman he is strongly attracted to is a real human. Having discovered that she is a 'replicant', a new dilemma kicks in: can he love her anyway?

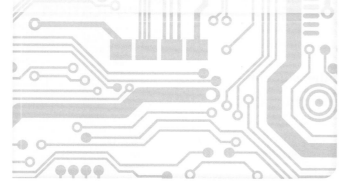

Participle clauses

▶ **GRAMMAR** REFERENCE p.163

3 Look at the underlined participle clauses (clauses that begin with a present or past participle) in the text and answer the questions.

1 Which participle clauses replace a relative clause?

2 Which participle clause expresses a reason and replaces a conjunction?

4 Find four more sentences in the article with participle clauses.

5 Match (1–6) to (A–F) to make sentences. Then rewrite the sentences using participle clauses.

Example: Tim had told everyone it was his birthday, so he received lots of messages and cards.

Having told everyone it was his birthday, Tim received lots of messages and cards.

1 I realised I was going to be late,

2 I hadn't slept a wink the night before

3 I was worried about finding myself in another tense situation with Andrea

4 I didn't want to have to be responsible for running the meeting,

5 Since I was convinced everyone knew about the situation with Andrea,

6 I was feeling very nervous as I walked into the room,

A so I tried not to look anybody in the eye.

B since I hadn't actually spoken to her since our last disastrous encounter.

C I decided it was pointless to behave as if nothing had happened.

D so I tried to find a taxi.

E and as a result, I was really tired.

F so I asked Victoria if she would chair it for me.

LANGUAGE TIP

Check that the subject of the participle clause and the main clause are the same. If they are not, many people will consider the sentence incorrect.

Picking up the phone, an unfamiliar voice greeted me. (This sounds as if the unfamiliar voice picked up the phone.)

6 Work in pairs.

Student A: turn to page 146.

Student B: turn to page 144.

Collaborative task and discussion (Parts 3 and 4)
negotiating and cooperating

▶ **EXAM** FOCUS p.183

1 ▶ 43 **Look at the Part 3 task and listen to Adam and Nadia discussing the questions. Choose the correct option in each sentence and discuss the reasons they give with a partner. Do you agree with their opinions?**

1 *Adam/Nadia* thinks that human pilots are preferable. Why?

2 Adam and Nadia say that robots *could/couldn't* be used to help look after the elderly. Why/Why not?

3 Adam and Nadia think that robots *would/wouldn't* be good at working in a pizza restaurant. Why/Why not?

Part 3

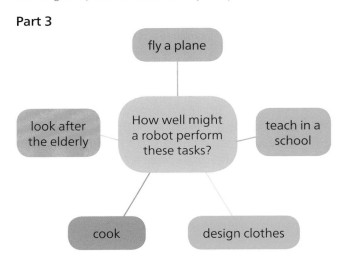

fly a plane

look after the elderly

How well might a robot perform these tasks?

teach in a school

cook

design clothes

2 **Look at Part 3 again. Discuss the rest of the tasks in pairs and decide which of the tasks a robot would perform the best. Remember to give reasons for your opinions.**

3 **Match phrases 1–6 to headings A–C.**

1 Isn't it sometimes the case that … ?

2 I would think that this is unlikely to hold true in all cases, but …

3 It's impossible to be categorical about something like this because …

4 I'm not entirely convinced that would be necessary.

5 … it's difficult to give a *yes* or *no* answer because…

6 I think it's also important to consider ….

A avoiding answering a question directly

B introducing a point

C challenging a point

4 **Take turns to answer the Part 4 questions. Use some of the phrases from Activity 3.**

Part 4

- Would you like to have a robot to help you at home?

- Some people believe that it will be possible for robots to feel human emotions. What do you think?

- Do you think there's a danger that people will become too dependent on robots?

- Should governments introduce strict regulations about the use of robots?

- Do you think science fiction helps people to understand the future better?

- Are you optimistic or pessimistic about the future of Artificial Intelligence? Why?

5 **Work in pairs. Turn to page 138 and do the activity.**

6 **Work in pairs. Turn to page 138 and discuss the Part 4 questions.**

Formal letter (Part 2)
including relevant information

▶ **WRITING** REFERENCE p.170

1 Work in pairs. Look at the exam task and the list of points a student made for inclusion in the letter. Decide which of the points you would and would not include.

> The language school where you study English is going to participate in an online service matching students to educational courses. You have been asked by the school director to write a letter to the person in charge of the website explaining why your school should be included. You should explain:
>
> - what your school or college specialises in.
> - what strengths your school or college has.
> - what kinds of students would enjoy or benefit from coming to study at your school or college.
>
> Write your **letter** in **220–260** words in an appropriate style.

- what kinds of students currently study at the school
- your opinion about these students
- what is not taught at the school
- other subjects you would like to see introduced
- why you can't offer some courses at the moment
- something your school is particularly proud of
- teachers' skills and qualifications
- what skills and qualifications students can expect to gain
- what you've heard people say about your school
- how your school compares to other schools

2 Look at the answer a student wrote for the task in Activity 1. Each of the three main paragraphs contains some irrelevant information. Find the information and discuss with a partner why it should not be included.

EXAM TIP

Don't go over the word limit. If you write too much, it is very likely that you will include irrelevant information.

3 Work in pairs. Turn to page 146 and do the activity.

Dear Sir or Madam,

I am writing to you on behalf of the Fenwick School. As you know, we hope to include an entry for our school on your website.

The Fenwick School offers language courses at all levels of proficiency. Although English as a foreign language teaching is an important part of our work, we also provide courses in other European languages, among them French, Italian, Spanish, Portuguese and Russian. Apparently, there is some discussion about offering Chinese at some time in the future but it is not currently available. In addition, we have courses in German for foreigners. One of the school's particular strengths is preparation for the official examinations in each of the languages we teach. Students have obtained excellent results in these examinations this year.

Standards of teaching at the school are very high. All the teachers are fully qualified and they also attend regular in-service training programmes. In addition to the teaching staff, there is a student welfare officer who helps students find accommodation. It can be very difficult to find accommodation here, so it is a good thing that the school provides such a service. Another excellent service the school offers is a complete social programme. This term alone we have had three trips to the theatre, two weekend excursions to nearby beauty spots and a party to celebrate the school's twenty-fifth anniversary.

I feel sure that anyone seeking to improve their level in any of the languages the Fenwick School offers would be delighted with the school. Although most students are in their early to mid-twenties, there are also older and younger people currently enrolled. The oldest student we've ever had was seventy-eight years old. In terms of nationalities, there is a very wide mix, though students from European and Latin American countries predominate.

We feel sure that you will want to include our school in the database for your educational matching service and look forward to hearing from you.

Yours faithfully,

K. Niemeyer

Klaus Niemeyer
Student Services Coordinator
The Fenwick School

1 Complete the second sentence so that it has a similar meaning to the first sentence, using the word in brackets.

1 Whatever she wears, she always manages to look amazing.

It .... she wears, she always manages to look amazing. (*matter*)

2 However hard I try, I always seem to forget Charlie's birthday.

It .... hard I try, I always seem to forget Charlie's birthday. (*difference*)

3 I made sure to take my umbrella as I had heard it was going to rain.

I made sure to take my umbrella .... to rain. (*having*)

4 I bought you some of those Belgian chocolates because I know how much you like them.

Knowing .... , I bought you some of those Belgian chocolates. (*how*)

5 She seems to take offence whatever you say.

She seems to take offence .... you say. (*regardless*)

6 I always make sure I have a good relationship with my neighbours irrespective of where I happen to be living.

I always make sure I have a good relationship with my neighbours .... to be living. (*wherever*)

7 Whatever we have for supper will be fine with me.

I .... have for supper. (*mind*)

8 You can come around whenever you like.

Any time .... is fine with us. (*would*)

2 Complete the sentences with one or two words.

1 I think they broke up because they were just not compatible .... one another.

2 Her views on all sorts of topics differ radically .... mine, but we're still good friends.

3 Nigel and Laura get on like a house ....

4 Tom and I used to be close, but we're just not .... the same wavelength anymore.

5 The new policy corresponds best .... the interests of families living in rural areas.

6 She's always making comments that have absolutely nothing to .... what we were saying.

3 Read the blog entry below and decide which answer (A, B, C or D) best fits each gap.

https://MyBlog/Set-up!

It was a set-up!

Just over four years ago I was set up on my first ever and only **(1)** .... date. My friend Simon had met a writer while doing a reading of his latest book in a local library. Convinced that his friend and I would be a perfect **(2)** ...., Simon passed on my email details and then came back and told me all about him.

The next **(3)** .... I knew, Simon and I were on Google, typing in his new friend's full name to see if any **(4)** .... of wives, girlfriends or long-term relationships appeared in any of his profiles. Having satisfied ourselves that the man in **(5)** .... was available, I sent him an email and we arranged to meet for coffee the following Sunday. We got **(6)** .... like a house on fire and though we're as different as **(7)** .... and cheese in all sorts of ways, we are essentially on exactly the same **(8)** .... Four years on, we now share our lives. And when anyone asks how we met, I say, quite proudly, 'We were set up.'

	A	B	C	D
1	surprise	secret	blind	unknown
2	fit	suit	partner	match
3	thing	time	moment	minute
4	information	idea	mention	rumour
5	interest	question	issue	mind
6	up	on	over	off
7	cream	butter	chalk	ham
8	wavelength	bandwidth	frequency	modulation

11 Face value

1 Work in pairs and decide if the statements are true (T) or false (F). Then turn to page 147 and check your answers.

1 Babies are born with the ability to smile.
2 Smiling uses fewer muscles than frowning.
3 There are ten different types of smile.
4 Smiling is a universal sign of happiness.
5 People who smile frequently live longer.
6 Smiling is a good way to relieve stress.
7 Men smile more than women.
8 Pretending to smile can increase stress.

Words to describe emotions

2 Work in pairs. Look at the words in the box and discuss the questions.

amusement astonishment bitterness confusion contentment delight
embarrassment exhilaration frustration hysteria indifference

1 Which of the emotions might you experience when
  • receiving a letter of rejection from a potential employer?
  • trying to communicate with someone whose English is difficult to understand?
  • celebrating getting your degree?
  • failing to understand a joke?
  • opening the exam results you'd been dreading to discover you'd actually done well?
  • copying your boss into a personal email by mistake?
  • doing a sky dive?
  • discovering just in time that you hadn't really lost your train ticket?
2 How likely are people to smile when experiencing these emotions?
3 What are the adjective forms that describe the emotion?

Open cloze (Part 2)

▶ **EXAM** FOCUS p.178

3 **Discuss the questions in pairs.**

1 Do you eat more when you are in a good mood or a bad mood?
2 Do you ever use food to reward yourself?
3 What do you eat as comfort food to cheer yourself up?

4 **Read the article and summarise the information.**

Good mood food

Research into the role of people's moods in shaping their eating patterns has, **(1)** .... very recently, almost always tended to focus on bad moods. The term 'emotional eating' referred to the way that negative feelings could trigger a binge. There are two theories about **(2)** .... a bad mood has this effect. The first is that many of us associate hunger **(3)** .... unpleasant emotions. The second is that we use food – especially sugar – **(4)** .... a drug to calm ourselves down.

It's now recognised that we don't **(5)** .... eat more when we're sad but also when we're feeling happy. This may seem obvious; we are, after all, conditioned from childhood to use excess calories to celebrate, **(6)** .... it's at a birthday party, at a wedding, or a take-away meal to reward ourselves at the end of a long week. What's **(7)** .... , food tastes better when we're feeling cheerful. This amazing fact is something that **(8)** .... anyone is aware of. Chocolate, it seems, enhances our sense of joy, while also providing comfort when we're down.

LANGUAGE TIP

Adverbs are often tested in this part of the test. Make sure you choose an adverb which makes sense and is also grammatically correct.
e.g. *He's* .... *got any money left from his inheritance. hardly/rarely/scarcely* all fit grammatically but *rarely* doesn't make sense in this context.

5 **Read the article again. For questions 1–8, think of the word which best fits each gap. Use only one word in each gap.**

6 **Work in pairs. Compare your answers to Activity 5. Then check your answers to questions 5, 7 and 8 by answering the questions.**

1 In question 5, what words in the sentence give a clue to the answer?
2 In question 7, do you need a word which means *in addition to* or *in contrast to*?
3 In question 8, do you need a word which means *a lot* or *not much*?

7 **Work in pairs. Take turns to describe a memorable meal at which you felt very happy.**

1 Work in pairs. In what situations do you laugh?

Example:

- *finding something someone's said funny*
- *wanting to make the other person feel good*

Multiple choice (Part 3)

▶ **EXAM** FOCUS p.182

2 ▶ 44 **You will hear a radio discussion between two reviewers called Mark Shaw and Diana Abel about a book on laughter by Robert Provine. For questions 1–6, choose the answer (A, B, C or D) which fits best according to what you hear.**

EXAM TIP

Don't worry if you can't answer a question the first time you listen – just move on to the next question. You will have another chance to answer any questions you've missed or aren't sure of during the second listening.

1 According to Mark, the idea that laughter is mainly used as a social lubricant

  A is a concept which people may be unwilling to accept.

  B needs further investigation.

  C has worrying implications.

  D contradicts opinions of other psychologists.

2 What surprised Diana about claims made in the book about male and female laughter?

  A the way men can be intimidated by women's humour

  B the changing role of laughter in relationships between the sexes

  C the difficulties faced by female comedians

  D the greater value women place on humour in relationships

3 Diana agrees with Provine that people should increase laughter by

  A choosing to socialise with light-hearted people.

  B preparing amusing stories to entertain friends.

  C refusing to take life too seriously.

  D trying to cheer people up who tend to be negative.

4 How has Mark and Diana's attitude to laughter changed after reading the book?

  A They find themselves more inclined to laugh.

  B They are more conscious of their own laughter.

  C They are more aware of people's reasons for laughing.

  D They find other people's laughter inappropriate.

5 Mark and Diana would both have liked Provine to include more information on

  A different kinds of humour.

  B the origins of laughter.

  C the negative aspects of laughter.

  D the physical effects of laughter.

6 Mark thinks the book will appeal to a non-academic audience because it

  A is written in a lively, conversational style.

  B will teach people about relationships.

  C contains fascinating stories.

  D can be used as a self-help guide.

3 Work in pairs and discuss the questions.

1 Do you think you laugh often enough?

2 How important do you think a good sense of humour is?

3 Do you ever laugh at jokes that you don't find funny?

4 When did you last have a fit of uncontrollable laughter?

4 Choose the correct alternative in each sentence.

1 He's not *admitting/advocating* attending laughter workshops.

2 People should *lighten/light* up and laugh at themselves more.

3 The effect it had on me was to monitor my own *impulses/reactions* to laugh – it made me less spontaneous, in a way.

4 But you can just skip those bits and move on to some of the lovely *anecdotes/reports* about the research.

5 Some of the accounts of the *contagious/dangerous* nature of laughter are really amazing. In some places, people couldn't stop laughing for days.

1 **What feelings do you think a dog is expressing when it does the following?**

putting ears flat   having ears pricked up
furrowed brow   eyes cast down
showing whites of eyes   wagging tail
having tail between legs

2 ▶ **45** **Listen to a woman telling a friend about some research into dogs' facial expressions she has read about. Which of the following statements are true, according to the research?**

1 Dog owners understood dogs' feelings the best.

2 Dogs and humans have a natural understanding.

3 Most people can also read other animals' emotions.

Passive forms

▶ **GRAMMAR** REFERENCE p.163

3 **Compare what the woman says with what was written by the researchers and answer the questions.**

1 Why is the passive used by the researchers?

2 What other differences do you notice between the spoken and written forms?

A 'They did an experiment recently which shows that people are able to tell how a dog is feeling by reading its facial expressions.'
An experiment was carried out recently which shows that people are able to tell how a dog is feeling by reading its facial expressions.

B 'The researchers think people may have a natural empathy with dogs.'
It is thought that people may have a natural empathy with dogs.

C 'They should do more research to find out if people can read other animals' emotions as well.'
Further research should be conducted to establish whether other animals' emotions can also be interpreted.

LANGUAGE TIP

The passive is often used after certain reporting verbs (*think, consider, hope, believe, need*, etc.).

*It **is thought** that humans and dogs may have a natural empathy.*

*Dogs **are considered to be** the most intelligent animals.*

4 **Rewrite the sentences using a passive modal structure.**

1 The test may have been confusing for the dogs.

2 The researchers must be surprised by the results.

3 Everyone should believe dog owners when they say they understand how their dog feels.

4 Most people can interpret a dog's emotions.

5 **Read the text. In what way are dogs similar to young children?**

6 **Complete the text using the passive form of the verbs in brackets.**

The researchers conducted the experiment by prompting the dog to display a range of emotions and taking a photograph of the different expressions. The results were a surprise because it **(1)** .... (*predict*) that dog owners would be better at interpreting the animal's facial expressions but this theory **(2)** .... (*not/support*) by the evidence.

In the past, dogs **(3)** .... (*consider*) to be incapable of experiencing complex emotions in the same way as humans. The opinions of scientists and philosophers, however, **(4)** .... (*always/dispute*) by dog owners, who could clearly see feelings such as joy, love and sadness regularly **(5)** .... (*display*) by their dogs. But more recently it **(6)** .... (*generally/accept*) that all the basic emotions of a two-and-a-half-year-old child **(7)** .... (*can/experience*) by dogs.
The familiar sight of a dog slinking off with its tail between its legs **(8)** .... (*always/associate*) with guilt. But dog lovers **(9)** .... (*may/force*) to accept this is impossible because it **(10)** .... (*now/believe*) that young children do not develop this particular emotion until the age of three or four.

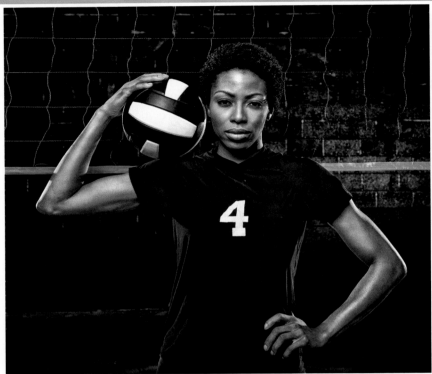

Cross-text multiple matching (Part 6)

▶ **EXAM** FOCUS p.180

1 **Work in pairs and discuss the questions.**

1 What do you think the portraits reveal about the people in the photos?

2 What skills do you think you need to be a professional photographer?

3 How do you usually feel about having your photograph taken?

4 Why do you think posting photos of yourself has become so popular?

2 **Read the reviews of a photography exhibition quickly and decide if they are mainly positive or negative. Would they encourage you to visit the exhibition? What would it be like to be the subject of one of Penn's portraits?**

3 **Look at question 1 in Activity 4 and answer the questions.**

1 What is Reviewer C's opinion of Penn's influence as a photographer? Underline the section of the review which refers to this.

2 Look at the other reviews and underline what they have to say about Penn's influence. Which reviewer has a very similar opinion to reviewer C?

3 Do any of the reviewers have a different opinion to reviewer C about Penn's influence?

4 **Read the reviews again. For questions 1–4, choose from the reviewers (A–D). The reviewers may be chosen more than once. Which reviewer**

1 shares Reviewer C's view of Penn's influence as a photographer? `1`

2 has a different view to Reviewer A about Penn's consistency over the years? `2`

3 has a similar view to Reviewer B about the effect of the background against which the portraits were taken? `3`

4 has a different opinion to the other reviewers regarding how well the portraits on display have been selected? `4`

EXAM TIP

One question may ask which writer has a different opinion to the rest on a particular issue. You need to underline the relevant parts in each text to identify this.

5 **Work in pairs and discuss the questions.**

How far do you agree that

1 a person's face can reveal their character?

2 people are judged too often on their appearance?

3 celebrities are too conscious of their image?

4 fashion photography is of little relevance to most people?

A What is most apparent from this exhibition of Irving Penn's portraits, which covers the photographer's entire career, is his commitment to quality and style. From the 1940s until his last work in 2007, he remained constant in his approach, never failing to deliver anything less than utter perfection. As his career progressed, Penn moved from classic fashion shots to focus more on portraits, investigating how far a person's character can be revealed by their face. He managed to shine a light on the inner qualities of his subjects by exaggerating an expression or gesture. The simplicity of the sets he used in all his portraits cleverly leaves his subjects nowhere to hide, exposing the individual behind the icon. For some the result is awkward but for others it is liberating and only serves to magnify their status. This thoughtfully assembled collection offers a fascinating insight into the true nature of some of the most significant cultural figures of the twentieth century.

B Irving Penn once wrote that 'very often what lies behind the façade is rare and more wonderful than the subject knows or dares to believe'. The exhibition displays portraits of some of the most celebrated figures of the last century, including John F. Kennedy, Pablo Picasso and Truman Capote. The less obvious points of his subjects' personalities are unashamedly portrayed by the photographer in characterless, bare surroundings. In showing the sitters without any of the trappings of celebrity, Penn successfully reveals qualities not seen in other portraits of these superstars. The development in style that takes place over Penn's fifty-year career is clearly shown, from his full-body images of the forties, to more intimate close-up portraits of later years. These all demonstrate that Penn's technical mastery is without equal. He undoubtedly created a style that later generations of photographers have found impossible not to imitate.

C *Irving Penn Portraits* at the National Portrait Gallery follows the progress of the American photographer's studio portraits from 1947–2007, emphasising the continuity of his vision, sensitivity to his subject and technical skill. It celebrates his interest in the power of photography (and its limitations) as a means of depicting the inner life of sitters and to discover, as Penn states, 'what lies behind the façade'. Penn's success lies in the importance of precision, attention to detail and meticulously planned composition. Penn is and will continue to be a giant in the world of photographic portraiture. But while he transformed the style of studio portraiture, his relevance also endures as a fashion photographer and the omission from this exhibition of some of his most iconic images for *Vogue* results in an incomplete portrayal of his achievements.

D As Penn's reputation inevitably begins to fade, those unfamiliar with his work might at first see only a collection of slightly out-of-date, black and white portraits. But a closer inspection will reveal how Penn turns the face into a landscape to be explored and discovered. Every feature is highlighted in a manner that most photographers appear incapable of capturing today. The portraits on display, spanning some fifty years, give a comprehensive summary of his work and provide a clear insight into the development in his confidence and style. The majority of these portraits were taken in his studio using a plain background and very few props. This helps to create a mood which, together with his expert use of light and shadow, make his images never less than exhilarating. Only in the last decade of his life does his work lose some of its magic: he experiments more with modern trends in lighting and appears to have been persuaded by celebrity publicists and fashion stylists to flatter his famous subjects.

6 **Choose the correct alternative in each sentence.**

1 The film *portrays/displays* the lives of two artists.

2 At the end of the story the family's secrets are *exposed/depicted*.

3 The paintings are *displayed/highlighted* in chronological order.

4 The portrait *highlights/exposes* the man's delight.

5 In his autobiography, the writer *reveals/portrays* the inspiration for his main character.

6 The paintings *depict/display* life in the early part of the nineteenth century.

7 **What is the noun form of the correct verbs in Activity 6?**

8 **Work in pairs and discuss the questions.**

1 Can you describe anything which has been revealed or exposed recently in the news?

2 How do you feel about people who display a lot of emotion?

3 What do you think your clothes reveal about you?

4 Which actor do you think would portray you in a film about your life?

Long turn (Part 2)

1 **Work in pairs and discuss the questions.**

1 What ideas and themes link the three pictures?

2 In what ways are they different?

3 What questions could an examiner ask about these pictures?

expressing certainty and uncertainty

▶ **EXAM** FOCUS p.183

2 ▶ **46** **Listen to the examiner's instructions and see how your ideas compare.**

3 **Underline the phrases for expressing certainty or uncertainty and tick the statements that you agree with. Compare with your partner.**

1 There's no doubt that sponsorship of major events is beneficial – otherwise companies wouldn't be prepared to pay for it.

2 I'm convinced that being sponsored by certain companies can damage the reputation of a sporting event.

3 Being associated with a prestigious event is undoubtedly extremely valuable to companies.

4 It's an undeniable fact that many sports could not survive without corporate sponsorship.

4 ▶ **47** **Listen to a candidate answering the follow-up question to Activity 2. Do you agree with her?**

5 **Listen again. What phrase does the candidate use to**

1 give herself thinking time?

2 give a speculative opinion?

3 avoid repeating words in the examiner's question?

6 **Work in pairs. Practise doing the task in Activity 4 using one of the pictures that the candidate didn't talk about. Try to use some of the phrases in Activity 3.**

7 **Work in pairs. Turn to page 139 and do Task 1. Then turn to page 142 and do Task 2.**

EXAM TIP

Don't just give a one- or two-word answer in response to your partner's pictures when you're asked to comment on them.

1 **Work in pairs and discuss the questions.**

1 What impression might you hope to create by wearing a suit?

2 How does wearing a suit make you feel?

3 Would you prefer a job where you could dress casually?

4 Why do you think many company dress codes are becoming less formal?

2 **Work in pairs. Read the text below quickly and discuss the questions.**

1 What type of person do you think would be interested in this text?

2 Where do you think this text was taken from?

A a business magazine

B a website for an expensive shop selling suits

C a fashion blog

3 What advantages of wearing a suit are mentioned? Do you agree with the writer's analysis?

4 Do you agree that most people judge on appearances and rely on first impressions when meeting someone for the first time?

3 **Is the text written in a formal or informal style? Find some evidence to justify your answer.**

SUITABLY ATTIRED

(1) .... the fact that a suit is universally recognised as the uniform of success, it goes without saying that if you want to be taken seriously in the business world, you need to wear a suit. Bankers, lawyers and politicians all depend on their attire to gain respect and credibility in public life. **(2)** ...., donning an impeccably tailored suit is a sign of affluence and good taste. It speaks volumes about the wearer even before a single word is uttered.

Linking adverbials

▶ **GRAMMAR** REFERENCE p.164

4 **Read the text again and cross out the linking adverbials that are not possible.**

	A	**B**	**C**
1	In view of	Apart from	Given
2	Additionally	Moreover	Alternatively
3	Furthermore	What's more	In contrast
4	Besides this	As well as this	Despite this
5	Even so	On the other hand	Alternatively
6	For this reason	On the contrary	Consequently

LANGUAGE TIP

Linking adverbials connect one sentence in a logical way to another. They usually appear at the beginning of a sentence and are followed by a comma. They help to make writing more cohesive.

5 **Which of the linking adverbials in Activity 4 are used to**

1 give extra information? (x6)

2 give a reason or result? (x4)

3 make a contrast? (x6)

6 **Work in pairs. Think of three reasons why employees in a company should not have to wear a suit to work. Use linking adverbials to explain your reasons.**

(3) ...., this advantage does not only apply to high-flying professionals. Those who lead more normal lives need to wear a suit at some point in order to boost their career chances. **(4)** .... most employers do judge on appearances and rely on first impressions, so it would be a mistake to wear scruffy jeans and a T-shirt to a job interview, even for a job where you would not be required to wear a suit. If you wear casual clothes, it could signify that you have a casual attitude. **(5)** ...., wear a suit and you display discipline, commitment and ambition. **(6)** ...., you would also be well advised to wear a suit should you be unlucky enough to find yourself appearing before a judge in court accused of a crime.

Since a well-tailored suit is considered the most effective way to win instant acceptance, it makes no sense not to wear one. A man or woman in a suit means business.

ACE BUSINESS SCHOOL

DRESS CODE

MEN

- **must wear:** formal suits in a dark colour, leather shoes
- **mustn't wear:** jeans or hoodies, sandals, flip-flops or trainers
- **optional:** a tie

WOMEN

- **must wear:** formal skirts/trousers
- **mustn't wear:** mini skirts, shorts, very high heels, large earrings

1 **Work in pairs and discuss the questions.**

1 Do you think the dress code for students at the business school in the poster above is reasonable?

2 Should pierced noses and tattoos be acceptable in college?

3 Should the dress code where you work or study be changed?

4 Is it acceptable for employers to tell employees how to style their hair?

Essay (Part 1)
planning your essay
▶ **WRITING** REFERENCE p.168

2 **Look at the exam task and write a plan including points 1–4.**

1 In the introduction, briefly describe the current situation and say why the college is considering introducing a dress code.

2 Choose which two advantages you are going to discuss and decide on the main point for each paragraph.

3 Think of some examples/evidence to support the main point in each paragraph.

4 Decide what points to use in your conclusion to support/reject the idea of introducing a dress code.

Your class has been involved in a discussion on whether a dress code should be introduced at the college where you are studying. You have made the notes below.

Advantages of proposed dress code
- image of college
- health and safety
- discipline

Some opinions expressed in the discussion:

'Wearing more formal clothes will prepare students for the workplace.'

'College isn't work or school, so students should be free to wear what they want.'

'Students are turning up to college in inappropriate clothes more frequently, so it's time for a dress code.'

Write an essay for your tutor discussing **two** of the advantages in your notes. You should **explain which of the advantages you think would be most important** for the college to consider in deciding whether to introduce a dress code, **giving reasons** to support your opinion.

You may, if you wish, make use of the opinions expressed in the discussion but you should use your own words as far as possible.

Write your **essay** in **220–260** words in an appropriate style.

---

3 **Write your essay.**

EXAM TIP

Remember to use linking adverbials to organise your ideas and to make it easy for the reader to follow your argument.

4 **Check your work using the checklist on page 166. Then swap with a partner. Check if they have used a range of linking adverbials and passive forms.**

1 Read the article and think of the word which best fits each gap. Use only one word for each gap.

Mirror, mirror on the wall

What can mirrors tell us about our self-image? Researchers have discovered that being aware of a mirror on the wall can influence the way we behave and, if this research **(1)** .... to be believed, always **(2)** .... the better.

The results of the research show that when there is a mirror present, people are more likely to work harder, be more cooperative and are less likely to cheat. In one experiment, participants **(3)** .... given a series of exercises to do and their performance was compared with a control group who did the same activities **(4)** .... a mirror present.

One possible explanation for the improved behaviour could be that mirrors make us more self-aware, which may lead us to give more consideration to our own behaviour and to think **(5)** .... we act, rather than acting on impulse. **(6)** .... greater level of self-awareness would seem, therefore, to have a positive impact on behaviour, if **(7)** .... because we like to have a positive self-image and prefer to see **(8)** .... in a favourable light.

2 Complete the sentences with the correct form of the word in brackets.

1 She reacted as if she were completely .... (*differ*) to the news. I don't think she cares at all.

2 Some people will always be .... (*content*), no matter how lucky they are.

3 The feeling of .... (*astonish*) was overwhelming – I just couldn't believe I'd won.

4 Trying to explain yourself in another language can be extremely .... (*frustrate*).

5 I was so .... (*relief*) when my magic trick actually worked – I really wasn't sure that it would.

6 Many people suffer from .... (*nervous*) before a job interview.

7 It's a .... (*delight*), if not very original, painting. It cheers you up just looking at it.

8 The audience didn't find the joke at all .... (*amuse*) – I think some of them were quite offended.

3 Complete the second sentence so that it has a similar meaning to the first sentence, using the word in brackets.

1 The original idea was to ban the wearing of jeans by the start of last term.

Originally, the wearing of jeans .... by the start of last term. (*have*)

2 Experts are convinced the painting was completed in the 16th century.

The painting .... completed in the 16th century. (*considered*)

3 Everyone had thought the painting was worth over £100 million.

The painting .... worth over £100 million. (*been*)

4 No one can do anything about students having tattoos if they want them.

There .... about students having tattoos if they want them. (*done*)

5 People want others to notice that they are doing the right thing.

People .... doing the right thing. (*seen*)

6 The audience were confused by the magician's trick.

The magician's trick .... the audience. (*confusion*)

4 Read the text and choose the correct alternatives.

SLAVES TO FASHION

(1) *Given/As well as* the fact that fashions change so frequently, it makes no sense to buy expensive clothes. **(2)** *Consequently/Even so*, many people, men included, spend far more than they can afford on designer clothes. **(3)** *Besides/Despite* this, some really dedicated followers of fashion are prepared to go so far as to get into serious debt in order to keep up with the latest trends. **(4)** *What's more/For this reason*, slavishly following the latest trends means not only that you have no individuality or personal style but also that you are likely to be broke.

12 Brilliant ideas

Sentence completion (Part 2)

▶ **EXAM** FOCUS p.181

1 Talk to a partner. Where would you go in search of brilliant ideas?

the internet   a library   a museum   social media

2 Work in pairs. Which things do not usually happen in science classes at school or university?

- taking notes
- jokes and laughter
- watching experiments
- chatting informally with the teacher/lecturer
- listening to music at the end

3 ▶ 48 You will hear a student called Max Bignall giving a presentation about a science club in New York. How many of the things in Activity 2 does he mention?

4 Listen again. For questions 1–8, complete the sentences below with a word or short phrase.

5 Do you think the Secret Science Club would work where you live?

sciencescene

The Secret Science Club

Max was surprised that one of the founders of the club was a **(1)** .... rather than a scientist.

The venue for the club is used for **(2)** .... on most weeknights.

Presenters at the club often conclude their presentations with **(3)** ...., which are popular with the audience.

The lecture given by an astrophysicist about **(4)** .... was one that Max particularly appreciated.

Max sometimes finds it difficult to understand the **(5)** .... which follow the lectures.

Max says that the way the club gives people the chance **(6)** .... with leading members of the scientific community is a huge benefit.

Max thinks this club follows the tradition of meetings which took place in coffee houses in **(7)** .... during the eighteenth century.

Max uses the word **(8)** .... to stress the club's attitude to scientific ideas.

Multi-part verbs
science and research

6 Work in pairs. If you wanted to compare various paper planes, how would you do it?

7 Read these instructions from a science blog on how to design a paper plane. Choose the most appropriate alternatives.

The perfect paper plane

Let us suppose you have developed some designs for paper planes and wish to **(1)** *find out/determine/know* which of these is best. Having **(2)** *watched/looked at/observed* paper planes in the past will allow you to **(3)** *get to/make/arrive at* a hypothesis – for example, that planes with wider wingspans fly further. You will then need to **(4)** *validate/check/try* your hypothesis by designing an experiment. This is relatively straightforward. You simply make some planes with **(5)** *different/varying/distinct* wingspans, throw them, measure how far they travel and record the distances. The planes should be thrown at least five times. You should record your results, **(6)** *plot/write/put* them on a graph and then examine your **(7)** *discoveries/findings/answers* before writing them up. In your conclusion, you should say whether your **(8)** *first/starting/initial* hypothesis has been confirmed or not. If it has not, it will need to be modified.

8 Replace the underlined verbs in the scientific statements below with the correct form of the multi-part verbs in the box.

---

carry out   look into   make clear   point out   put forward
set out   take into account   take issue with

---

1 They <u>conducted</u> a study of perceptions of temperature.

2 The research group are currently <u>investigating</u> the effects of first language on the recall of childhood experiences.

3 They were finally able to <u>clarify</u> the distinction between learning and acquisition.

4 They <u>propose</u> a new model for the description of the universe.

5 They fail to <u>consider</u> a series of contributing factors.

6 I <u>indicate</u> several flaws in the methodology.

7 We <u>intended</u> to examine the stripe distribution in tabby cats.

8 We <u>contest</u> the statement by Burbrook and colleagues.

9 Decide which other patterns you can use with the multi-part verbs.

Example: They carried out an experiment.
A *They carried an experiment out.* ✓
B *They carried it out.* ✓
C *They carried out it.* ✗

1 I plan to look into the reasons for the differences.
A I plan to look the reasons into for the differences.
B I plan to look them into.
C I plan to look into them.

2 He pointed out the error.
A He pointed the error out.
B He pointed it out.
C He pointed out it.

3 She put forward a new theory.
A She put a new theory forward.
B She put it forward.
C She put forward it.

10 Work in pairs. Write sentences using all the patterns possible with these multi-part verbs and nouns. Can you use the same patterns with all the verbs? Why/Why not?

take into account (certain factors)
count on (getting a grant)
turn down (a job offer)

11 Work in pairs. Discuss how you would design studies to test these hypotheses.

1 People of all ages buy more in clothing shops if there is loud music playing.

2 Five-year-olds who have never used a tablet before will learn to use one more quickly than fifty-year-olds.

LANGUAGE TIP

Some phrasal verbs can be split by a full object though we sometimes avoid this for reasons of emphasis, e.g.
*She **put** several valuable suggestions **forward**.*
*She **put forward** several valuable suggestions.*
The second sentence emphasises *valuable suggestions*.

1 Answer the questions. Then compare your answers with a partner.

1 What are the health benefits of taking a nap during the day? Do you ever do this?

2 Do you remember your dreams? What do you think we can learn from dreams?

3 Have you ever woken up and tried to write down whatever it was you were dreaming? Did it help you to remember your dream?

2 Read the magazine article about two famous scientists. How would they answer the last two questions you discussed in Activity 1?

Cohesion

▶ **GRAMMAR** REFERENCE p.164

EXAM TIP

In the Writing paper you are tested on your ability to write coherently and cohesively. When parts of a text are logically connected, readers perceive the text as coherent. Cohesion devices (reference, substitution, ellipsis, conjunction and lexical cohesion) mark those logical connections explicitly.

3 Underline the different ways Otto Loewi and John Eccles are referred to in the article, including pronouns and repetitions of their names (examples of reference and lexical cohesion).

4 Find words or phrases with a similar meaning to *nap* and *question* in paragraph 1. Find another word for *wrote* in paragraph 3 (examples of lexical cohesion).

5 Look at paragraph 2 and find two examples of ellipsis. Which word has been left out in both cases?

6 Complete the last two paragraphs of the article with words to link the paragraphs, sentences and clauses.

7 Work in pairs. Do you think it is better to sleep on a problem or to try to solve it immediately? Can you name any scientists who have won the Nobel Prize? Why were they awarded the prize?

DREAM DISCOVERIES

Taking a quick nap not only refreshes you but can also reveal the answer to a question that's been nagging you or a problem you haven't been able to solve while awake. In the case of two famous neurophysiologists, not just a short siesta but a full night's sleep was required to allow them to meet the challenges they confronted.

German-born Otto Loewi and Australian John Carew Eccles both devoted their scientific careers to researching the way in which signals are transmitted in the brain. While one scientist struggled to find an experimental design to prove his theory that transmission was chemical rather than electrical, the other sought a means of accounting for experimental evidence of electrical activity. Both found what they were looking for in dreams.

Loewi had hit a wall with his research when he woke from a dream one night in April 1920. Realising that what he had dreamt was significant, he jotted a few notes down on a thin piece of paper and then went back to sleep. He woke again with a start a few hours later, aware that whatever it was he had written down was of vital importance to his work. To his horror, however, he realised he could neither decipher his own handwriting nor remember anything about the dream. The next night he went to bed again and read for a few hours before going to sleep. He woke suddenly at two in the morning with a vivid picture of an experimental design he knew would test and ultimately prove his theory.

Over a quarter of a century later and on the other side of the world, John Eccles was struggling to make sense of a mass of new experimental evidence. **(1)** .... Loewi, he went to bed one night with this problem on his mind and woke a few hours later, aware that **(2)** .... he was sleeping, a theory that explained the evidence had come to him. Eccles knew the story of Loewi's dream and the near tragic loss of the experimental design that had ultimately won him the Nobel Prize, **(3)** .... he forced himself to stay awake **(4)** .... he had checked every detail of the theory he had dreamt about against the experimental data. Eccles went on to win the Nobel Prize in 1963.

You may not be in the running for the Nobel Prize **(5)** .... if you've got a problem to solve, try sleeping on it. Make sure, **(6)** .... , that you've got a pen and paper handy and can read your own handwriting. If not, you might forget the solution.

All parts
improving your performance

▶ **EXAM** FOCUS p.182

1 ● 49 **Listen to two candidates doing Part 1 of the Speaking test. One of the candidates does not perform as well as the other. Which candidate is this, Gustave or Maria? How could they improve?**

2 ● 50 **Listen to Maria and Gustave talking about the pictures in Part 2 and answer the questions.**

1 Is there anything that Maria should do but doesn't, or does do but shouldn't?

2 Is Gustave's answer to the examiner's question long enough?

3 **Work in pairs.**

Turn to page 139 and do Task 1.
Then turn to page 143 and do Task 2.

4 ● 51 **Listen to Gustave and Maria doing Part 3 and tick the strategies they use to complete the task. Are there any other strategies you think they should use?**

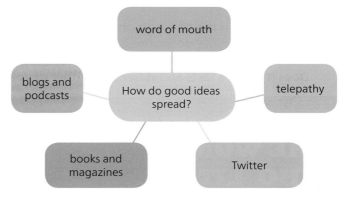

- Discuss each of the prompts in detail.
- Initiate the discussion.
- Involve the other person in the discussion.
- Follow up on what the other person says.
- Avoid long silences by using words like 'right' or 'OK'.

5 **Work in pairs. Turn to page 139 and do the activity. Give yourself a mark out of 5 for each of the following and then check to see if your partner agrees with your evaluation.**

- Accurate use of a range of grammatical structures
- Use of varied vocabulary
- Fluency and use of linking devices
- Pronunciation including intonation and sentence and word stress
- Ability to initiate, negotiate and respond effectively

6 ● 52 **Listen to Gustave and Maria doing Part 4 of the test and discussing some of the examiner's questions below. Which of the two candidates performs well? How could the other candidate have done better?**

- How important is it for people to learn about the history of science at school?
- Some people say they don't see the point of scientific research. Why do you think this is?
- Whose responsibility should it be to inform people about science – scientists or the media? Why?
- Science departments at universities often find it easier to get funding than other departments. Do you think this is right? Why/Why not?
- Which do you think is more important for success in any career – talent or hard work?

1 **Work with a partner and discuss these questions.**

1 What qualities do you need to become a scientist?

2 How many Nobel Prize winners can you name?

3 Which is more important in scientific achievement: hard work or talent?

2 **The woman in the photograph is the famous scientist Marie Curie. Write down three things you know about her and compare your list with a partner. Now read the text. Does it include facts about her life neither of you mentioned?**

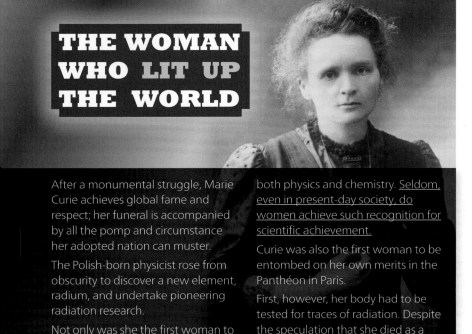

THE WOMAN WHO LIT UP THE WORLD

After a monumental struggle, Marie Curie achieves global fame and respect; her funeral is accompanied by all the pomp and circumstance her adopted nation can muster.

The Polish-born physicist rose from obscurity to discover a new element, radium, and undertake pioneering radiation research.

Not only was she the first woman to win the Nobel Prize, she was also the first person to win two Nobel Prizes. Furthermore, no other scientist ever won the prize in more than one scientific field. Curie won prizes for both physics and chemistry. Seldom, even in present-day society, do women achieve such recognition for scientific achievement.

Curie was also the first woman to be entombed on her own merits in the Panthéon in Paris.

First, however, her body had to be tested for traces of radiation. Despite the speculation that she died as a result of radiation poisoning, in fact the levels were quite low. A more likely cause was X-ray poisoning sustained during her service in mobile X-ray units in the First World War.

Emphasis with inversion

▶ **GRAMMAR** REFERENCE p.165

3 **Look at two sentences from the text and the alternative ways of expressing the same ideas. What is different about their impact on the reader?**

1A Not only was she the first woman to win the Nobel Prize, she was also the first person to win two Nobel Prizes.

B She was the first woman to win the Nobel Prize and the first person to win two Nobel Prizes.

2A Seldom, even in present-day society, do women achieve such recognition for scientific achievement.

B Even in present day society women seldom achieve such recognition for scientific achievement.

4 **What is the difference in the grammatical form of the sentences from the text and the alternative sentences in Activity 3?**

LANGUAGE TIP

You are more likely to find structures with subject–verb inversion in more formal or literary written contexts than you are in speech. Inversion tends to occur with negative adverbials.

Hardly had he arrived when Jo rushed in.

5 **Rewrite the sentences using inversion. Start with the word given.**

1 This city has seldom been in greater need of energy-efficient public transport than it is today.

Seldom ....

2 We had just ordered our meal when the waiter rudely asked us if we would mind paying the bill.

Scarcely ....

3 I have rarely seen such a brilliant display of artistry and expertise.

Rarely ....

4 You have failed to hand in your essay on time and you have also copied several paragraphs directly from the internet.

Not only ....

5 You should not let people who don't respect the dress code into the club under any circumstances.

Under no circumstances ....

6 She posted the letter and then began to regret what she had said.

No sooner ....

7 My client has never revealed the contents of this document to the media.

At no time ....

8 I had only just finished the assignment when my boss asked me to do something else for her.

Hardly ....

6 **Work in pairs. In which situations would you expect to hear or read the sentences in Activity 5?**

Key word transformation (Part 4)

▶ **EXAM** FOCUS p.179

1 Complete the second sentence so that it has a similar meaning to the first sentence, using the word given. Do not change the word given. You must use between three and six words, including the word given.

1 I regret not having written down that amazing dream I had. **ONLY**

If .... that amazing dream I had.

2 I'm convinced that I was woken up by some kind of noise. **MUST**

It .... some kind of noise that woke me.

3 I only managed to recall the contents of my dream by going back to sleep. **ONLY**

It .... back to sleep that I managed to remember the contents of my dream.

4 The dream I had that night would later change the course of medical science. **WAS**

The dream I had that night .... the course of medical science.

2 Which of the grammatical points in the box is being tested in each of the sentences in Activity 1?

emphasis with inversion   future in the past
hypothetical meaning   introductory *it*
modal verbs   verb patterns

3 Look at the sentences and the answers. There is one word missing in each answer. Add the missing word.

1 I had only just arrived when he insisted we leave. **SOONER**

No <u>sooner had I arrived</u> he insisted we leave.

2 I cannot remember ever having seen him before. **RECOLLECTION**

I have <u>no recollection ever</u> having seen him before.

3 I'm phoning because my daughter is too ill to talk to you. **BEHALF**

I'm phoning <u>on behalf my daughter</u>, who is too ill to talk to you.

4 If you tell yourself you will remember your dreams, you often do. **DETERMINED**

If <u>you determined to remember</u> your dreams, you often do.

EXAM TIP

Make sure you do not leave out any of the missing words. Remember that there will always be at least three words and as many as six words, including the given word.

4 Look at the sentences and the answers. The second sentence does not have a similar meaning to the first sentence. Make the necessary changes so that the meanings are similar.

1 Research has shown that frightening experiences are forgotten more readily than painful ones. **DIFFICULT**

According to research, <u>it is more difficult to forget</u> frightening experiences than painful ones.

2 Sue decided that it was not a good idea to return the dress to the boutique. **TAKE**

Sue decided that she should not <u>take the dress to</u> the boutique.

3 I only realised that Michael and Tim were brothers when I saw them together last week. **STRUCK**

It had <u>always struck me that</u> Michael and Tim were brothers until I saw them together last week.

4 I adore getting clothes for my birthday. **WHEN**

I adore <u>people when they give me</u> clothes for my birthday.

5 Complete the second sentence so that it has a similar meaning to the first sentence, using the word given. Do not change the word given. You must use between three and six words, including the word given.

1 I regret sending him that email. **WISH**

I .... him that email.

2 Alison would have come to the party unless something had happened to her. **MUST**

Something .... to Alison or she would have come to the party.

3 I managed to get to bed before midnight for once. **SUCCEEDED**

For once .... to bed before midnight.

4 I resolved the problem by talking to his mother. **DID**

What I .... to talk to his mother.

5 There is a rumour that the head of department will be retiring in the spring. **BE**

The head of department is .... in the spring.

6 Don't ever say anything to John about the new scheme. **CIRCUMSTANCES**

Under .... to John about the new scheme.

1 Turn to page 148 and do the quiz. Compare your answers with a partner. How many questions did you answer?

Gapped text (Part 7)

▶ **EXAM** FOCUS p.180

2 Read the article about Nikola Tesla. How many of the quiz questions in Activity 1 can you answer as a result of reading the article?

3 Read the article again. Six paragraphs have been removed from the article. Choose from the paragraphs A–G the one which fits each gap (1–6). There is one extra paragraph which you do not need to use.

EXAM TIP

When you have chosen an option (A–G) for each gap, read the whole text through with your chosen paragraphs in place to double-check that it makes sense.

4 Look at the underlined words and phrases in the article and the paragraphs and choose the correct meaning. Underline the words that help you work out which is the correct meaning.

1 pip him at the post   **A** accuse him of something
                            B narrowly beat him

2 edging   **A** gradually advancing
              B cutting

3 eulogising   **A** criticising   **B** praising

4 pleas   **A** requests   **B** declarations

5 panned   **A** evaluated negatively
              B described fully

6 got wind of   **A** discovered   **B** preferred

Vocabulary

expressions with *matter*

5 Choose the correct alternative in each sentence.

1 Astrophysicists are still trying to solve the puzzle of *grey/dark* matter in the universe.

2 As a matter of *truth/fact*, I'd never heard of Tesla until you told me about him.

3 She couldn't take the money. It was a matter of *principle/honour*.

4 It can only be a matter of *time/waiting* before someone is seriously injured.

5 As a matter of *enquiry/interest*, where was Tesla born?

6 Can't it wait? It's hardly a matter of *life and death/living or dying*.

A

It was not the first time Tesla had seen a rival pip him at the post, nor was it to be the last. If his contemporary fans are to be believed, he was responsible for any number of inventions and discoveries from X-rays to radar to dark matter in the universe.

B

Donors purchased all kinds of Tesla merchandise, ranging from glossy photos at twenty dollars through to guest passes to something called a 'Tesla event' at a thousand. It seems their desire to tangibly express their devotion to the eccentric genius knew no bounds.

C

Tesla fans often demonise his great rival, casting their hero as innocent victim. They also tend to exaggerate Tesla's inventive genius and attribute to him alone discoveries that were the result of generations of hardworking scientists and engineers edging towards solutions to problems.

D

If, like me, you have never seen one of these, I should tell you that it's the same machine that electrifies the monster and brings it to life in Frankenstein movies. It was in fact an expensive project involving a giant version of the device that was Tesla's undoing.

E

Conflicts like this occurred throughout his life perhaps because he was in some ways the quintessential mad scientist. He slept only two to three hours a night and had obsessions such as a loathing for round objects, human hair, jewellery and numbers not divisible by three.

F

We also have Tesla to thank for the fact that enough electricity comes out of sockets to power our appliances. But to achieve this goal he had first to win what is sometimes called 'the war of the currents' against the man who gave him a job but was later his most vehement detractor.

G

It would seem that Tesla's hugely loyal fan-base is largely made up of geeky young people who play real-time strategy games. To publicise their hero they have developed literally hundreds of sites devoted to eulogising his work.

NIKOLA TESLA:
the ultimate geek?

Frances Mulrennan tells us what she learnt about an extraordinary man.

I had actually never heard of Nikola Tesla until I happened to read that his fans had responded to <u>pleas</u> to fund a Tesla museum by pledging donations of $900,000 only a couple of days after the appeal was launched. The group promoting the project now have even more funds than they thought they needed. But who were the people who so rapidly answered the call?

1 [   ]

There are biographies and articles and a film, largely <u>panned</u> by the critics, starring the singer David Bowie. There is even a car called the Tesla. Given his notoriety, I now wonder how it was possible for Tesla to have escaped my attention. But that he did, even though he was once very famous and is still in the news. When you consider that many children know about him because of something called the Tesla coil, often used in science demonstrations, my ignorance is more surprising still.

2 [   ]

It was intended to be the key element in a plan to transmit energy to the entire world and to create a transatlantic wireless telecommunications system. The scheme's potential profitability meant that Tesla was able to attract investment, to the tune of almost the same amount as the current funding for the museum. But when shareholders <u>got wind of</u> the fact that a competitor of Tesla's, the Italian inventor Marconi, had successfully transmitted a long-distance radio signal, they lost faith in the project and refused to fund it further.

3 [   ]

The most controversial of all was the electric light bulb. Thomas Edison, of course, usually gets the credit for this, the most ubiquitous of twentieth-century inventions. But Tesla, who was employed by Edison, played a major role in turning it into a workable device that could be sold to consumers.

4 [   ]

Why they had such intense antipathy towards one another remains unclear. Whatever the motives, Edison became a passionate defender of direct current, or DC – the sort that comes out of an ordinary battery and is still used in cars – believing it to be the way forward for electrical power generation and distribution. To his great irritation, Tesla was eventually able to show that alternating current (AC) was far more efficient.

5 [   ]

It is true, though, that Tesla was a man of exceptional talents. Yet even as a young man, he was extremely volatile, challenging the opinions of one of his professors at a prestigious Austrian technical university. The professor refused to back down and soon after, Tesla dropped out of the course.

6 [   ]

Even so, and despite these strange habits, for the work on electricity alone he deserves our gratitude. I for one am certainly glad I came to learn a little more about this quite remarkably gifted man.

6 Has there ever been a situation where you were not given credit for something you did? How did you feel?

Essay (Part 1)
linking phrases and conjunctions
▶ **WRITING** REFERENCE p.168

1 Complete the advice for writing essays with *Do* or *Don't*. Compare your answers with a partner.

1 .... give your own opinion immediately.
2 .... have a balanced approach.
3 .... give your own opinion at the end.
4 .... use connectors to link your ideas.
5 .... use ideas from the task input to support your arguments but change the wording.
6 .... involve the reader by using rhetorical questions.
7 .... use a formal register and present your ideas in a clear, objective way.
8 .... use bullet points.

2 Look at the exam task and a candidate's essay. Find examples in the essay of each of the good pieces of advice in Activity 1.

Your class has attended a panel discussion on what methods governments should use to encourage an appreciation of scientific research. You have made the notes below.

Methods governments could use to encourage an interest in science
- media coverage
- adult education
- greater financial investment

Some opinions expressed in the discussion

'Science reporting in the media often emphasises less useful research.'

'Some older adults didn't enjoy their science classes at school, so they won't want to go to science classes now.'

'The problem is that politicians don't understand the importance of science.'

Write an essay for your tutor discussing **two** of the methods in your notes. You should **explain which method you think is more important** for governments to consider, **giving reasons** to support your opinion.

You may, if you wish, make use of the opinions expressed in the discussion but you should use your own words as far as possible.

Write your **essay** in **220–260** words in an appropriate style.

Methods to encourage an interest in science

Nowadays we frequently hear people complaining about government spending on scientific research. This lack of appreciation is the result of insufficient information about scientists and the work they do. As long as this lack of information persists, people will continue to view investment in scientific research negatively. Closer connections between the scientific community and the general public need to be forged to overcome this problem. But how might this be achieved?

One possible approach would be to increase media coverage. The government could insist that journalists emphasise scientific findings the public see as necessary and of benefit to them. While this would almost certainly give scientific research a more positive image, it implies placing restrictions on the freedom of the press. This is not an easy task. Nor is it one that most members of a civil society would find acceptable.

A second tactic the government might take is to extend the excellent science teaching in our secondary schools to the adult education sector. A potential difficulty here is that some adults might feel uncomfortable about returning to formal education because of bad memories of their school days. Nevertheless, any resistance might be overcome by holding free lectures on science at science museums and possibly even in bars and cafés rather than in classrooms and lecture theatres.

In my view, the second of these two approaches should be implemented. Provided this were done efficiently, members of the public would have closer informal contact with scientists and thus a change in attitude would certainly come about. Rather than demanding cutbacks, we may even find that members of the public start to ask why more money is not being spent.

3 Find four linking words or phrases in the essay. Which one introduces

1 the first idea?
2 a contrasting idea?
3 an opinion?
4 a result?

EXAM TIP

To do well in the writing paper, you must demonstrate that you can use a range of complex language, such as vocabulary and structures, as well as using a variety of conjunctions, linking words, etc.

4 Turn to page 148 and do the exam task. Make sure you have followed all the advice in the checklist on page 166.

1 Complete the multi-part verbs in the sentences.

1 They .... out a study of how people interpret facial expressions.

2 The theory she put .... was not taken seriously until many years later.

3 They .... issue with some of the things he had said during the meeting.

4 He tried to take all the different factors .... account.

5 It took her several months to arrive .... a good design for the new light fitting.

6 I don't care what he does, he'll never get her to back ....

2 Complete the second sentence so that it has a similar meaning to the first sentence, using the word in brackets. Do not change the word given. You must use between three and six words, including the word given.

1 I only managed to buy my own place after years of sharing with other people.

Only after years of sharing with other people .... my own place. (*did*)

2 The neighbours are really noisy and they are not very friendly either.

Not .... really noisy, they are also not very friendly. (*only*)

3 You shouldn't ever put your full address on a luggage label.

At .... put your full address on a luggage label. (*time*)

4 It will be six years since I moved here next Saturday.

By next Saturday I will .... six years. (*for*)

5 You shouldn't tell anyone about this under any circumstances.

Under .... tell anyone about this. (*no*)

6 I closed the door and immediately realised I had left my keys inside the house.

No .... the door than I realised my keys were inside the house. (*sooner*)

3 Read the story and think of the word which best fits each gap. Use only one word in each gap.

All's well that ends well

Carla introduced David to the people she had met in France. **(1)** .... was sure **(2)** .... would get on like a house on fire. She suggested they all go out for dinner together and **(3)** .... couples agreed to meet that evening at 8.30. Carla offered to book a table in a restaurant. **(4)** .... there were several dozen good restaurants in town, **(5)** .... of them had a table that night at 8.30. One of the head waiters suggested that Carla should call back at 8.00 to see if there had been any cancellations and, as luck would have it, there was **(6)** .... Carla asked the head waiter to reserve the table in her name and he promised he **(7)** .... When they got to the restaurant, however, there was no record of Carla's booking at all. Her friends thought she should make a formal complaint but she decided not **(8)** .... They found a very good place two doors down the street, **(9)** .... their evening was certainly not ruined. In fact, it was one of the most enjoyable evenings any of them had ever **(10)** ....

PROGRESS TEST 4

Multiple-choice cloze (Part 1)

1 For questions 1–8, read the text below and decide which answer (A, B, C or D) best fits each gap. There is an example at the beginning (0).

Classic comedy: *When Harry met Sally*

Since its **(0)** *A, release* in 1989, *When Harry met Sally* has **(1)** .... a lasting place in the affections of audiences around the world. Director Rob Reiner could never have predicted that the film's central question, 'Can men and women really be friends?' would have such wide **(2)** .... It won the **(3)** .... of audiences and critics alike, with Nora Ephron **(4)** .... a nomination for best screenplay at the Academy Awards. The film **(5)** .... the relationship of the two main characters, Harry (Billy Crystal) and Sally (Meg Ryan), over the course of twelve years. At first it seems they are completely **(6)** .... to each other; she's a romantic optimist, while he's cynical and **(7)** .... in commitment. Unlike the characters, however, audiences will not be deceived by their seeming incompatibility, aware that the laws of romantic comedy dictate that love **(8)** .... prevails.

0	**A** release	**B** rise	**C** emergence	**D** origin
1	**A** remained	**B** gained	**C** continued	**D** reached
2	**A** appeal	**B** charm	**C** fame	**D** popularity
3	**A** celebration	**B** success	**C** approval	**D** recognition
4	**A** holding	**B** collecting	**C** taking	**D** receiving
5	**A** portrays	**B** displays	**C** reveals	**D** demonstrates
6	**A** inappropriate	**B** unsuited	**C** unfit	**D** inadequate
7	**A** lacking	**B** faulty	**C** missing	**D** insufficient
8	**A** absolutely	**B** exactly	**C** inevitably	**D** truly

Open cloze (Part 2)

2 For questions 1–8, read the text below and think of the word which best fits each gap. Use only one word in each gap. There is an example at the beginning (0).

Designed to inspire

The Melbourne Brain Centre is one example of a new trend **(0)** *in* science building design emerging in universities **(1)** .... the world. Instead of the isolating partitions and cubicles intended to promote competition, the architects who designed the Brain Centre set **(2)** .... to promote openness and collectivity. Both are qualities which, **(3)** .... to historian of innovation Steven Johnson, have **(4)** .... a far greater contribution to scientific advancement. Johnson's analysis of innovative thinking highlighted the importance of creating an environment in **(5)** .... ideas can develop. In the case of the Brain Centre, **(6)** .... includes cafés and lounges throughout the building and laboratories, which are open spaces **(7)** .... equipment and conversation can be shared. The walls of lounges are covered in a markable surface so that two researchers talking about their work can jot their thoughts down **(8)** .... having to interrupt the flow to look for pen and paper. In short, the Brain Centre is an environment designed to inspire.

Word formation (Part 3)

3 **For questions 1–8, read the text below. Use the word given in capitals at the end of some of the lines to form a word that fits in the gap in the same line.**

Just testing

It is not actually possible to fail a

(0) ~personality~ test but many people   **PERSONAL**

react **(1)** .... if they feel the   **INDIGNATION**

results don't match their own ideas

of their strengths and **(2)** ....   **ABLE**

What is simply an interpretation of

the results is sometimes understood

as a **(3)** .... or even an outright   **CRITICISE**

attack. Those who find themselves

repeatedly turned down for jobs on

the basis of test results may start

to feel that the tests are simply too

(4) .... and may even decide to   **DEMAND**

try and cheat on the next test they

do. This is harder to do than you

might think. Someone analysing test

results would immediately become

(5) .... if they were to notice   **SUSPECT**

that a candidate had answered

inconsistently. Finding a series of

(6) .... between a candidate's   **MATCH**

answers will make it obvious that the

person taking the test is **(7)** ....   **TRUST**

The best advice, then, is to make

your **(8)** .... as authentic as   **RESPOND**

you can.

Key word transformation (Part 4)

4 **For questions 1–6, complete the second sentence so that it has a similar meaning to the first sentence, using the word given. Do not change the word given. You must use between three and six words, including the word given.**

Example:

We're going to camp whether or not it's raining.

EVEN

We're going to camp w~even if it's~ raining.

1 It would be a good idea for you to talk to the careers advisor first.

SUGGEST

I .... to the careers advisor first.

2 Michael doesn't see that he is in the wrong and he refuses to discuss the situation.

ONLY

Not .... fail to see he is in the wrong, he also refuses to discuss the situation.

3 They sometimes tell the people who arrive late that they can't enter the theatre.

PREVENTED

People arriving late .... the theatre.

4 Although the painting is worth much more, it was recently sold for only £10,000.

BEING

The painting was recently sold for only £10,000, ... much more.

5 Just as I got to the theatre, they announced that the concert was sold out.

HAD

Hardly .... when they announced that the concert was sold out.

6 People think that Edison invented the light bulb.

THOUGHT

Edison .... the light bulb.

Support for Speaking tasks

Unit 1, Speaking and Use of English focus, Activity 4

Take turns to take the role of examiner and candidate. Ask and answer the questions.

1 **Choose one or two questions from the list.**

- Where are you from?
- What do you do there?
- How long have you been studying English?
- What do you enjoy most about studying English?

2 **Choose one or more questions from the list.**

- What has been your most interesting travel experience?
- What did you like most about the area where you grew up?
- Who has more influence on your life – your friends or your family?
- Do you prefer to get the news from newspapers, television or the internet?
- Do you ever wish you were rich and famous?

Unit 2, Speaking and grammar focus, Activity 7
Task 1

Student A: Here are your pictures. They show people putting up messages. I'd like you to compare two of the pictures and say why the people might be putting up the messages and what sort of reaction they might get.

Student B: Do you think putting up messages is a good way to help people remember things?

> - **Why are the people putting up the messages?**
> - **What sort of reaction might they get?**

Unit 3, Speaking focus, Activity 5

Work in groups of three. Take it in turns to take the roles of examiner and candidates.

Examiner: Listen to check how well the candidates respond to and expand on each other's ideas.

Candidates: Look at the task and follow the examiner's instructions. Remember to respond to and expand on your partner's ideas.

Examiner's instructions

For Part 3, say:

Now I'd like you to talk about something together for about two minutes. Here are some habits we often think make people seem youthful and a question for you to discuss. First, you have some time to look at the task. (Pause for fifteen seconds.) Now talk to each other about how much these things can help a person seem youthful.

When the candidates have spoken for two minutes, say:
Now you have about a minute to decide which habit would have the greatest long-term benefit. (Give the candidates one minute to decide.)

For Part 4, ask two of these questions:

- *How important do you think it is for older people to maintain a youthful appearance?*
- *Some people find it difficult to do enough physical activity once they grow older. Why do you think this is?*
- *Whose responsibility should it be to care for the elderly: families or the state?*
- *Which do you think is more important for an older person: spending time with their family or with other older people?*
- *Some people say that youth is wasted on the young. What do you think?*

Unit 4, Speaking focus, Activity 6
Part 3

Talk about something together for about two minutes. Here are some factors which affect young people's ability to do well at a sport and a question for you to discuss.

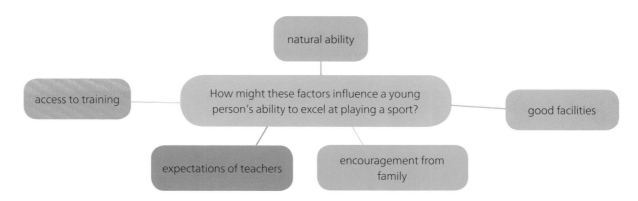

Talk to each other about how these factors influence a young person's ability to excel at playing a sport.

Part 4

- How easy do you think it is to recognise talent in a child?
- What risks might there be if young people are pushed too hard to excel at something?
- Should parents always have high expectations of their children?
- Do you think schools should encourage competition among children?

Unit 5, Use of English and Speaking focus, Activity 8

Task 1

Student A: Here are your pictures. They show people doing things in unusual places. I'd like you to compare two of the pictures and say what might be difficult about doing these activities in places like these.

Student B: Which of these activities would surprise other people most? Why?

> **What might be difficult about doing these activities in places like these?**

Unit 6, Speaking focus, Activity 7

Task 1

Student A: Here are your pictures. They show people using different types of memory aids. I'd like you to compare two of the pictures and say what kind of information these things can help people remember and how effective they might be.

Student B: Which sort of memory aid do you think is most useful for students? Why?

> - **What kind of information can these things help people remember?**
> - **How effective might they be?**

Unit 7, Speaking focus, Activity 7

Work in groups of three.

Student A: You are the examiner. Choose a question to ask. Then listen to the candidates' answers, thinking about the points on the checklist.

Students B and C: You are the candidates. Follow Student A's instructions.

Examiner's questions

- Do you think there should be more careful regulation of advertising?
- Were people able to make up their own minds about products and services before there was so much advertising?
- How have the internet and social networking changed the way products are marketed and advertised?
- Do you agree with bans on advertising aimed at certain groups, e.g. young children, or products, e.g. cigarettes?
- Do you think marketing and advertising are appropriate ways to use psychology and linguistics research?

Examiner's checklist

Did the candidate

1 say enough?
2 avoid basic errors like lack of agreement between subject and verb, double negation, etc.?
3 use clear intelligible pronunciation?
4 respond naturally to what the other candidate said?
5 use expressions for justifying an opinion?
6 use expressions for agreeing and disagreeing?

Unit 8, Speaking focus, Activity 7
Task I

Student A: Here are your pictures. They show people arriving at an airport. I'd like you to compare two of the pictures and say what the purpose of the people's trip might be and how they might be feeling about their trip.

Student B: Give your partner feedback on his/her performance using the General marking guidelines on page 185.

> - **What might the purpose of the people's trip be?**
> - **How might they be feeling about their trip?**

Unit 9, Speaking focus, Activity 7
Task 1

Student A: Here are your pictures. They show people doing things that are usually learnt from a teacher. I'd like you to compare two of the pictures and say why people might prefer to learn these things on their own and what difficulties they might have.

Student B: Who do you think looks the most confident? Why?

> • **Why might people prefer to learn these things on their own?**
> • **What difficulties might they have?**

Unit 10, Speaking focus, Activity 5
Part 3

Talk about something together for two minutes. Here are some methods which people might use to try to make new friends and business contacts and a question for you to discuss.

Talk to each other about how useful these methods might be when trying to make new friends and business contacts.

Unit 10, Speaking focus, Activity 6
Part 4

- Some people prefer to make new friends exclusively through being introduced to them by others. Why do you think this is?
- Many people keep the same friends they had at school or university throughout their lives. Why do you think this is?
- Do you think there is too much emphasis on linking up via social networking sites with people who share your interests? Why/Why not?
- It is sometimes said that fate chooses our relatives but that we choose our friends. Do you agree?

Unit 11, Speaking focus, Activity 7

Task 1

Student A: Here are your pictures. They show people looking at things carefully. I'd like you to compare two of the pictures and say why the people might be enjoying looking at these things and what they might learn from these experiences.

Student B: Do you think it's better to look at things carefully on your own or with other people?

> • **Why might the people be enjoying looking at these things?**
> • **What might they learn from these experiences?**

Unit 12, Speaking focus, Activity 3

Task 1

Student A: Here are your pictures. They show people using recent inventions. I'd like you to compare two of the pictures and say why people might find inventions like these useful and what reactions they might get from other people when they use them.

Student B: Give your partner feedback on his/her performance using the General marking guidelines on page 185.

> • **Why might people find inventions like these useful?**
> • **What reactions might they get from other people when they use them?**

Unit 12, Speaking focus, Activity 5

Talk to each other about something for about two minutes. Here are some kinds of scientific research that people do. Talk to each other about how important these kinds of research are for contemporary society.

- research into how the brain works
- surveys of work and leisure habits
- How important are these kinds of scientific research for contemporary society?
- observation of galaxies and stars
- research into plant and animal life
- creating cleaner energy sources

Now you have about a minute to decide which kind of research would have the greatest long-term benefit.

Unit 2, Speaking and grammar focus, Activity 7

Task 2

Student B: Here are your pictures. They show people giving information. I'd like you to compare two of the pictures and say how important it is to give this information clearly and what might happen if the information is misunderstood.

Student A: Do you think it's always necessary to have important instructions written down?

> - **How important is it to give this information clearly?**
> - **What might happen if the information is misunderstood?**

Unit 5, Use of English and Speaking focus, Activity 8

Task 2

Student B: Here are your pictures. They show people doing things that can be beneficial. I'd like you to compare two of the pictures and say how these activities might be beneficial to the people and what might be easy or difficult about doing them in settings like these.

Student A: Which activity do you think requires the most concentration? Why?

> - **How might these activities be beneficial to the people?**
> - **What might be easy or difficult about doing them in settings like these?**

Unit 6, Speaking focus, Activity 7
Task 2

Student B: Here are your pictures. They show people holding objects of sentimental value. I'd like you to compare two of the pictures and say what memories the objects might bring back and how long the people might keep the objects for.

Student A: Do you think people have more sentimental objects as they get older?

> - **What memories might the objects bring back?**
> - **How long might the people keep the objects for?**

Unit 8, Speaking focus, Activity 7
Task 2

Student B: Here are your pictures. They show people packing to go away somewhere. I'd like you to compare two of the pictures and say how difficult it might be for the people to choose what to pack and how organised they need to be.

Student A: Give your partner feedback on his/her performance using the General marking guidelines on page 185.

> - **How difficult might it be for the people to choose what to pack?**
> - **How organised do they need to be?**

Unit 9, Speaking focus, Activity 7
Task 2

Student B: Here are your pictures. They show people doing activities to help them learn to work as a team. I'd like you to compare two of the pictures and say why these activities might help people learn to work as a team and what difficulties they might have.

Student A: Which group do you think are enjoying the activities most? Why?

> • **Why might these activities help people learn to work as a team?**
> • **What difficulties might they have?**

Unit 11, Speaking focus, Activity 7
Task 2

Student B: Here are your pictures. They show people who have to wear a uniform doing their jobs. I'd like you to compare two of the pictures and say why the people need to wear the uniforms and how they might feel about wearing them.

Student A: Do you think some people look more responsible wearing a uniform?

> • **Why do the people need to wear the uniforms?**
> • **How might they feel about wearing them?**

Unit 12, Speaking focus, Activity 3
Task 2

Student B: Here are your pictures. They show people working in environments designed to encourage creativity. I'd like you to compare two of the pictures and say how these environments might make people more creative and what difficulties people might have working in environments like these.

Student A: Give your partner feedback on his/her performance using the General marking guidelines on page 185.

> • How might these environments make people more creative?
> • What difficulties might people have working in environments like these?

Communication activities

Unit 1, Listening focus, Activity 5

Work in pairs. Take it in turns to ask and answer the questions.

1 Have you ever ordered something from *room service*? What did you order?

2 Are there any drinks that you prefer at *room temperature*? Why/Why not?

3 Do you know anyone who lives in a flat or house where there is *no room to swing a cat*? How do they feel?

4 Which is more important to you: living somewhere that is nice and *roomy*, having a good view or living somewhere near great entertainment facilities? Why?

5 Would you be attracted to a job that offered you free *room and board*? Why/Why not?

6 Do you ever pay for a special seat on a plane to make sure you'll have enough *leg room*? Is it worth the money?

Unit 10, Grammar focus, Activity 6
Student B

1 Check that Student A has the correct answers for sentences 1–3.

1 The people on the beach saw a man ~~who was~~ waving frantically as he was swept out by the strong current.

2 There are only fifteen places so some people ~~who~~ apply**ing** to attend the course will inevitably be disappointed.

3 The bandage ~~which was~~ protecting the cut from infection had to be replaced every two days.

2 Decide which words you can cut to turn the relative clauses in the sentences into participle clauses. Do you need to make any other changes? Check your answers with Student A.

Example: I had just arrived at the party when I saw a girl ~~who was~~ wearing exactly the same outfit as me.

4 Her prime concerns when she has been looking for a partner have always been status and wealth.

5 The film, which was released last Tuesday, has received some very damning reviews.

6 Anyone who wishes to raise an issue for discussion during the meeting should contact the secretary at least a week beforehand.

3 Work with Student A to create a story that includes either sentences 1 or 4.

Unit 4, Writing focus, Activity 6

Look at the exam task and plan your introduction. Decide together what information should be included.

1 the actions you have chosen to discuss

2 analysis of which action is more important

3 reasons why you think the actions are important

4 why governments should promote health and fitness among young people

5 other action the government could take

Your class has attended a panel discussion on the action governments can take to promote health and fitness among young people. You have made the notes below.

Action to promote health and fitness among young people
- Improve teaching in schools.
- Improve attitudes to competitiveness.
- Improve the image of sports.

Opinions expressed during the discussion

'There need to be specialist sports teachers for children and students of all ages.'

'Some young people are put off by the pressure to compete.'

'A lot of young people don't think it's cool to take part in sports.'

Write an essay for your tutor discussing **two** of the actions in your notes. You should **explain which action is more important, giving reasons** to support your opinion. You may, if you wish, make use of the opinions expressed during the discussion but you should use your own words as far as possible. Write your **essay** in **220–260** words in an appropriate style.

Unit 6, Grammar focus, Activity 8

Which two of the buildings should be saved for posterity? With your partner, put them in order of importance and say why the two you have chosen have the greatest historical significance.

Unit 6 Vocabulary focus, Activity 7
Student A

Play the word association game with Student B. Say an adjective from the box and ask what ideas Student B associates with the adjective. Then listen to Student B's adjective and say what ideas you associate with it.

changeable   comforting   illogical   irresponsible
unbelievable

Unit 7, Writing focus, Activity 2
Survey results

1   I like to look at most of the advertisements I am exposed to.
    Agree: 52%   **Disagree:** 37%   **Neither:** 11%

2   Most advertising insults my intelligence
    Agree: 48%   **Disagree:** 39%   **Neither:** 13%

3   In general, I feel I can trust advertising.
    Agree: 38%   **Disagree:** 51%   **Neither:** 11%

4   Products usually live up to the promises made in their advertisements
    Agree: 50%   **Disagree:** 34%   **Neither:** 16%

5   In general, I like advertising.
    Agree: 54%   **Disagree:** 35%   **Neither:** 11%

Unit 9, Grammar focus, Activity 6
Student B

1   Student A promised to invite you to the cinema last night but didn't. Listen to Student A explain what happened.

2   You borrowed student A's tennis racket last week and forgot to return it. Call Student A now to apologise and make your excuses. Use *I was going to, I was planning to* and *I would have.*

Unit 9, Listening focus, Activity 5
Student A

Take turns with Student B to match the first half of the sentences 1–6 with the second (A–F).

1   I made a mental
2   I'll put a bit of oil on that hinge. That should do
3   I meant to get some coffee from the supermarket but it completely slipped

A   up a mental image of a place where you felt perfectly happy?
B   up, which can be rather embarrassing.
C   brain to remember which street she lived in but I had no idea really.

Unit 10, Grammar focus, Activity 6
Student A

1 Decide which words you can cut to turn the relative clauses in the sentences into participle clauses. Do you need to make any other changes?

Example: I had just arrived at the party when I saw a girl ~~who was~~ wearing exactly the same outfit as me.

1 The people on the beach saw a man who was waving frantically as he was swept out by the strong current.

2 There are only fifteen places so some people who apply to attend the course will inevitably be disappointed.

3 The bandage which was protecting the cut from infection had to be replaced every two days.

2 Check your answers with Student B. Then check that he/she has the correct answers for sentences 4–6.

4 Her prime concerns when ~~she has been~~ looking for a partner have always been status and wealth.

5 The film, ~~which was~~ released last Tuesday, has received some very damning reviews.

6 Anyone ~~who~~ wish~~es~~**ing** to raise an issue for discussion during the meeting should contact the secretary at least a week beforehand.

3 Work with Student B to create a story that includes either sentences 1 or 4.

Unit 10, Writing focus, Activity 3

Look at the exam task and decide what programme of studies you have been following.

> Your school or college takes part in an exchange programme with another institution in another country. You have decided to apply to go on an exchange visit and are required to write a letter to the director of the host institution, explaining why they should accept you as a student. You should explain:
>
> - what programme of studies you have been following at your home institution.
> - why you are a suitable candidate for an exchange programme.
> - what benefits you expect to gain from taking part in the programme.
>
> Write your **letter** in **220–260** words in an appropriate style.

Student A: plan the section on why you are a suitable candidate for an exchange programme.

Student B: plan the section on what benefits you expect to gain.

Look at each other's plans and write your letter.

Unit 11, Vocabulary and Use of English focus, Activity 1

Answers

1 T
2 F (It takes twelve muscles to smile and eleven to frown.)
3 F (There are nineteen.)
4 T
5 T
6 T
7 F
8 F (It can make you feel better.)

Unit 6 Vocabulary focus, Activity 7

Student B

Play the word association game with Student A. Listen to Student A's adjective and say what ideas you associate with it. Then say an adjective from the box and ask what ideas Student A associates with it.

excitable imaginative incomprehensible irresistible unthinkable

Unit 8, Speaking focus, Activity 8

Imagine you are travelling in Thailand. Together choose the best souvenir to buy for

1 your grandmother/grandfather.
2 your ten-year-old brother/sister.
3 your boyfriend/girlfriend.
4 your boss.

Unit 9, Grammar focus, Activity 6

Student A

1 You promised to invite student B to the cinema last night but you forgot. Call student B now and make your excuses. Use *I was going to*, *I was planning to* and *I would have*.

2 Student B borrowed your tennis racket last week and forgot to return it. Listen to Student B explain what happened.

Unit 9, Listening focus, Activity 5

Student B

Take turns with Student A to match the first half of the sentences 1–6 with the second (A–F)

4 I've got two friends – one called Andy and one called Sandy – and I often get their names muddled
5 I was racking my
6 Can you conjure

D the trick and stop the noise.
E my mind. I'll have to go back and get some.
F note to call the bank the next morning.

Unit 2, Listening focus, Activity 1

● If you answered yes to four or more questions, you are an introvert.

● If you answered no to four or more questions, you are an extrovert.

● If you have a mixture of yes and no answers, you have tendencies to be both an extrovert and an introvert, depending on your mood.

Unit 12, Reading focus, Activity 1

Quick quiz

1 Who is normally credited with having invented the radio?
2 Who is normally credited with having invented the electric light bulb?
3 What are the two major types of electric current used today?
4 Which type is used to power cities?
5 Which type is used in most cars?
6 Who invented the radar?

Unit 12, Writing focus, Activity 4

Look at the exam task.

1 Work in pairs and plan an outline for the essay.
2 Write your essay and make sure you have followed all the advice in the checklist on page 166.
3 Show your essay to other students and see if they can find any other mistakes or make suggestions for how your essay could be improved.

You have attended a Science Club lecture on how schools could encourage young people to train for careers in science. You have made the notes below.

Ways in which schools could encourage young people to train for careers in science
- enjoyable science lessons
- careers advice
- guest lectures from professional scientists

Some opinions expressed in the discussion

'Kids should be able to design their own experiments.'

'A lot of the careers advice given is already out of date.'

'A lot of scientists are too busy to spend time visiting schools.'

Write an essay for your tutor discussing **two** of the methods in your notes. You should **explain which method you think is more important** for governments to consider and provide reasons to support your opinion. You may, if you wish, make use of the opinions expressed in the discussion but you should use your own words as far as possible. Write your answer in **220–260** words in an appropriate style.

Grammar reference

Unit 1

1 Verbs in perfect and continuous forms

Tense refers to the time when the action of the verb occurs. The action can occur in one of three time periods: past, present or future. They form a time line.

Past   Present   Future

I ate. → *I eat.*   → *I will eat.*

Aspect refers to how we view the action described by the verb with respect to time. We can view the action of the verb as occurring either across or between those periods of time. That is, the times on the time line can be extended (progressive aspect) or combined (perfect aspect).

2 Simple aspect

The action is viewed as a fact.

*I **don't eat** meat.*

2.1 Present simple

1 for routine or regularly repeated actions (often with adverbs and expressions of frequency like *always, usually, often, sometimes, rarely, never, every Saturday morning, twice a week*).

*We **go** for a walk most afternoons.*
*She **doesn't go** out on weeknights.*
*I rarely **go** to bed before midnight.*

2 for present habits.
*I usually **get** the tram to work.*

3 for permanent situations.
*They both **come from** the same village in Devon.*
*They **live** in a side street off the Ramblas.*

3 Continuous aspect

The action is continuous.
*When Sam called, I **was eating**.*

3.1 Present continuous

We use the present continuous when we use dynamic (action) verbs to talk about

1 actions happening now.
A: *Where's Terry?*
B: *She's in the kitchen – she's **making** a cup of tea.*

2 changing/developing situations.
*Inma **is losing** weight.*

3 temporary situations.
*He's **working** as a cleaner until he can find a better job.*

4 annoying or surprising habits, with *always*.
*I'm **always forgetting** to charge my mobile.*
*She's **always buying** her grandchildren little presents.*

5 plans and arrangements in the future.
*Are you **doing** anything next weekend?*

4 Perfect aspect

The action happened at some unknown time between then, the past, and now, the present time of speaking.
*I **have eaten** a lot today.*

4.1 Present perfect simple

We use the present perfect simple

1 to talk about states, single or repeated actions over a long period of time up to the present (*often with ever/ never, often/always*).
*I've **always dreamt** of visiting New York.*
*Have you **ever been** to Ireland?*
*I've only **been** skiing once since I moved to Spain.*
*He's **missed** at least ten of the classes this term.*
*This is only the second time I've **travelled** by plane.*
*It's one of the most disgusting meals I've **ever eaten**.*

2 to talk about recent single actions with a present result (often with *just, already, yet*).
*I've **already started** making spaghetti for dinner, so I don't want to go out.*
*Have you **finished** reading 'The Road to Riverton' yet?*
*I've **just got back** from Australia.*

> **Watch out!** In American English it is acceptable to use the past simple in sentences like these.
> *Did you eat yet?*
> *I already ate.*

3 to talk about an unfinished period of time up to the present (often with *for/since, this week/month/year*).
*Irene **has lived** in Abu Dhabi for just over a year.*
*They've **been** married since early last year.*
*I've always **hated** long-haul flights.*
*She's **refused** to eat meat since she saw a film about animal rights.*
*We **haven't seen** him for a couple of months.*

4.2 Present perfect continuous

We use the present perfect continuous

1 to talk about a recent activity when the effects of that activity can still be seen.
A: *Why are you crying?*
B: *I've **been chopping** onions.*

2 to emphasise how long an action has been going on for, or that it has been repeated many times.

I've been trying to get through to Max all morning but he doesn't have his phone switched on.

I've been working on this essay for over two weeks.

3 to suggest that an activity is temporary.

I've been working in advertising for the past ten years but now feel it's time for a change.

4 to suggest that an action is not complete.

I've been trying to teach myself to play the piano but I'm still pretty terrible.

5 We tend to prefer the present perfect simple for talking about more permanent situations.

She's lived in Rome since she was a child.

We prefer to use the present perfect continuous for more temporary situations.

She's been living out of a suitcase for months, so she'll be glad to get home.

> **Watch out!** Sometimes there is little difference in meaning between the present perfect simple and the present perfect continuous. It is simply a difference in emphasis.
>
> *Isabel has played/has been playing the piano since she was five.*

See also page 161 for future perfect forms (Future in the past).

Exercise

Complete the sentences using the correct present form of the verb in brackets.

1 I .... difficulty sleeping for the last couple of months. (*have*)

2 Karl .... from home at the moment. (*work*)

3 Rafaella .... in Sweden, France and Portugal. (*live*)

4 My neighbours .... about our dog barking. (*always complain*)

5 I .... the oddest message from Karen. (*just have*)

5 Stative and dynamic verbs

There are two categories for verbs in English: stative verbs and dynamic verbs.

1 Dynamic verbs can be used in simple and progressive aspects. They describe habitual activities or activities taking place at the moment.

Tim does Pilates.

Tim is doing Pilates at the moment so he can't come to the phone.

2 Stative verbs usually refer to a state or condition which is quite static or unchanging. They can be divided into verbs referring to emotions, knowledge, possession, communication and the senses. Stative verbs cannot normally be used in the continuous.

*Tina really **loves** her brother Nigel.* (emotion)

*I **don't know** where they live.* (knowledge)

*Alexander **owns** a flat in London and a house in the country.* (possession)

*I **promise** I won't tell a soul.* (communication)

*That cheese **smells** awful.* (senses)

> **Watch out!** Some verbs have stative and dynamic meanings. We only use them in continuous forms with their dynamic meaning, but not with their stative meaning.
>
> *I'm feeling a bit run-down.* (dynamic; *feel* = experience a feeling or emotion)
>
> *I feel that the situation will improve in the near future.* (stative; *feel* = have an opinion)

Exercise

Three of these sentences contain errors. Find the errors and correct them.

1 I'm loving living in London at the moment. It's great.

2 They're having three children: Hanna, Charlie and Aurora.

3 She denies having had anything to do with the robbery.

4 This soup tastes a bit strange.

5 He's not understanding anything about technology.

6 Conjunctions

We use conjunctions to join ideas within a sentence. They may come at the beginning or in the middle of a sentence. They improve the cohesion of a text.

1 Conjunctions which are used to make a contrast include *although, while, whereas, yet.*

*The task wasn't difficult, **yet***
While/Although the task wasn't difficult, } *Tom found he couldn't complete it on time.*

*Tom found himself unable to complete the task on time, **whereas** Harry finished it quickly.*

2 Conjunctions which are used to add information include *and* and *nor.*

*He wasn't afraid of taking risks **and** he didn't worry*
***nor** did he worry* } *about the potential consequences.*

3 Conjunctions which are used to give a condition include *as long as, provided that, if, unless* and *if only.*

***As long as/Provided (that)** she earned enough money to cover her bills, she didn't care about becoming rich.*

***Unless** he improves his performance,*
***If** he doesn't improve his performance,* } *he won't be promoted.*

***If only** he would have a bit more confidence, he would do really well.*

4 Conjunctions which are used to give a reason include *as, because, since* and *so.*

As he hadn't had time to study, he didn't do as well as he'd hoped in the exam.

Exercise

Complete the sentences with the conjunctions in the box.

as (x2)   if only   nor   provided that   whereas   yet

1 I knew it would have changed a lot .... I still longed to go back.

2 Simon always had his head in a book .... his brother spent most of his time watching television.

3 She should be able to join us for dinner, ... her plane arrives on time.

4 .... the plumber still hasn't come, we won't be able to use the bathroom today.

5 .... Jessica were here. She would know what to do.

6 Nigel loves hiking, ... does his girlfriend Georgia.

7 I don't eat meat, ... does my partner.

Unit 2

1 Narrative tenses

1.1 Past simple

Narrative forms are used when describing events in the past.

We use the past simple

1 to talk about a finished event that happened at a specific time in the past.

*I **spoke** to my sister this morning.*
*She **met** Bill in early 1981.*

2 to describe a sequence of finished events in chronological order.

*She **stood up**, **looked** around the room and **began** to speak.*

3 to talk about habits in the past.

***Did** you **play** tennis when you were younger?*

4 to talk about states in the past.

*When I **was** a baby, I **suffered** from persistent earaches.*
*The museum **housed** a huge collection of artefacts from all over the Mediterranean Basin.*

5 in reported speech.

*She claimed she **knew** nothing about the robbery.*

1.2 Past continuous

We use the past continuous

1 to describe an action in progress in the past, often to set the scene for a particular event.

*He **was lying** in a hammock with a hat over his eyes.*

2 to talk about temporary situations in the past.

*Susan **was studying** architecture in the early 1970s.*

3 to talk about an event that was in progress in the past and was interrupted.

*I **was** just **falling** asleep when the phone rang.*

4 to talk about actions in progress at the same time in the past.

*While I **was flying** back from Australia, she **was trying** to get in touch with me on my mobile.*

5 to talk about anticipated events that did not happen.

*They **were planning** to get married but then he met someone else.*

1.3 Past perfect

We use the past perfect

1 to refer to a time earlier than another past time, when this is needed to make the order of events clear.

*Everyone **had been invited** to the meeting so I don't understand why she claimed not to know about it.*

*By the time I got to Doha, I **had** already **missed** my connecting flight.*

> **Watch out!** Be careful not to overuse the past perfect. It is not necessary with *before* or *after*, which make the sequence of events clear. Once we have established the time sequence, we can revert to the past simple.
>
> *I **dusted** the shelves before I **vacuumed** the carpet.*

2 in reported speech.

*They said they **had met** before.*

1.4 Past perfect continuous

We use the past perfect continuous to talk about an action in progress over a period of time that concludes in the past.

*I **had been living** in London for about a month when I met William.*

2 Other verb forms to talk about the past: *used to* and *would*

We use *used to* + bare infinitive to talk about past habits and states that do not occur now or which are no longer the case.

*Everyone **used to get** milk delivered but now we all buy it in the supermarket.*

*What did your grandmother **use to do** before she retired?*

*I **didn't use to enjoy** sport very much at school but now I love it.*

> **Watch out!** The past participle (used in the negative and question form) is ***use.***

We use *would* to talk about past habits and repeated actions but NOT about past states, thoughts, emotions, etc.

Exercise

Decide if one or both verbs are possible.

1 I *didn't realise/hadn't realised* that I *left/had left* my keys in my other bag until I *got/had got* to work.

2 My sister and I *got on/used to get on* really well when we were children but we *would/used to* argue a bit when we *went/were going* on long car journeys.

3 *Wasn't there/Didn't there use to be* a cinema across the road from your flat?

4 I *hadn't been living/hadn't lived* in Santa Cruz for very long when I *met/I had met* my friend Irene.

5 Jack *had been thinking/was thinking* about getting a new laptop when his girlfriend *had given/gave* him one for his birthday.

3 Defining and non-defining relative clauses

3.1 Defining relative clauses

Defining relative clauses contain essential information. If the relative clause is the object of the sentence, the relative pronoun can be omitted.

*We met in a restaurant **(which/that) a friend had recommended**.*

If the relative clause is the subject of the sentence, the relative pronoun can't be omitted.

*The man **who/that owns it** is from Turkey.*

1 The relative clause defines or identifies the person, thing, time, place or reason.

*Chris is the man **who I met on the train**.*

*That's the park **where we used to play football**.*

2 *That* can be used instead of *who* or *which*.

***The person who/that told me** asked me to keep it a secret.*

3 The relative pronoun can be left out if it is the object of the verb in the relative clause.

***The book** (which/that) **you lent me** is really good.*

4 No commas are used before and after the relative clause.

3.2 Non-defining relative clauses

Non-defining relative clauses follow either the subject or object of a sentence. They are used to provide extra information.

*This phone, **which (NOT that) I only bought six months ago**, keeps freezing.* (follows subject)

*They repaired it at the phone shop, **which (NOT that) is on New Street**.* (follows object)

1 The relative clause gives extra information which can be omitted.

2 *That* cannot be used instead of *who* or *which*.

3 Commas are used before and after the relative clause.

*The shop, **where I worked as a student**, is closing down.*

*The bank manager, **whose wife is a teacher at my school**, is very helpful.*

> **Watch out!** Leaving out the commas in a non-defining relative clause can change the meaning of a sentence.
>
> *The doctor, who treated me when I had flu, is retiring.*
>
> *The doctor who treated me when I had flu is retiring. (The other doctors are not retiring.)*

3.3 Prepositions in relative clauses

Prepositions can come before or after the relative pronoun, depending on whether the sentence is formal or informal.

*The person **to whom I spoke** told me the vacuum cleaner would be delivered this morning.* (formal)

*Mrs Evans, **who I talked to just now**, sends her regards.* (informal)

Exercise

Choose the correct pronoun.

1 The manager, *whose/which* number I tried to call, just rang me back.

2 My neighbour, with *whose/whom* I've had lots of arguments, turned out to be a really kind person.

3 My passport was in my car *which/where* I'd left it the night before.

4 I had to walk to work, *that/which* was why I was late.

5 It was a friend *whose/that* told me about this restaurant.

6 My grandfather, *that/who* will be 90 soon, still walks 5 km every day.

Unit 3

1 Future forms

1 We use *will* + *infinitive*
   - for predicting something based on our belief or our knowledge of characteristic behaviour.
   *This website **will give** you lots of useful information.*
   - for promises, threats, offers and requests.
   *I promise I **won't tell** anyone.*
   *I'**ll book** the restaurant if you want.*

2 We use *going to* + infinitive or the present continuous to talk about plans and arrangements that have already been decided.
   *She's decided she'**s going to get** another job.*
   *Where **are** you **meeting** Max this evening?*

3 We use *going to* + infinitive to talk about things that are certain to happen because there is present evidence.
   *I know I'**m going to enjoy** this module. It's on my favourite topic.*

4 We use *will/shall* + infinitive to talk about future actions decided at the time of speaking.

*I know! I'**ll get** her that new Kate Atkinson novel.*

5 We use the future continuous (*will/shall* + *be* + *-ing*) to say that an action will be in progress at a definite time in the future.

*I'**ll be living** in my own apartment by this time next year.*

6 We use the future perfect (*will/shall* + *have* + past participle) to describe something that will be completed before a definite time in the future.

*By the end of the month, I **will have completed** my dissertation.*

2 Future time expressions

1 followed by the present simple

*It won't be long **until** I start my new job.*

*It's only a matter of time **before** he hears the news.*

2 followed by *will*

***Within** the next six months she'll be a qualified doctor.*

***In twenty-five years' time** there will be less air pollution.*

3 followed by the future continuous

***Ten years from now** I'll be doing the same job.*

4 followed by the future perfect

***By the time** I'm twenty-five I'll have worked in several different countries.*

5 followed by the past simple

***It's about/high time** I left home.*

Exercise

Complete the sentences using the correct form of the verb in brackets.

1 I .... dinner if you like. (*cook*)

2 That .... Tim. He often phones at this time. (*be*)

3 What time .... Kim for dinner on Friday? (*we/meet*)

4 I know what I .... her for her birthday! One of those inflatable travel pillows. (*get*)

5 This time next week I .... on a beach in Lanzarote. (*lie*)

6 By this time next year he .... more than fifty novels. (*read*)

7 Ten years from now my parents .... (*retire*).

8 By the year 2040 robots .... a lot of the work people do now. (*do*)

3 Introductory *it*

1 We use *it* as introductory subject to avoid beginning a sentence with an infinitive or *-ing* form.

***It** would probably be better to give her a gift voucher for Christmas.*

***It**'s been lovely having you to stay with us.*

2 to emphasise a relative clause (cleft sentence)

***It was Julia who** gave Sally a bag for her birthday.* (the emphasis is on *Julia*)

***It was a bag that** Julia gave Sally for her birthday.* (the emphasis is on *a bag*)

***It was Sally who** Julia gave a bag to.* (the emphasis is on *Sally*)

3 when the subject of a clause is another clause

***It**'s terrible just how many young people are unemployed.*

***It**'s likely that his plane will be delayed.*

***It**'s always a relief when the cool weather arrives.*

4 We use *it* as introductory object in the structure: subject + verb + *it* + adjective + infinitive/clause.

***I find it very strange** the way you never tell me where you're going.*

***They made it perfectly clear** that they wanted a window and an aisle seat on the plane.*

> **Watch out!** We do not normally use subject + verb + *it* + adjective + infinitive/clause if there is no adjective.
>
> *I find the way Joe keeps telling us what to do really annoying.*

Exercise

Put the words in the correct order to create sentences with introductory *it*.

1 lovely visit to Lisbon it again was

2 how many shocking young people litter in the street it drop is

3 inevitable almost it that is finish will not time on the assignment I

4 didn't want made clear very Fiona it that birthday presents she any

5 so smoothly run negotiations Eva was it made who the

6 Wednesday arranged we on it meet to was that

Unit 4

1 Verb patterns: *-ing*/infinitive

1.1 Common verbs followed by the *-ing* form

These are some common verbs we use with the *-ing* form: *admit, appreciate, avoid, consider, delay, deny, detest, dislike, enjoy, escape, face, feel like, finish, forgive, give up, imagine, involve, keep, mention, mind, miss, postpone, practise, prefer, put off, recommend, regret, resent, risk, suggest, understand.*

*I **regretted telling** him what had happened.*

1.2 Common verbs followed by object + -ing form

These are some common verbs we use with object + -ing form: *discover, forbid, notice, observe, overhear, prevent (from)*.

They **discovered him sitting** by the road.

1.3 Common verbs followed by the infinitive

These are some common verbs we use followed by the infinitive: *afford, agree, appear, arrange, ask, attempt, bear, begin, care, choose, consent, decide, determine, expect, fail, forget, happen, hate, help, hesitate, hope, intend, learn, like, love, manage, mean, offer, prefer, prepare, pretend, promise, propose, refuse, remember, seem, start, swear, try, want, wish*.

He **intended to tell** her the truth.

1.4 Common verbs followed by object + infinitive

These are some common verbs we use followed by object + infinitive: *advise, allow, ask, cause, command, encourage, expect, forbid, force, get, hate, help, instruct, intend, invite, leave, like, mean, need, oblige, order, permit, persuade, prefer, press, recommend, remind, request, teach, tell, tempt, trouble, want, warn, wish*.

He **persuaded me to help** him.

Her parents **forbade her to drive** the car.

1.5 Common verbs followed by object + infinitive without *to*

These are some common verbs we use with object + infinitive without *to*: *let, make, hear, help*.

He **made me tidy** my room.

> **Watch out!** In passive sentences, *make, hear* and *help* are followed by an infinitive with *to*.
>
> She **was made to pay** the money back.
>
> Passive forms are usually followed by the infinitive.
>
> We **were advised to go** home.

2 Verbs followed by -ing form or infinitive with a difference in meaning

Common verbs that we use with different meanings when followed by the -ing form or infinitive are *remember, forget, regret, stop* and *try*.

- We use *remember/forget* + -ing when the action or event took place before the remembering or forgetting.

  I **remember meeting** him at a party. (I met him and I now remember that.)

- We use *remember/forget* + infinitive when the action or event took place after the remembering or forgetting.

  I **remembered to ring** the doctor. (I remembered and then I rang the doctor.)

- *regret* + -ing means 'be sorry about an action in the past'.

  I **regret selling** my car.

- *regret* + infinitive means 'be sorry about a present situation'.

  I **regret to inform** you that your car has been stolen.

- *stop* + -ing means 'give up doing or cease to do something'.

  I **stopped drinking** coffee because it kept me awake at night.

- *stop* + infinitive means 'stop doing something in order to do something else'.

  We **stopped to have** a coffee on the way home.

- *try* + -ing means that the action is an experiment which may or may not be successful.

  Try studying at a different time of day – it might suit you better.

- *try* + infinitive means 'make an effort even though the action may be difficult or impossible'.

  Try to study for at least three hours a day.

3 Common verbs followed by -ing form or infinitive with little difference in meaning

Common verbs that we use with the -ing form or the infinitive with little difference in meaning are: *attempt, begin, continue, love, prefer, see* and *start*.

I continued **working/to work** hard.

Exercise

Which of the verbs A–E fits in each sentence? Sometimes more than one answer is possible.

A persuaded	**C** suggested	**E** forced
B prevented	**D** intended	**F** regretted

1 They .... her from quitting college.

2 He .... me to see the film.

3 I .... never to see him again.

4 My mother .... not finishing her degree course.

5 We were .... to get off the train.

6 No-one .... travelling to the island by boat.

4 Modal verbs

4.1 Possibility

1 We use *can* or *could* for theoretical possibility.

  Can/Could there **be** life on other planets?

2 We use *may/might/could* + infinitive to talk about possibility in the present or future.

  He **may be** on holiday. (strong possibility)

  They **might/could be** waiting at the station. (less possible)

3 We use *may/might/could* + *have* + past participle (perfect infinitive) to talk about the possibility of past events.

*He **might have decided** to go home early.*

*She **could have been** a great athlete.*

4.2 Certainty (deduction)

1 We use *must* to say that we are sure about something in the present or past.

*That **must be** the new teacher.* (present)

*He **must have been** asleep because he didn't hear the phone ringing.* (past)

2 We use *can't* or *couldn't* (but not *mustn't*) in negative sentences.

*That **can't be** your mum. She looks so young!* (present)

*They **can't/couldn't have forgotten**. I only reminded them this morning.* (past)

4.3 Obligation, prohibition and necessity

1 We use *must/mustn't* to talk about present and future obligations/prohibitions imposed by the speaker, often on him/herself.

*I **must finish** my assignment this weekend.*

*You **mustn't forget** to go to the bank.* (prohibition)

2 We use *have to/have got to* to talk about present and future obligations that are imposed by someone other than the speaker.

> **Watch out!** *Have got to* is more common in British than American English.
>
> *I **have (got) to see** my tutor on Monday.*

3 We use *had to* to talk about past and reported obligations of all kinds.

*They told us we **had to apply** for the course by 31 March.*

4 We can also use *need to* to talk about obligation and necessity.

*Do we **need to send in** a hard copy?*

4.4 Lack of obligation or necessity

1 We use *needn't, don't need to* and *don't have to* to talk about lack of obligation in the present or future.

*You **don't need to/needn't** pay me back until next month.*

2 We use *needn't* + *have* + past participle to say that somebody did something but that it was unnecessary.

*Sam **needn't have offered** to pay for our dinner at the restaurant.*

3 We use *didn't need to* + infinitive to say that something wasn't necessary without saying whether the person did it or not.

*You **didn't need to bring** a sleeping bag with you.*

4.5 Ability

1 We use *can/could* to express typical situations or behaviour.

*It **can be** difficult to find a summer job.*

2 We use *can/be able to* for present and future ability.

*Many children **can type** before they can write.*

3 We use *can* for the future where there is a sense of opportunity.

*They **can visit** the museum while they're here.*

4 We use *could/couldn't* and *was/were able to* to talk about general past ability.

*I **couldn't swim** until I was seven.*

5 We use *could/couldn't* + perfect infinitive to talk about unfulfilled ability in the past.

*I **could have learnt** to ski but I preferred skating.*

4.6 *should*

1 We use *should* to talk about obligations and duties in the future, present and past or to give advice. *Ought to* is sometimes used instead of *should* but is more formal.

*You **should speak** English in class.*

2 We often use *should* + *have* + past participle to criticise our own or other people's actions.

*I **should have told** him myself.*

Exercise

Choose the correct alternative to complete the sentences.

1 Tom wasn't feeling well so he *might have decided/must decide* not to go to the match.

2 Sophie *must have been/could have been* a really great tennis player but she didn't practise enough.

3 It *must be/can't be* time for lunch. I'm starving!

4 Rob *needn't have/couldn't have* worried so much about the exam. He got top marks.

5 We *should have/can't have* got there earlier because all the tickets were sold out by the time we arrived.

6 You *mustn't/couldn't* be so critical of Johnny, he's doing his best.

Unit 5

1 Substitution and ellipsis

We avoid repetition of words or expressions that have already been used by means of substitution and ellipsis.

1.1 Substitution

Substitution involves using other words such as *it, one, do, there, that, so, neither* and *not*.

*We've been to Laos several times, but as Iain hadn't been **there** he decided to join us on our last trip.*

*Bill doesn't like Chinese food and **neither do I**.*

A: *Would you like a coffee?*

B: *I'd love **one**.*

A: *Would you like to come to an exhibition opening on Thursday?*

B: ***That** sounds great.*

A: *Will we get the work finished by Sunday?*

B: *I hope **so**.*

A: *After flying all that way, she won't feel like doing much more than going to bed.*

B: *I suppose **not**.*

1.2 Ellipsis

Ellipsis involves leaving out words to avoid repetition. We do this

- after *and*, *but* and *or*.

  She felt hurt and ~~she felt~~ angry about what they had said about her.

  They were pleased but ~~they were~~ a little embarrassed about receiving such an expensive gift.

  I'm thinking of getting her a bag for her tablet or perhaps ~~getting her~~ a top.

- at the end of a verb phrase.

  She wanted to spend more than ten days in Melbourne but she couldn't.

  She said she was going to talk to an accountant and she has.

- with infinitives.

  She didn't want to give the puppies away but her mother said she had to.

  He doesn't play the piano much now. He used to, though.

Exercise

Complete the second part of each dialogue with one of the words/phrases in the box.

do that it neither nor not one so some there

1 A: I don't like fish.

  B: .... do I.

2 A: Are they chocolates you're eating?

  B: Yes. Would you like .... ?

3 A: Do you fancy watching *Game of Thrones*?

  B: I'd rather .... It's too violent.

4 A: Will you be in class tomorrow?

  B: I suppose .... We've got a test, haven't we?

5 A: Have you done the homework for tomorrow?

  B: I've done .... but I haven't finished .... all yet.

6 A: I'm thinking of hitchhiking around Europe next summer.

  B: I wouldn't .... if I were you. It's a bit dangerous.

7 A: People tell me Oporto is really beautiful.

  B: I wouldn't know. I've never been ....

8 A: Jenny can't ride a bicycle.

  B: .... can Sally.

2 Hypothetical meaning

2.1 *wish*

1 We use *wish* + past simple to express a wish for circumstances to change in the present. When *wish* is followed by a form of the verb *be*, we often use *were* instead of *was*, especially in more formal styles. We use this structure when we want our own situation (or the situation of the person who is doing the wishing) to be different.

*I **wish** Kathy **lived** here.*

*Don't you **wish** you **spoke** another language?*

*I **wish** he **was**/**were** a little more open-minded.*

*We all **wish** the economy **wasn't**/**weren't** so unstable.*

2 We use *wish* + *would* to talk about other people's irritating habits.

*I **wish** my brother-in-law **would sell** that old car.*

*I **wish** he **wouldn't complain** about the weather all the time.*

> **Watch out!** This form is rarely used with *I* or *we*. To talk about wishes we have for ourselves, we use *could*.
>
> *I **wish** I **could buy** a new computer.*

3 We use *wish* + *could* to talk about an ability we would like to have or a habit we would like to change.

*I **wish** I **could learn** to be a bit tidier.*

4 We use *wish* + past perfect to refer to things we are sorry about in the past or to express regret.

*I **wish** I **had started** learning Spanish when I was younger.*

*She **wishes** she **hadn't lost** her temper.*

2.2 *if only*

We use *if only* with the same verb forms as *wish* when our feelings are stronger. We often use it with an exclamation mark (!). We also use it with *would*/*wouldn't* to criticise someone else's behaviour.

*If only I **could take back** the dreadful things I said!*

*If only the neighbours **would stop** making so much noise!*

*If only I **had** never **left** my home town!*

2.3 *it's time*

We use *it's time* with the past simple to talk about the present or future. We mean that the action should have been done before. For emphasis, we can also use *it's about time* and *it's high time*.

*It's (**about**) time you **went** to bed. You've got an early start tomorrow.*

*It's (high) time we **left** for the airport. We're supposed to check in an hour and a half before the flight.*

2.4 would rather

1 We use *would rather* + past simple to talk about preferences in the present and future.

I'd rather you didn't mention this to Alex.

Would you rather I came back a bit later?

I'd rather we didn't eat out tonight. I'll cook something here.

2 We use *would rather* + past perfect to say what we wanted to happen in the past.

I'd rather you hadn't invited Tim. He doesn't get on well with Eleanor.

I'd rather you had informed me of your decision sooner.

> **Watch out!** We don't use *would rather* + past simple or past perfect when we are talking about our own preferences for ourselves or other people's preferences for themselves. In these cases we use *would rather* + infinitive without *to*.
>
> *I'd rather fly than catch the train.*
>
> *They'd rather take a taxi.*

Exercise

Complete the sentences with the correct form of the verb in brackets.

1 I wish you .... (*stop*) drumming your fingers on the table like that. It's driving me crazy.

2 I'd rather we .... (*not take*) the underground to the airport. It's always too crowded.

3 It's high time you .... (*tidy up*) your bedroom. It's a real mess.

4 If only I .... (*turn back*) the hands of time.

5 I bet they wish they .... (*spend*) all that money on the renovations.

6 Sally wishes she .... (*not have to*) go to the dentist tomorrow.

Unit 6

1 Comparing

1.1 Regular comparative and superlative forms

1 With adjectives ending in one syllable, we use *-er* and *-est* (*-ier*, *-iest* for adjectives ending in *-y*).

*His criticism was **harsher** than necessary.*

*It's the **funniest** story I've ever read.*

2 With longer adjectives, adjectives ending in *-ful/-less/ -ing* and adverbs which have the same form as the adjective, we use *more/less* and *the most/least*.

*I thought the film was **more/less enjoyable** than the book.*

*The guidebook was **more/less useful** than I expected.*

*The train left early but the bus left even **earlier**.*

*The objects in the exhibition could have been displayed **more imaginatively**.*

***The most/least impressive** building in the town is the old castle.*

3 To compare two equivalent things, we use *as … as*.

*The film is **as believable as** the book.*

1.2 Intensifying and modifying comparisons

We can use the following words to intensify and modify comparative forms.

***considerably/far/much/a lot/a great deal** more/less interesting than*

***very much** bigger/better*

***more and more** difficult*

***a bit/slightly/a little** higher*

***no** worse than*

***not any** quicker*

***just/quite/easily** as interesting as*

***almost/not quite** as crowded as*

***not nearly/nowhere near** as useful as*

***by far** the best*

1.3 like in comparisons

1 We use *like* + noun to describe similarity.

*He's tall **like** his father.*

2 We use *nothing like as* to emphasise the difference between two things.

*Driving is **nothing like as** fast as going by train.*

> **Watch out!** *As* is only used in comparisons in the phrases *as … as* and *not so/as … as*.

Exercise

Complete the sentences.

1 It was .... far the most interesting play I've ever seen.

2 People are .... near as friendly in the city as they are in the country.

3 The film was .... much better than I'd expected.

4 This job is a .... deal harder than my last job.

5 Driving is .... so much fun as it was in the past.

6 Their house is very old, ... yours.

2 Modifying adverbs

We can use adverbs to make adjectives, other adverbs and verbs stronger (intensifiers) or weaker (modifiers).

1 We can use these adverbs before gradable adjectives (i.e. adjectives that can be used in the comparative) and adverbs: *bitterly, barely, deeply, somewhat, seriously, really, extremely, practically, entirely, pretty, completely, quite, scarcely, totally, very.*

*We were **bitterly** disappointed when our holiday was cancelled.*

*He answered the question **somewhat** abruptly.*

2 Some modifying adverbs collocate with certain adjectives.

bitterly *cold/ashamed/disappointed/divided*

barely *alive/legible/comprehensible*

completely *serious/open/honest*

deeply *serious/painful/sorry*

entirely *convinced/clear/satisfactory*

pretty *doubtful/hopeless*

perfectly *capable/aware/reasonable/normal/safe/ straightforward/sure*

seriously *alarmed/worried/hurt*

3 Extreme or absolute (non-gradable) adjectives include: *amazing, devastating, disastrous, fantastic, freezing, furious, immense, impossible, staggering.* We can use the following adverbs with extreme adjectives: *absolutely, totally, really, utterly, pretty, quite.*

*The building was **utterly** immense.*

> **Watch out!** When used with non-gradable adjectives, *quite* means *absolutely*, not *fairly*.

Exercise

Decide if it is possible to use one or both modifiers in each sentence.

1 It's *practically/absolutely* impossible to know when he's joking.

2 He was *seriously/totally* worried when he lost his car keys.

3 I find listening to politicians makes me *really/utterly* annoyed.

4 I'm *somewhat/extremely* sorry I broke your phone.

5 He was *bitterly/seriously* disappointed when his team lost.

6 Their house is *quite/perfectly* immense.

Unit 7

I Conditionals

See also *Hypothetical meaning* in Unit 5, page 156.

1.1 Zero conditional

FORM *if* + present simple + present simple in the main clause

USE to describe a general truth

*If you **heat** water, it **boils**.*

Alternatives to *if*

***Unless** they **are** cornered or startled, snakes **do not** normally **attack** people.*

***When** older people **are** dehydrated, they often **experience** a decrease in cognitive function.*

1.2 First conditional

FORM *if* + present simple + future in the main clause

USE to describe what is possible or likely in the present or future

*She**'ll be** absolutely thrilled **if** it **turns out** that you can go back to Australia in November.*

We can also use *if*, etc. + present continuous/present perfect + future or imperative in the main clause to talk about possibility or likelihood in the present/future.

*You **won't get** the grant unless you**'ve managed** to get really good references.*

***If** you**'re visiting** Santa Cruz in February, you **will be** able to enjoy the carnival.*

1.3 Second conditional

FORM *if* + past simple/continuous + *would/could*, etc. + infinitive in the main clause

USE

1 to talk about something

- that is contrary to the present facts or seen as very unlikely to happen

  ***If** I **was/were** in your shoes, I**'d** seriously **consider** emigrating.*

  ***If** I **was/were** prime minister, I **wouldn't cut** education and health care spending.*

- that is very unlikely to happen in the future

  *I **wouldn't take out** a loan unless I **knew** I would have no difficulty whatsoever paying it back.*

2 to give advice

  *I**'d try** and eat less bread **if** I **were** you.*

1.4 Third conditional

FORM *if* + past perfect + *would/could*, etc. + *have* + past participle in the main clause

USE to describe something in the past that could have happened but didn't or that shouldn't have happened but did

*I **wouldn't have said** anything about it **if** I**'d had** any idea he would make such a fuss.*

*She **could have had** a stopover in Dubai **if** she **had flown** with the other airline.*

1.5 Mixed conditionals

It is possible to have sentences that mix conditionals in

- an *if* clause referring to the past with a main clause referring to the present or future.

  ***If** I **had finished** my law degree, I **would** probably **be** a lawyer now.*

  ***If** we **hadn't been asked** to help, we **could go** home now.*

- an *if* clause referring to the present or future with a main clause referring to the past.

  ***If** you **don't like** hot weather, you **shouldn't have booked** to go to Córdoba in July.*

*If you've got to get up so early tomorrow, you **ought to have gone** to bed by now.*

1.6 Modal verbs in conditional sentences

Modal verbs (*can, could, might*, etc.) can be used in all types of conditional sentences.

*I **might pop in** to see you **if** I **can persuade** Jo to drive me.*

*If she **had** more support, she **could set up** her own business.*

*If I **hadn't been** late, we **might** never **have met**.*

Exercise

Two of these sentences contain errors with conditionals. Find the sentences and correct the errors.

1 If you do that again, I would scream.

2 Our dog doesn't bark unless he thinks there's a threat of some kind.

3 The whole family will be really pleased to see you if you can manage to visit some time this year.

4 If I were you, I wouldn't told her what he said.

5 The customers wouldn't have made such a fuss if you had listened patiently to their complaint.

6 If she had thought more carefully before sending the email, they would probably still be together now.

2 Conditionals: advanced features

2.1 Conditional linking words and alternatives to *if*

Common conditional linking words are: *if, as/so long as, unless, even if, whether, providing, provided (that), on condition that*. When the clause with the conditional linking word is at the beginning of the sentence, there is a comma. When the main clause begins the sentence, there is no comma.

If you lay the table, I'll serve the dinner.

As long as you can check your email, we can stay in touch.

I won't stay late unless they need me to.

They're holding the carnival even if it is cold and wet.

I'll attend the meeting provided that I can get time off.

In the event of cancellation, a full refund will be provided.

I hope Val emails me today. Otherwise, I'll have to call her.

> **Watch out!** *In case* is used to describe things we do as precautions against what might happen.
> *I'll book a later flight in case I miss the connection.*

2.2 Formal style

1 In more formal styles we can omit *if* but we have to place the auxiliary verb before the subject.

Had I known you were not going to be available, I would have called the meeting for another day.

Had I not booked a return ticket, I would be able to stay for another month.

Were Tim my son, I would not hesitate to help him.

2 *if + should* is common in formal letters. For even greater formality, omit *if* and begin the sentence with *should*.

If you should require any further information, please do not hesitate to contact us.

Should you wish to contact me, I can be reached at the above address.

2.3 *if + (should) happen to*

We use *if + (should) happen to* to suggest that something is more unlikely or just a chance possibility. *Should* and *happen* can be used together.

If you should happen to run into my old friend Simon, do say hello to him from me.

If you happen to pass a post office, could you get me a couple of stamps?

2.4 *suppose/what if … ?*

Suppose means *what if … ?* and it is used with

1 the present simple to describe something that may possibly happen or may have happened.

Suppose someone hears us.

Suppose someone tells her what you said.

2 the past simple to talk about something that is imaginary or which is unlikely to happen in the future.

Suppose Caroline found out about the letter. What would you do?

Suppose you got a great job abroad. Would you emigrate?

3 the past perfect to talk about something that could have happened in the past but didn't.

Suppose we had never met. Do you think you would have married Silvia?

Suppose you had been born in another country. How would your life have been different?

2.5 *if + will/would*

We use *if + will/would* to make requests more polite. In this case the auxiliary *will/would* means 'be willing to'.

If you will just bear with me for a few moments, I'll tell the head of department that you are here.

If you would be kind enough to supply the additional documentation, we will then be able to offer sound advice on your investments.

Exercise

Choose the correct alternative to complete the sentences.

1 *On condition that/In the event of/* fire break the glass and press the button.

2 *Provided that/Otherwise* I can get an early train, I'll be at the airport by 10.30.

3 They swim every day of the year *even if/whether* the temperature drops below freezing.

4 I took out travel insurance *unless/in case* my luggage gets lost.

5 I hope you feel better in the morning. *Provided that/Otherwise* you should see a doctor.

6 *Whether/If* you like it or not, I'm going to India next Christmas.

7 *Had/Should* you wish to apply for the position, enclose a complete CV with your application.

8 If you *should/would* see Diana, tell her I was asking after her.

Unit 8

1 Reported speech

1.1 Changes in reported speech

1 If the report is after the time the thing was said or written, the verb form generally changes as follows.

Direct speech	Reported speech
present simple/continuous *'I haven't got time to finish the report now,' said Jack.*	past simple/continuous *Jack said (that)* **he didn't have** *time to finish the report immediately.*
past simple/continuous *'I worked there for ten years,' said Kate.*	past simple/continuous or past perfect simple/continuous *Kate said (that) she* **had worked** *there for ten years.*
present perfect simple/continuous *'I've decided to apply for a new job,' Helen told me.*	past perfect simple/continuous *Helen told me (that) she* **had decided** *to apply for a new job.*
will *'I'll show you where the manager's office is,' she said.*	would *She said (that) she* **would show** *me where the manager's office was.*
must (obligation) *'You must have a permit,' he said.*	had to *He said (that) we* **had to have** *a permit.*
can *'I can play the violin quite well,' said Ian.*	could *Ian said (that) he* **could play** *the violin quite well.*

2 The verb form does not need to change when:
- the information being reported is unchanged.
  'Sea temperatures are rising,' said the lecturer.
  The lecturer told us (that) sea temperatures are rising.

- the information being reported happened recently.
  'I'll tell you about it tomorrow,' she said.
  She said (that) she'll tell me about it tomorrow.
  (It's still the same day.)

- the information being reported contains the modals *would, could, might, ought to* and *should* or *must* for logical deduction.
  'I think he must be late,' she said.
  She said (that) she thought he must be late.

- the information being reported contains the past perfect.
  'He had already been invited to the reception,' she said.
  She said (that) he had already been invited to the reception.

3 Other changes that occur in reported speech are shown in the table below.

Direct speech	Reported speech
tomorrow	*the next day, the day after, the following day*
now	*at that time/moment, immediately, then*
yesterday	*the day before, the previous day*
last week	*the week before, the previous week*
here	*there*
this morning	*that morning*
today	*that day*
next Friday	*the following Friday, the Friday after*
(two hours) ago	*(two hours) before/earlier*

1.2 Reported questions

1 Reported *Yes/No* questions

When there is no question word in the direct speech question, we use *if/whether*. The word order is the same as in the statement. The verb tense and other changes are the same as for other types of reported speech.

'Could I borrow your notes?' she asked.

She asked **if/whether she could borrow** *my notes.*

2 Reported *wh-* questions

The *wh-* word is followed by statement word order (subject + verb). The verb tense and other changes are the same as for other types of reported speech.

'Why did you leave that job?' she asked him.

She asked **him why he had left** *that job.*

Exercise

Report these statements.

1 'You must work harder if you want to pass the test this Friday,' our teacher told us.

....

2 'Can I make an appointment for tomorrow afternoon?' Lily asked the doctor.

....

3 'I've made up my mind that I don't want to go to university,' Erica said.

....

4 'Matt's been living in Athens since last summer,' Julie informed everyone.

....

2 Verb patterns with reporting verbs

1 verb + infinitive

agree, claim, decide, offer, promise, refuse, threaten

*We **refused to go** to the meeting.*

2 verb + object + infinitive

advise, beg, encourage, invite, order, permit, persuade, remind, tell, warn

*She **persuaded me to lend** her some money.*

3 verb (+ *that*) + clause

accept, admit, claim, doubt, explain, promise, recommend, say, suggest

*She **recommended (that) we should visit the museum**.*

4 verb + object + (*that*) + clause

promise, remind, tell, warn

*He **warned us (that) he might be late**.*

5 verb + -*ing*

admit, deny, recommend, regret, suggest

*He **suggested visiting** the museum.*

6 verb + preposition + -*ing*

apologise for, insist on, object to

*She **apologised for forgetting** my name.*

7 verb + object + preposition + -*ing*

accuse sb of, blame sb for, congratulate sb on, discourage sb from, forgive sb for

*She **discouraged him from going** to university.*

8 verb + *wh*- word + infinitive

describe, explain, know, wonder

*She **explained where to find** the library.*

9 verb + object + *wh*- word + infinitive

ask, remind, tell

*The manager **told us what to expect** in the interview.*

Note: It's not necessary to report statements word for word. The information can be summarised.

'I think it would be a really good idea for you to apply for the job in Paris,' said Emma's dad.

Emma's dad encouraged her to apply for the job in Paris.

3 Impersonal reporting verbs

Impersonal reporting verbs are used in formal written English to report general opinions. Verbs such as *believe, consider, expect, suggest* can be used.

It is believed that migration will increase substantially in the next ten years.

Exercise

Complete the sentences.

1 'Please don't forget to phone me as soon as you arrive,' said my mum.

My mum reminded ....

2 'Have you taken my keys again?' my brother said.

My brother accused ....

3 'It's Dan's fault that we missed the plane,' Kerry said.

Kerry blamed ....

4 'I wish I'd never emigrated to Australia,' said Rob.

Rob regretted ....

5 'Ella told me the party would be terrible, so I didn't go,' Amy said.

Ella discouraged ....

6 'It's not fair that we have to work such long hours,' said Jon.

Jon objected ....

Unit 9

1 Future in the past

We often talk about the past and events or intentions which were in the future at that time.

1 We use the past continuous to talk about future events from a past perspective.

*The lecture **was starting** in fifteen minutes, so I didn't have time for lunch.*

*I **was aiming** to complete the report before I went on holiday.*

2 We use *be going to* + infinitive to talk about unfulfilled intentions in the past.

*I **was going to call** you but my phone ran out of battery.*

3 We use *would*

• to refer to future events that did actually happen.

*The business **would become** one of the most successful in the city.*

• to make predictions about the future from a past perspective.

*I knew there **would be** a lot of questions to be answered.*

4 We use *was/were about to* to refer to future events that did not actually happen. In this case it is usually followed by the past participle.

*The company **was to have opened** three further shops by December. (but something went wrong)*

5 We also use *was/were to* to refer to future events that did happen. In this case it is usually followed by the infinitive.

*Adele **was to become** a best-selling artist by the age of twenty-two.*

Exercise

Use one word to complete the future in the past sentences.

1 We .... aiming to complete the project by 2019 but our plans were far too ambitious.

2 No one predicted that our classmate Simon .... to go on to become a famous surgeon.

3 The small restaurant business my grandfather started in the 1960s .... become world famous before we sold it in 2020.

4 The government was to .... eliminated the tax on solar energy by this time last year but they changed their minds.

5 They said the weather was .... to get better today but it's still cloudy and cold.

6 She knew he .... be upset when he found out about her travel plans.

2 Advanced features

1 We use *was/were about to* + infinitive and *was/were thinking of* + *-ing* to describe future actions which were interrupted.

*I **was about to call** you when you called me!*
*I **was thinking of calling** you when you called me!*

2 Other ways we use to refer to unfulfilled intentions/ events that did not happen include *was/were due to*, *was/were meant to*, *was/were supposed to*.

*Her plane **was due to leave** at 11.00 but there was a very long delay and they didn't take off till after 12.00.*
*The children **were meant to go** back to school this week but the weather is so bad we've been told to keep them at home.*
*The meeting **was supposed to start** at 3.30 but the client arrived over an hour late.*

Exercise

Rewrite the sentences using the word in bold and making any other necessary changes.

1 I was thinking of going for a walk when it started to rain. **ABOUT**

2 Weren't you meant to leave for Australia on the twentieth? **DUE**

3 She was about to step out in front of the oncoming traffic when someone pulled her back on to the pavement. **GOING**

4 The students should have received their exam results today. **SUPPOSED**

5 According to the timetable the train was due to leave at 19.10 but we're still in the station. **WOULD**

6 Kathy wasn't to be told anything about the surprise party. **KNOW**

Unit 10

1 whoever, whatever, etc.

1.1 *-ever* words in separate clauses

We use *however, whatever, whenever, wherever, whichever* and *whoever* to mean 'it doesn't matter/no matter how/what/when, etc.' or 'it doesn't make any difference how/what/when, etc.'.

***However** hard I try, it's just never good enough.*
***Whatever** you do, don't breathe a word about the surprise party to Bea.*
*I wouldn't go to a place like that, **whoever** invited me.*
***Whenever** we went out together, we had a great time.*
***Wherever** I go in the world, I always take my laptop.*

1.2 *-ever* words: additional meanings

- We use *whatever* (and the very formal *whatsoever*) as a pronoun and determiner with the meaning 'any (thing) that'.

  *I'll do **whatever** I can to persuade you not to leave.*
  ***Whatever** he says makes her laugh.*

- We also use *whatever* as a dismissive and impatient reply to a question, suggestion or explanation. It can sound rude.

  A: *Do you think I should ask Jane to marry me?*
  B: *Whatever.*

  We can make it sound less impolite by adding a clause or making a complete sentence.

  A: *Would you prefer lasagne or spaghetti bolognese for supper tonight?*
  B: *Whatever is easiest for you.*

- *Whatever* can also be used as an emphatic form of *what*. It can imply a criticism or surprise.

  ***Whatever** were you thinking of telling Leonard I thought his experiment was stupid!*

  However, whenever, wherever and *whoever* are all used as emphatic forms of *how, when, where* and *who*, with similar meanings to *whatever*.

  ***However** did someone like that get the job? He's hopeless!*
  ***Whenever** did you learn Tibetan? I had no idea you spoke it.*
  ***Wherever** did you get that shirt? It looks terrible on you!*
  ***Whoever** do you think you are, talking to me like that?*

- *Whenever* can also mean 'at any time' or 'every time that'.

  *I go to the beach **whenever** I can.*

- *Whenever* can also mean 'I don't know exactly when'.
  *Last month – or **whenever** it was we had the meeting – I explained that I was going away.*
- The other *-ever* words can be used with similar functions and meanings.
  *I'm willing to go and live **wherever** I can find a job.*

Exercise

Complete the sentences with the words in the box.

however   whoever   whatever   whenever   wherever

1 I would never let anyone talk to me like that, ... important they were.
2 .... we talk about politics, my dad loses his temper.
3 .... I go, my dog always follows me.
4 .... wrote this article doesn't understand anything about it.
5 If you're worried about anything you can always call me, ... time it is.

2 Participle clauses

We can use participle clauses (*-ing* and *-ed* clauses) in place of relative pronouns to make writing more concise.

2.1 *-ing* forms

An *-ing* participle has an active meaning. It can replace relative clauses which have an active verb.
*This is the letter **referring to** the loan. (= which refers to …)*
*There was a large cat **sitting** in the middle of the living room floor. (= which was sitting …)*

2.2 *-ed* forms

An *-ed* participle has a passive meaning. It can replace relative clauses which have a passive verb.
*The gallery, **designed** by a local architect, houses a collection of contemporary art. (= which was designed …)*

2.3 Other uses of participles

1 after conjunctions
  ***Before going** to bed, I made a list of all the things I had to do.*

2 to express reason, condition, result, etc., in place of adverbs
  ***Realising** that I wouldn't be able to see her before I left, I phoned and left a message on her answering machine. (= Because I realised …)*
  ***Having decided** to visit Rome in the spring, he enrolled in an intensive Italian course. (= After he had decided …)*
  ***Seen** from a distance, he looks much younger than he actually is. (If/When you see him …)*

Exercise

Decide what changes you need to make to include a participle clause in each sentence.

1 Having been brought up in several countries, he could speak five languages fluently.
2 After we had seen the film, we wanted to read the book.
3 There were hundreds of people who were waiting in the queue for tickets to the show.
4 The machine, which was invented at the end of the 19th century, still works today.
5 Once I had understood the problem, it made it much easier to find a solution.

Unit 11

1 Passive forms

We use the passive form in all structures. To form the passive, use the appropriate tense of the verb *be* + past participle.
*The project **will have been completed** by the end of the week. (future perfect)*
*The flowers **must have been sent** by Jim. (modal verb)*

We use passive forms to talk about actions, events and processes when the action, event or process is considered more important than the agent (the person responsible for the action, event or process). Passive forms are frequently used in academic writing and in business reports.

1.1 Impersonal passive reporting verbs

We often use reporting verbs such as *believe, claim, report, say* and *think* in impersonal passive structures in formal situations, when we don't know or don't wish to specify the subject.

- *it* + *be* + past participle of reporting verb + *that*
  ***It is thought that** a solution will be found. (present)*
  ***It was claimed that** the idea had been stolen. (past)*
- subject + *be* + past participle of reporting verb + infinitive
  ***An announcement is thought to be** imminent.*

Exercise

Rewrite the sentences using a passive form.

1 Students must show their identity card when entering the building.
2 You need to send the form by next week.
3 They'll finish the job today.
4 No-one expected her to win the election.
5 They should have invited Tom to the party.
6 Everyone agreed that the meeting should be cancelled.

2 Linking adverbials

We use linking adverbials to connect one sentence in a logical way to another. They usually appear at the beginning of a sentence and are followed by a comma. They help to make writing more cohesive.

1 Linking adverbials used to give extra information include: *additionally, as well as, besides* (*this*), *furthermore, moreover, what's more.*

   We decided there was little to be gained by waiting any longer. **Besides**, *there was a storm coming.*

2 Linking adverbials used to give a reason or result include: *for this reason, consequently, as a result, in view of, given.*

   We decided there was little to be gained by waiting any longer. **Consequently**, *we managed to catch the last train home.*

3 Linking adverbials used to make a contrast include: *on the contrary, on the other hand, in contrast, alternatively, despite this, even so.*

   We decided there was little to be gained by waiting any longer. **Despite this**, *we ended up wasting another half an hour trying to agree what to do next.*

For a list of useful linking words and phrases, see Writing Reference, page 167.

Exercise

Choose the correct linking adverbial.

1 Living abroad would be the adventure of a lifetime. *On the other hand/Besides*, it might be terribly lonely.

2 *As well as/As a result of* having to look after three young children, she also had to manage two part-time jobs.

3 Her parents gave her a car and threw a huge party for her 18th birthday. *What's more/Consequently*, she was given a lot of money for her gap-year trip.

4 The restaurant was very over-priced and we had to wait ages for a table. *In view of this/Even so*, I'd still recommend it.

5 There's no point trying to persuade him to do the sensible thing; he won't listen. *For this reason/Despite this*, we've decided to let him make his own mistakes.

Unit 12

1 Cohesion

1.1 Coherence and cohesion

We say that a text is coherent if we can see logical connections between the various parts of the text. We indicate these connections by using cohesive devices.

1.2 Cohesive devices

There are two types of cohesion: grammatical cohesion and lexical cohesion. Grammatical cohesion includes reference, substitution, ellipsis and conjunction. Lexical cohesion involves links between the vocabulary items in the text, such as collocations, repetitions or the use of synonyms, antonyms, etc.

1 Reference

Reference is the use of pronouns and determiners to refer back or forward to full forms used earlier or later in the text.

Ralph spent **all morning** washing the **car**. **It** needed a clean and **he** knew **this** was the only time **he** had available.

Jane saw **him** walking towards her – **Richard Johnson**, the boy **she** had met the summer before.

2 Substitution

We use substitution to avoid repeating certain words in a sentence. Substitution can be used to replace a noun, a verb or even a phrase.

I was making **a sandwich** *for Sue, but she said she didn't want* **one**.

We had planned **to take the scenic route** *but we were advised that* **to do so** *would add an extra hour to our journey.*

3 Ellipsis

When we use ellipsis, we simply omit the words that we wish to avoid repeating.

A: *Are you coming to the party?*

B: *I'll try* (to come to the party) **but I'm not sure I can** (come to the party).

A: *Frances isn't staying with Patricia after all.*

B: **Why** (is Frances) **not** (staying with Patricia)?

4 Conjunction

We use conjunction to link ideas in a text.

- Coordinating conjunctions include *and, or, but, so, nor* and *yet.*

  I love living here **yet** *I still feel homesick from time to time.*

  I'm not keen on football, **nor** *is Amy.*

- Subordinating conjunctions include: *after, although, as, as far as, as if, as long as, as soon as, as though, because, before, if, in order that, since, so, so that, than, though, unless, until, when, whenever, where, whereas, wherever* and *while*. We use them to link a subordinate clause to a main clause.

  As far as *I'm concerned, he can take over responsibility for the work next week.*

  Alfonso offered to help me with the translation **so that** *I could spend more time with my children.*

Exercise

Complete the sentences and dialogues using a single word.

1 **A:** I loved Selma Hayek's latest movie.

   B: I haven't seen .... yet.

2 There .... were, my old friends from university who I hadn't seen for three years.

3 Make sure you bring your ID to the test. Failure to .... so may result in your not being allowed into the exam room.

4 **A:** Don't forget to buy some milk when you go to the supermarket.

   B: I .... I promise.

5 **A:** Ian won't speak to Carla.

   B: Why .... ?

6 I love spicy food. .... does William.

2 Emphasis with inversion

2.1 Negative adverbs/adverbial expressions

We can put a negative adverb or adverbial expression at the beginning of a clause for emphasis. When we do this, there is inversion of the auxiliary and subject.

__Under no circumstances should you share__ your password with others.

__At no time did she consider__ any other possibility.

__Not until__ she had failed to make contact for over twenty-four hours __did they contact__ the police.

2.2 Restrictive words and expressions

We can also put certain restrictive words or expressions at the beginning of the clause for emphasis. We are more likely to use inversion in formal or literary contexts.

__Hardly had I arrived__ in Paris __when__ I received a call telling me I had to return home urgently.

__No sooner had I sat down__ to have a cup of tea __than__ the telephone rang.

__Seldom have I felt__ so moved by a piece of orchestral music.

__Little did I know__ that they were planning to replace me as project leader.

__Never had his wife looked__ more beautiful.

__Only when__ I saw him again __did I realise__ just how good a friend he had been.

__Not only have you missed__ several classes, you have also failed to submit all the written work.

Exercise

Put the words in the correct order to form sentences.

1 been angry so have I seldom

2 got hardly into bed had neighbours loud music playing started when the I

3 she told understand did I when only me how she felt gone wrong what had

4 time no at attempt he did discuss to it us with

5 towels down our than put the sun behind went a cloud sooner no we had

6 circumstances no say anything under should you Gary to about this

Writing reference

Contents

Checklist

When you have finished the first draft of a piece of work, check that you have:

- done everything you were asked to do in the task input.
- used appropriate language for your target reader consistently in your answer.
- used appropriate layout for the task (headings, paragraphs, etc.).
- used a range of structures and vocabulary, even if you have chosen to use bullet points in part of your answer.
- used different language from the language of the input to avoid register problems.
- made links between paragraphs and between sentences in paragraphs.
- checked the accuracy of your grammar, spelling and punctuation.

Have a mental list of the kinds of errors you tend to make and pay particular attention to looking for these errors.

Read your work at least three times and look for a different aspect of the answer each time, e.g. the first time check for clarity of message and general organisation, the second time check for grammar and punctuation and the third time for spelling.

1 Useful linking words and phrases

1.1 Time sequencers

Examples include *after a while, eventually, later, no sooner, hardly, at first, at last, scarcely, when.*

*We didn't see them arrive but, **eventually**, they got there, apologising for not having been there to meet us.*

***Scarcely** had I time to put down my suitcase **when** my partner asked me to help him load some new software.*

1.2 Listing points

Examples include *firstly, first of all, to begin with, secondly, thirdly, then, finally, lastly.*

***Firstly**, I will discuss the attitudes to older people among my peers. I will **then** go on to explain why these attitudes need to be changed. **Finally**, I will offer some proposals of how these changes might be achieved.*

1.3 Adding information/emphasising

Examples include *additionally, moreover, furthermore, in addition, what's more, as well as, besides, not only ... but (also), on top of that, to make matters worse, in fact, as a matter of fact, seldom, rarely.*

***Not only** has the cost of the scheme proved to be prohibitive **but** no suitable site has been found.*

***Seldom** have we had to confront such important challenges as those we face today.*

1.4 Reasons, causes and results

Examples include *in view of the fact that, given the fact that, due to, owing to, for this reason, consequently, in consequence, since.*

***Due to** the increased fire danger, people are asked to avoid lighting fires in the open.*

***In view of the fact that** no suitable candidate was available here in Spain, we had to advertise the position abroad.*

*I was late for my appointment. **Consequently**, I had to wait over half an hour before the dentist could see me.*

1.5 Contrast

whereas, while

- *Whereas* and *while* are used to compare things, people or ideas and show how they are different. They are used in the same way as *but*.

  *Being self-employed means that you are entirely responsible for your own professional development, **whereas/while** if you work for a company or institution, you can expect staff training to be provided.*

- *While* is also used in the same way as *although*.

  ***While** there may well be arguments in favour of single-sex education, it is important to examine its limitations.*

in contrast

In contrast links two contrasting ideas in separate sentences. It is normally used at the beginning of a sentence.

*Skiing requires a lot of expensive equipment. **In contrast**, running only involves a pair of good trainers.*

even so

Even so means 'although I know that is true'. It can be used to begin a new sentence or after *but* in the second clause of a single sentence.

*I already own an e-reader and a laptop, so I don't actually need a tablet . **Even so**, I think I'll get one.*

On (the) one hand, ... On the other hand, ...

These expressions are used to introduce opposite points in a discussion.

***(On the one hand,)** if you have a gap year before you start university, you will gain experience of the world. **On the other hand,** you will take longer to finish your studies and get out into the job market.*

nevertheless/however

Nevertheless and *however* are used when saying something seems different or surprising after your previous statement. *Nevertheless* is usually used at the beginning or end of the sentence. *However* can be used in the middle of a sentence if it is separated from the rest of the sentence by commas.

*Studies have demonstrated a link between stress and a shortened lifespan. **Nevertheless**, little evidence has been provided that stress in the workplace is harmful.*

*The team had considerable success earlier in the season. Since then, **however**, they have suffered a series of embarrassing defeats.*

2 Model answers with hints and useful phrases

2.1 Essay

(Part 1)

For work on essays, see pages 14, 46, 66, 120 and 130.

TASK

Your class has attended a panel discussion on what methods the government should use to encourage people to buy products produced in your region or country. You have made the notes below.

Methods governments could use to encourage consumption of local products
- advertising campaigns
- education
- economic subsidies

Some opinions expressed in the discussion

'People are not aware of what is produced locally and what comes from outside.'
'Local products are often among the most expensive. They should be cheaper.'
'The producers won't use the subsidies properly.'

Write an essay for your tutor discussing **two** of the methods in your notes. **You should explain which method you think is more important** for governments to consider and **provide reasons** to support your opinion. You may, if you wish, make use of the opinions expressed in the discussion but you should use your own words as far as possible. Write your answer in **220–260** words in an appropriate style.

USEFUL LANGUAGE

Introducing the topic
- *Some people claim that* museums are a waste of money.
- *It is often said that* children should be taught more history at school.
- *We often hear that* more should be done to prevent food wastage.

Linking ideas
- *While it is true that* spending money is good for the economy, it may not always be a good thing to spend too much.
- Not only do people eat far more than they need to *but they also* throw away a horrifying amount of perfectly good food every day.
- *That may well be so but, surely,* people throw away food because they are simply unaware of the dreadful moral and economic cost of such a practice, both for themselves and for others.
- *In fact,* there is a growing demand for greater controls on food advertising.

Giving opinions
- *I can honestly say that* I would wholeheartedly support such a plan.
- *In my view,* the first of these approaches is likely to prove the more successful.
- *As I see it,* no one solution can be applied to such a complex issue.

Concluding
- *On balance,* I feel that more money should be spent on preserving history.
- *Taking everything into consideration, there is a clear case for* cutting the budget for the arts.

Model answer

Promoting locally produced goods

Members of the local business community often complain about the lack of support for locally produced goods. The public's indifference to local products is both the result of a lack of awareness and the huge variety of imported goods available. There is clearly scope for the government to do something about this situation. In this essay I will discuss two possible approaches that could be taken.

The first of these is a public service advertising campaign. This would alert people to the many benefits of buying local goods. The campaign could be supported by labelling products as locally made. While this would almost certainly lead to a greater level of awareness of the advantages of buying locally, more could still be done to make local goods more competitive in terms of price.

A second tactic could be to offer subsidies so that goods can be sold more cheaply. There are some drawbacks to this approach, however. Where, for example, is the guarantee that the producers would use this funding appropriately? This issue can be addressed by introducing a system of quality control. The public could thus rest assured that the local products offer good value for money.

In my view, advertising and subsidising local products must go hand in hand. Once awareness has been raised, community spirit might well lead people to choose local products. If, into the bargain, they see that they are superior in terms of quality and price, there will be far less temptation to buy products from abroad.

DO state the problem at the beginning of your essay.

DON'T start with your own opinion or by giving your conclusion – make sure that your essay leads to the logical conclusion.

DO have a balanced approach.

DO involve the reader by using rhetorical questions.

DO remember to use a semi-formal register and to present your ideas objectively.

DO give your opinion in the final paragraph.

2.2 Formal letter

For work on formal letters, see page 110.

TASK

Your town or region has applied to be included in an international database on language learning. You have been asked by the president of the local council to write a letter to the person in charge of the database, explaining why your town or region should be included. You should explain:

- what languages are spoken in your town or region and why they are important.
- what facilities there are for learning these languages.
- what opportunities there are for leisure and cultural activities to help students practise these languages.

Write your **letter** in **220–260** words in an appropriate style.

USEFUL LANGUAGE

Beginning the letter

If we know the person's title and name:

- *Dear Dr Smallwood,*
- *Dear Professor Carmichael,*
- *Dear Ms Wilkinson,* (if we know the person is a woman)
- *Dear Mr Johnson,* (if we know the person is a man)

If we are writing to a specific person (e.g. the director of a college) but we do not know the person's name, title or gender:

- *Dear Sir or Madam,*

If we do not know who will read our letter or when in the future our letter will be read (e.g. a letter of reference for a colleague):

- *To whom it may concern,*

Opening phrases

- *I am writing with regard to …*
- *I am writing in reply to …*
- *I have been asked to write to you concerning …*
- *In response to your letter of 15 January, I am writing to …*

Ending the letter

- *I very much hope you will consider …*
- *I am sure you will see …*
- *I look forward to receiving your response to …*
- *I look forward to hearing your views on …*
- *Yours sincerely,* (when we have begun the letter with the person's title and name)
- *Yours faithfully,* (when we have begun the letter with **Dear Sir or Madam** or **To whom it may concern**)

Model answer

DO begin by identifying the situation you are writing about.

DO use this way of opening your letter if you don't know the person's name.

Dear Sir or Madam,

I am writing to you on behalf of the Macquarie Valley local council. As I believe you are aware, we are keen for our region, Macquarie Valley, to be included in the International Language Learning Database.

Although English is the official language in our country, Macquarie Valley is a perfect context to study a number of other languages. As a result of immigration from Latin America and China, Macquarie Valley boasts large communities of Spanish and Mandarin speakers. As is well known, these languages are of increasing importance internationally and may even come to rival English in the future.

DO make links between paragraphs.

DON'T use the same language as the input.

To satisfy the growing demand for these languages, our educational institutions provide many opportunities for formal study. The universities all offer degree courses and there are also private language schools, many of which now also teach English plus Spanish or Mandarin. In addition, home stays can be arranged with families or single people who are speakers of these languages.

DO make links between points within the paragraph.

Aside from these more formal ways of studying, there are also many opportunities for informal contact with native speakers. One such is taking one of the walking tours of the area, which are popular with locals and tourists alike. The thriving theatre and music scenes are also excellent vehicles for extending one's knowledge of the language and culture and for meeting others.

DO say what you want the result of your letter to be in the final paragraph.

Macquarie Valley has a great deal to offer the language student. We very much hope you will consider us for inclusion in the database and look forward to hearing from you.

Yours faithfully,

Nina Strefford

Nina Strefford

If you have not used a name at the beginning of your letter, DO end it like this.

2.3 Informal letter/Email

For work on informal letters or emails, see page 98.

TASK

Read part of an email from a friend who is planning to come and visit your country.

> Of course, I'd really like to see as much as I can, but with so little time (only a week) I wonder if that's feasible. Do you have any suggestions on where to go and what to do in your country?

Reply to the email message offering your friend some advice. Write your **email** in **220–260** words in an appropriate style.

USEFUL LANGUAGE

Beginning the letter/email

- *Thanks so much for your letter/email. It was really great to hear from you.*
- *Sorry not to have written/been in touch for so long/such a long time.* I've been really busy lately.
- *I thought I'd better drop you a line/write to let you know ...*

Ending the letter/email

- *I think that's all my news for the moment. Do write soon and let me know* what you've been doing.
- *Once again, thanks very much for* being so nice to Susie ...
- *Can't wait to* see you *on the twenty-fourth/next week in* Cambridge ...
- *Don't forget to say hi to ... from me.*
- *Give my love to ...*

Apologising

- *I'm really/terribly/awfully sorry* about what happened the other night.
- *Sorry I didn't manage to* see you last time I was in ...

Inviting

- *How about* meeting up for a cup of coffee/coming over for a meal *some time?*
- *Why don't we* try to get together some time soon?
- *I was wondering if you might like to* get together with ... next time you're in town.

Responding to an invitation

- *Thanks very much for* inviting us to your party. We're really looking forward to it.
- *I was really excited when I got your invitation. Unfortunately,* I've just realised it's the same weekend as my cousin's wedding, so *I won't be able to make it/it doesn't look as if I'm* going to make it.

Making a request

- *I was wondering if you happen to* know anywhere in Dublin we could stay.
- *If you've got a spare moment, do you think you could* find out when the music festival is on this year?

Referring to a previous letter/email

- *Do you remember* that sports centre *you mentioned in your last letter?*
- *You said in your letter that* you were thinking of applying for a scholarship.
- *Last time you wrote, you asked* how Tina was getting on.
- *You know that* course *I told you* I had applied for? *Well, ...*

Model answer

Dear Samuel,

I thought I'd better reply as quickly as possible since I see you're actually leaving next Monday. I'm so excited. I can't wait to see you.

You're right that in such a short time it won't be possible to see everything. You'd need at least six months for that! What I would do is to explore one area in depth. I have to say that Victoria, where I live, would be an excellent choice.

You could start by spending a couple of days in Melbourne and then rent a car and head for the Great Ocean Road. It's a really spectacular road that follows the coastline and stretches for over 250 kilometres. If I were you, I'd plan to spend a couple of days driving along, stopping for the night in Lorne or Apollo Bay.

You asked about things to do and I have to say it's hard to know where to begin. While you're in Melbourne, I'd definitely try to visit the National Gallery of Victoria and the South Bank complex, which is nearby. There are some great bars and restaurants there. On your drive along the Ocean Road you'll see all the famous surf beaches but it's also a great area for walking. There are hundreds of tracks through the rainforest. I think you'd really enjoy that too.

Well, I'd better stop now. Give me a call as soon as you get in and we'll meet up somewhere. I might even join you on the Ocean Road trip.

All the best,
Alex

DO begin by telling your friend why you've decided to write.

DO expand upon the task input.

DO divide your letter into paragraphs, each of which should cover a different element from the task input.

DO close your letter by mentioning the next time you will see or speak to the person you are writing to.

DON'T finish your letter with *Yours sincerely/faithfully*. DO use an appropriate INFORMAL phrase. There are various ways of closing letters. For very close friends and relatives you can use *With (all my love*, *Love* or *Lots of love*; with friends use *All the best*; with people you still don't know very well use *(With) best wishes*.

2.4 Report/Proposal

For work on reports, see pages 34 and 78. For work on proposals, see pages 24 and 88.

> **TASK**
>
> Your local council is conducting an enquiry into the volume of visitors to the centre of your town or city with a view to encouraging more people to make greater use of shops, restaurants, cafés and entertainment facilities there. You agree to write a report describing the existing situation, including factors which discourage people from coming to the city centre and recommending ways of attracting more visitors.
>
> Write your **report** in **220–260** words in an appropriate style.

Model answer

DO use headings and bullet points. This will make it clear to your reader that your report is not an essay or a review.

DO state the purpose of your report at the beginning.

DO use a relatively formal and impersonal style.

DO use the task input as a guide for how to divide your report into sections.

DO include a sentence summarising your opinion at the beginning of the final section of your report.

DO use bullet points. DON'T overdo it, though. If you use them in more than one section, you won't be able to show the full range of structures and vocabulary you know.

Visitors to our city centre

Introduction

The principal aims of this report are to provide an overview of the volume of visitors using services in our city centre and to identify factors which deter people from using them. The final section makes recommendations as to how the situation could be improved.

Current situation

I conducted interviews with a random selection of shoppers and customers in local restaurants and cafés. Fewer than half regularly visited the city centre. Among those who did make frequent use of what is on offer, most cited the pedestrianised Mitchell Mall as their favourite area. Smaller numbers enjoyed shopping or dining around Holmes Square, though several people said they found the traffic noise disagreeable.

Factors preventing greater use of city-centre services

There was a clear division between those who regularly visited the city centre and those who did so infrequently. The latter cited traffic congestion and pollution along with inflated prices for goods as factors that acted as a deterrent. For those who frequently came into town, on the other hand, the pedestrianised area and the outdoor cafés were a major attraction.

Recommendations

Clearly, more could be done to attract people to our city centre. I would make the following recommendations:
- extend the pedestrianised area to include the streets surrounding Holmes Square so as to capitalise on what is already an attractive area.
- encourage shops, cafés and restaurants to offer discounts to regular customers.
- maintain access to the pedestrianised areas for cyclists.

This final recommendation will encourage those who currently cycle into town to continue to do so, while reducing noise and pollution from motor traffic.

Although reports and proposals have a similar layout, reports are based on current circumstances or situations whereas proposals are action plans for the future. You give more space to the current situation in a report and more space to recommendations for future action in a proposal.

USEFUL LANGUAGE FOR A REPORT

Stating the purpose of the report

The principal aim/objective/purpose of this report is to provide a description of/present results of/assess the importance of …

In this report I will provide a description of/present results of/assess the importance of …

This report describes/provides an assessment of/presents results of …

Describing how you got your information

I conducted interviews with local council officers/*a survey of* all current members of the sports club …

Shopkeepers in the High Street responded to an online questionnaire.

I visited three of the most popular restaurants: Oregano, the Beach on Broad Street and Frank's Fish Shack …

High Street shoppers were invited to attend a focus group …

Reporting your results

Most of those responding to the survey stated that/expressed the opinion that …

According to one *interviewee, Mr Ross Peters, the traffic problem is …*

A large/considerable/significant proportion of those surveyed/respondents/informants said that …

Nearly three quarters of the shopkeepers (74 percent) had seen an improvement in the situation …

Presenting a list

The arguments against banning cars in the city centre altogether are the following:

1 …

2 …

The following were the main reasons given for supporting the ban: firstly … , secondly …

Points our informants mentioned in favour of/against the scheme were:

1 …

2 …

There are several ways in which locals and tourists alike might be drawn back to the city centre:

1 …

2 …

Making recommendations

Taking all the factors mentioned into account/In light of the results of the survey/questionnaire/focus group sessions creating a bicycle track would appear to be the most viable solution/option/approach.

I would therefore recommend the immediate implementation of the scheme.

USEFUL LANGUAGE FOR A PROPOSAL

Stating the purpose of the proposal

The principal objectives/aims of this proposal are to …

This proposal is intended to …

In this proposal I describe/evaluate/present/assess …

Background information

Comments made at the end of the questionnaires suggest …

Following a survey among families of young children …

Concerned *members of the local community* were invited to attend …

A number of concerns with regard to the most recent street party were expressed by locals.

Making recommendations and suggestions

A working group should be set up *by …*

There should be *an enquiry into …*

I recommend that *a larger survey should be conducted before a final decision is reached …*

Final recommendations

The results of the survey/questionnaire suggest that the introduction of heavier fines would seem to be the best option/choice/solution.

If these recommendations are implemented, the situation is bound to improve.

Unless these suggestions are implemented, it is unlikely that there will be any improvement in the short term.

2.5 Review

For work on reviews, see page 56.

TASK

The editor of your college English language magazine has asked you to write a review of two films you have seen recently, saying why one of the films is likely to be of particular relevance and interest to students at the college and why you believe the other is not worth watching.

Write your **review** in **220–260** words in an appropriate style.

USEFUL LANGUAGE

Concert

types of group or musician: *hip hop/indie/rock/heavy metal artist/band/group/musician, (bass/lead/rhythm) guitarist, (backing/lead) singer, drummer, folk singer/guitarist, country and western singer, jazz band/quartet/trio/singer, orchestra, quintet/quartet/ensemble/soloist/violinist/cellist*

elements: *auditorium, cantata, concerto, hall, lyrics, piece, tune, score, song, stage, symphony, theatre*

people: *composer, conductor, songwriter*

Exhibition

types: *painting, sculpture, photography, design, handicrafts*

elements: *gallery, catalogue, displays*

Book

Fiction

types: *fantasy, historical, mystery, romance, science fiction, thriller, whodunit*

elements: *atmosphere, author, character, dialogue, novelist, plot, setting, writer*

Non-fiction

types: *coffee-table book, cookbook, travel book, textbook, manual*

elements: *author, chapter, editor, illustration, index, glossary, section*

Film

types: (as for fiction +) *adaptation, animation, comedy*

elements: *animation, costume, design, photography, role, screenplay, script, set, special effects, soundtrack*

people: *actor, cinema-photographer, cast, director, producer, scriptwriter*

Play

types: (as for film +) *drama, farce, musical*

elements: *act, costume, design, lyrics, music role, scene, set, stage*

people: (as for film +) *composer, playwright*

TV programme

types: *chat show, current affairs programme, debate, documentary, drama, series, soap opera, situation comedy*

people: *actor, cast, compere, director, host, presenter, producer, scriptwriter*

Background information

- *'Sisters on Holiday' is Greta Johnson's* **first novel/first/second film/starring role/third individual exhibition**.
- *'Word World Three'* **opened at** *the Photographer's Space last week and* **I went along to have a look**.

A brief account of the plot

- **Set in** *late twentieth-century Honolulu,* **the film tells the story of …/recounts events in** *the lives of the Waikiki beach boys.*
- **In the context of the period after the Great Depression**, *the novel explores themes of alienation and intimacy.*
- **The series begins with** *the wedding of the two principal characters, Tyler Melville and Charlotte Burbrook.*

Criticism

- **The script seemed rather conventional/predictable/contrived** *to me.*
- **The plot struck me as completely bizarre/absurd/incomprehensible.**
- **The director has succeeded in creating a film that is both believable and thoroughly engaging.**
- **The characters are appealing and true to life.**
- **The dialogue is witty/stilted/natural/artificial.**
- **The dancers were quite brilliant/thoroughly amateurish.**
- **Andrea LoBianco's sets were a particular strength/weakness of the production.**

Recommendations

- *I would strongly encourage you not to miss/not to waste your money on* 'The rites of autumn'.
- *I would definitely recommend seeing/visiting/reading/having a look at* 'Santa Cruz as it once was'.

Model answer

DO give your reader the structure of your review at the beginning.

DO start by raising a question in your readers' minds.

DON'T give the ending away. It will ruin your readers' enjoyment of the film or book.

DON'T just tell the story. Give your assessment of what you have seen or read.

DON'T forget to cover all the points mentioned in the task input.

DO make comparisons.

DO use specific vocabulary for films, books, exhibitions or concerts.

DO include a final recommendation or evaluation at the end of your review.

End-of-course film night: my recommendations

I have seen two films that I considered as possible candidates for our end-of-term film night: 'Life before Life' and 'No More Midnight'. I enjoyed them both, but only one of them is right for our end-of-course film night, in my opinion.

'Life before Life' has many merits but is not the best film for our particular purposes. It has had rave reviews, partly because it stars Edwin Kamashila and the director, Sam Pickering, never fails to please the critics and audiences. The trouble is that the film is just too slow, particularly for a group of students at the end of the academic year. Over half the film involves intense discussions between Kamashila's character, Rupert, and his girlfriend, Carrie. I won't reveal whether they decide to stay together, but I fear the film would put many in our audience to sleep.

'No More Midnight', on the other hand, had me on the edge of my seat throughout. The cast are not as well known as Kamashila, but they do a great job of portraying the anxieties of a family waiting for news of a missing daughter. There's tremendous suspense but a good dose of humour, too. This makes for a film which is both utterly involving and entertaining.

I'm a fan of Pickering's films and I liked 'Life before Life' but not nearly as much as 'No More Midnight'. If we want to ensure that our audience can sit back, relax and forget about the exams, then this is definitely the film for us. Let's keep 'Life before Life' for the beginning of next semester.

Exam focus

Contents

Reading and Use of English
(1 hour 30 minutes)

Part 1 (Multiple-choice cloze)

What is being tested?

Part 1 tests your knowledge of vocabulary, including words with similar meanings, collocations and fixed phrases.

What do you have to do?

- Read a text with eight missing words.
- Choose the correct word to fill the gap from a set of four options.
- Mark the correct letter, (A, B, C or D) on your answer sheet.

Strategy

1 Read the title and the text quickly to get a general understanding of what it's about, without trying to fill any of the gaps.

2 Read the text again. Stop at each gap and try to predict what the missing word might be.

3 Look at the options for each gap carefully. Try putting each of the options in the gap to see which one fits best.

4 Check the words on either side of the gap to see if the option you have chosen goes with these.

5 Read the whole text again to make sure the options you have chosen make sense. Do not leave a blank; make a guess if necessary.

6 Transfer your answers to the answer sheet.

Part 2 (Open cloze)

What is being tested?

Part 2 tests your knowledge of grammar and lexico-grammatical items such as auxiliary verbs, articles, prepositions, pronouns, phrasal verbs, etc.

What do you have to do?

- Read a text with eight missing words.
- Put one word in each of the eight gaps.
- Write the correct word on your answer sheet.

Strategy

1 Read the title and text quickly to get a general idea of what it is about, without trying to fill any of the gaps.

2 Think about what kind of word is missing (e.g. preposition, article, pronoun).

3 Write in the missing words in pencil. Only write one word in each gap.

4 When you have finished, read through the whole text again. Check it makes sense and check the spelling.

5 Transfer your answers to the answer sheet.

Part 3 (Word formation)

What is being tested?

Part 3 tests vocabulary and your knowledge of how words are formed using prefixes and suffixes and by making internal changes to the word. You will have to identify what part of speech is required in each gap and write the correct form (e.g. noun, adjective, adverb).

What do you have to do?

- Read a text with eight gaps.
- Use the word in capital letters at the end of each line with a gap to form a word which fits the gap. This could be a noun, an adjective, an adverb or a verb. For example, you may need to change the word at the end of a line from a noun to an adjective with a negative prefix.
- Write your answers on the answer sheet.

Strategy

1 Read the title and the text quickly to get a general idea of what it is about.

2 Read the text again. This time stop at each gap. Think about whether the missing word is positive or negative, plural or singular, a noun, verb, adjective or adverb. Use the words before and after each gap to help you decide.

3 Write the correct form of the word in the gap.

4 Read the text again to make sure your answers make sense and the words are spelt correctly.

5 Transfer your answers to the answer sheet.

Part 4 (Key word transformation)

What is being tested?

Part 4 tests your knowledge of grammatical structures as well as vocabulary and shows examiners that you can express yourself in different ways.

What do you have to do?

- Complete six sentences using three to six words (including the key word) so that they have a similar meaning to the first sentence. You will usually have to change two things.
- Write your answers on the answer sheet.

Strategy

1 Read the first sentence and the key word. Work out what it is testing (e.g. you may need a passive form in the future).

2 Identify what is missing from the second sentence.

3 Think about what kind of words need to be used with the key word.

4 Write down the missing words. Do not change the key word in any way.

5 Make sure you have not written more than six words (contractions, e.g. *don't*, count as two words) and that you have not changed the meaning at all.

6 Check your spelling and that the sentences make sense.

7 Transfer your answers to the answer sheet.

Part 5 (Multiple choice)

What is being tested?

Part 5 focuses on your ability to understand a long text in detail. The questions may test understanding of detail, the main idea and the writer's opinion, attitude or purpose. You may be asked to deduce meaning from context and to follow features of text organisation such as examples, comparisons and reference.

What do you have to do?

- Read a text and six questions. Each question has four possible answers (A, B, C or D) and follows the order of the text.
- Choose the correct option for each question, based on the information in the text.
- Mark the correct letter, (A, B, C or D) on your answer sheet.

Strategy

1 Read the rubric and the title and sub-heading of the text.

2 Skim the text to get a general idea of what it is about.

3 Read each question and highlight the key words. (Do not worry about the four options yet.)

4 Highlight the part of the text that the question relates to.

5 Read the text carefully. When you find a part of the text you have highlighted, look at the question and the four options and decide on the answer. The meaning will be the same but the language will be different.

6 Choose the best answer and then check that the other options are definitely wrong.

7 Make your decision. If you are not sure, choose the one that seems most likely.

8 When you have completed all the questions, transfer your answers to the answer sheet.

Part 6 (Cross-text multiple matching)

What is being tested?

Part 6 focuses on understanding the opinion and attitude of four different writers across four short texts. The questions test your ability to identify where the writers may have similar or different opinions to each other about a specific issue.

What do you have to do?

- Read four short texts (A–D) and four multiple matching questions. The texts are independent of each other but all talk about the same topic.
- Identify the opinion or attitude expressed in each question and decide whether the opinions in the four texts (A–D) are the same or different.
- Write the correct letter for each answer on your answer sheet.

Strategy

1 Read the four questions and underline the key words.

2 For each question, underline the section of the text (A–D) referred to (e.g. *Writer A's opinion about*) and make sure you understand the writer's point of view.

3 Read the other texts and underline the sections which talk about the same issue.

4 Find the text which has a similar or different opinion/ attitude to the writer referred to in each question.

5 One question may ask you to identify the writer who has a different point of view on a specific issue to the other three writers. Check where this issue is mentioned in each text and identify the writer who expresses a differing view to the rest.

6 Check your answers again before transferring them to the answer sheet.

Part 7 (Gapped text)

What is being tested?

Part 7 tests your understanding of coherence, cohesion and text structure, as well as your global understanding.

What do you have to do?

- Read a text from which six paragraphs have been removed and placed in a jumbled order before the base text. You must decide where paragraphs A–G have been taken from. (There is one paragraph you do not need to use).
- Read the seven paragraphs and decide which paragraph best fits each gap.
- Mark your answers on your answer sheet.

Strategy

1 Read the title to get an idea of the topic.

2 Read the base text carefully to make sure you understand what it is about and to get a sense of the coherence of the passage.

3 Read before and after each gap and predict what information is missing from each gap.

4 Underline any textual clues (nouns, pronouns, linking words, etc.) which will help you to identify the missing paragraph.

5 Read the seven paragraphs and look for textual clues that will connect them to the gaps. Look for topic words, synonyms and reference words.

6 If you are not sure which paragraph to choose for one gap, go on to the next gap and return to it later.

7 Read through the completed text. Check that it makes sense and that you haven't used any paragraph more than once.

8 Try the extra paragraph in each gap again, just to check that it doesn't fit.

9 Transfer your answers to the answer sheet.

Part 8 (Multiple matching)

What is being tested?

Part 8 tests your ability to find specific information in a number of short texts, as well as an understanding of the writer's opinions and attitudes.

What do you have to do?

- Read four to six short texts around the same theme or one longer text divided into four to six paragraphs.
- Match ten questions or statements to the text or paragraph that they relate to. The text does not follow the same order as the questions.
- Write the correct letter for each answer on your answer sheet.

Strategy

1 Read the title of the text and any sub-headings.

2 Skim the text quickly to get an idea of what the text is about.

3 Read the questions carefully and highlight key words.

4 Scan each section of the text to find the information in the questions. You do not need to read in detail. Look for words or phrases which are similar in meaning to the words or phrases in the questions but don't just choose a paragraph because it contains the same words as in a question or statement.

5 Highlight possible answers in pencil. You may find similar – but not exactly the same – information in other sections.

6 Read the information carefully to check that it is an exact answer to the question.

7 Leave any questions that you are not sure about but always go back and answer them as you will not lose marks for a wrong answer. Choose the most likely answer.

8 When you have finished, transfer your answers to the answer sheet.

Writing
(1 hour 30 minutes)

Part 1 (Essay)

What is being tested?

Part 1 tests your ability to write coherently and to communicate ideas effectively in a semi-formal written style.

What do you have to do?

- Write an essay based on information and notes that you are given.
- Write between 220 and 260 words.

Strategy

See Writing reference on page 168.

Part 2 (Choice of task)

What is being tested?

Part 2 tests your ability to communicate your ideas effectively in an appropriate written style for the task which you have selected.

What do you have to do?

- Choose one task out of the three tasks you are given.
- Write one of them using an appropriate format and style. The task could be an email or letter, a report or proposal, or a review.
- Write between 220 and 260 words.

Strategy

See Writing reference on pages 170–177.

Listening
(approximately 40 minutes)

Part 1 (Multiple choice)

What is being tested?

In Part 1 the focus of the questions may test the main idea, the purpose, the attitude or opinion of the speakers.

What do you have to do?

- Listen twice to three short dialogues, each on a different topic, involving two speakers.
- Answer two multiple-choice questions about each of the three dialogues.
- Write the correct letter (A, B or C) on your answer sheet. (You are given five minutes at the end of the test to transfer your answers from the question paper to the answer sheet.)

Strategy

1 Read the questions and options and highlight the key words before you listen. (You are given some time to do this.)

2 The first time you listen, mark the answer you think is best.

3 Check your answers the second time you listen and make sure the options you have chosen answer the questions correctly. If you aren't sure, choose the answer you think is most likely – you may be right.

4 Transfer your answers to the answer sheet.

Part 2 (Sentence completion)

What is being tested?

In Part 2 the focus is on your understanding of detail, specific information and opinion.

What do you have to do?

- Read eight sentences with gaps about the recording.
- Listen twice to a monologue. It may be part of a radio report or a talk on a topic.
- Complete eight sentences with the exact word/words from the recording.
- Write your answers on your answer sheet.

Strategy

1 Before you listen, read the sentences carefully and highlight key words. Think about the kind of information that's missing. You have some time for this.

2 As you listen, try to complete the sentences. The sentences are in the same order as the information on the recording. Write a word or short phrase to complete each sentence. You should only write the words you hear and you should not change these words.

3 If you can't complete a sentence the first time you listen, leave it blank.

4 The second time you listen, complete any remaining sentences and check your answers. Don't leave any of the gaps blank; guess if you aren't sure.

5 Check your spelling and grammar (e.g. singular, plural) is correct and that the sentences make sense.

6 Be careful not to make any mistakes when you copy your answers onto the answer sheet at the end of the test.

Part 3 (Multiple choice)

What is being tested?

In Part 3 the focus of the questions will be on understanding the opinions and attitudes of the speakers in a longer dialogue.

What do you have to do?

- Listen to an interview or a conversation on a topic, usually between two or three speakers.
- Answer six multiple-choice questions.
- Write the correct letter, (A, B, C or D) for each answer on your answer sheet.

Strategy

1 Before you listen, read the introduction to the task to get information about who the speakers are and what they will talk about.

2 Read the questions and options and highlight the key words. Think about the kind of information you need to listen for.

3 Listen for paraphrases of the words and phrases on the recording and choose one of the options, A, B, C or D. If you are not sure of the answer, continue answering the other questions and come back to it in the second listening.

4 During the second listening, check the options you have chosen. Make sure you have chosen an option which answers the question correctly. The information in the other options may also be true but it may not be the right answer to the question. If you aren't sure, choose the one that seems most likely.

5 Transfer your answers to the answer sheet.

Part 4 (Multiple matching)

What is being tested?

Part 4 tests understanding of informal speech. The focus is on gist, attitude and opinion.

What do you have to do?

- Listen to five short monologues on a related topic twice.
- There are two tasks, each containing eight statements. Match one statement from each task to each of the five monologues. There are three extra statements in each task which do not match any of the monologues.
- Write the correct letter (A–H) for each answer on your answer sheet.

Strategy

1 Read the rubric carefully. This tells you what topic the speakers will talk about.

2 Read the sentence. Highlight key words or phrases in each statement.

3 The first time you listen, try to identify the main idea of what the speaker is talking about and mark the statement which you think matches most closely. Listen for paraphrases or synonyms for key words in the statements. But be careful as you may hear similar words repeated in several texts because they are all on the same topic.

4 During the second listening, check that the statements match exactly what the speaker says. Don't choose a statement just because it contains a word from the monologue.

5 Transfer your answers to the answer sheet.

Speaking
(approximately 15 minutes)

Part 1 (Interview)

What is being tested?

Part 1 focuses on your general interaction and your social language skills.

What do you have to do?

- The examiner will ask you and the other candidate for some personal information.
- You will be asked different questions about things such as what you do in your spare time, your work/studies and your future plans.
- This will take around two minutes.

Strategy

1 Avoid giving one-word answers. Add detail but not too much.

2 Try to sound interesting. Don't speak in a monotone.

3 Speak clearly. Try to speak confidently and look relaxed.

4 If you don't know a word, say it in another way. Don't leave long pauses.

5 Listen carefully both to the examiner and to your partner.

6 If you don't understand the question, ask for it to be repeated.

7 Give relevant, personal answers but don't speak for too long.

Part 2 (Individual long turn)

What is being tested?

In Part 2 the focus is on your fluency and your ability to organise your ideas and express yourself clearly. You will have to make comparisons and speculate about the situations in the pictures.

What do you have to do?

- You are given three pictures on the same topic. You listen to the task, which is also printed on the page with the pictures.
- The examiner will ask you two questions about the pictures. You must answer the questions by comparing two of the pictures. You can choose which pictures you want to talk about.
- You are given one minute to do both parts of the task.
- You then listen to the other candidate speaking and look at their pictures. When they have finished, you have to give a short answer to a question related to the topic.

Strategy

1 Listen carefully to the instructions. It's important that you understand exactly what you need to talk about. Ask the examiner to repeat the instructions if necessary but remember that the instructions are also written above the pictures.

2 Summarise the main similarities and any differences between two of the pictures. Talk about general ideas and don't be tempted just to describe the pictures or go off topic. You will need to speculate and give your opinion, especially about the second part of the task.

3 Make sure you answer both questions.

4 Keep talking for the whole minute. Use paraphrases and 'fillers' if necessary. The examiner will say, 'Thank you,' when the minute is finished.

5 Listen carefully while the other candidate is speaking, and look at their pictures but don't interrupt. When the examiner asks you a question related to the pictures, give a short answer.

Part 3 (Collaborative task)

What is being tested?

Part 3 tests your ability to negotiate with the other candidate to reach a decision. You will be expected to give your opinions and evaluate ideas, as well as listen and respond to your partner's ideas.

What do you have to do?

- Work with the other candidate to discuss something together.
- The examiner gives you both a task and a task sheet with some ideas to discuss. The task is also written on the page and you have some time to look at the task.
- The task may involve solving a problem, negotiating, agreeing and disagreeing. Discuss the task with the other candidate for two to three minutes.
- The examiner will then give you another instruction asking you to discuss something related to the topic and to make a decision together. You have about a minute for this.

Strategy

1 Read and listen carefully to the instructions. Use the time given to look at the task. Ask for clarification if you do not understand.

2 You should discuss each of the prompts in some detail but don't spend too long on any one idea.

3 One of you should start the discussion. Then take turns to give your opinions, agree, disagree, etc.

4 Turn-taking skills are important. Avoid dominating the discussion or interrupting rudely. It is important to involve and encourage your partner, and follow up on what they say.

5 Explain things in a different way if you can't think of a word or phrase and don't leave long pauses. Use words such as *right* or *OK* to 'fill the gaps'.

6 Try to use a range of functional language, such as asking for and reacting to opinions, agreeing and disagreeing, suggesting, speculating, opening and summarising the discussion.

7 You should be prepared to compromise in the second part of the task in order to reach a decision.

Part 4 (Discussion)

What is being tested?

Part 4 gives you the opportunity to show the examiner that you can discuss a topic in more depth, develop and expand your ideas, and justify your opinions.

What do you have to do?

- In this part of the test, the examiner asks you both questions which develop the topic in Part 3 and may lead to a more general discussion.
- You may add to what the other candidate has said or disagree with their ideas.
- The discussion will last for around four minutes.

Strategy

1 If you don't understand the question, ask the examiner to repeat it.

2 Give opinions and express your feelings about issues. Give reasons or examples to justify your opinions.

3 Listen to what the other candidate says and ask questions or give follow-up comments.

4 Take the opportunity to use a range of language but don't dominate the discussion.

General marking guidelines

Writing

Band	Content	Communicative Achievement	Organisation	Language
5	All the necessary information is included. Has a very positive effect on the reader.	Communicates complex ideas in a consistently effective way.	Organises ideas skilfully. Text is easy to follow. Uses a range of linking words effectively to make text coherent.	Uses a range of complex vocabulary accurately and appropriately. Able to produce both advanced and more basic grammatical forms confidently with minimal errors.
4	A mix of bands 3 and 5			
3	Most of the necessary information and/or some irrelevant information is included. Has a satisfactory effect on the reader.	Generally communicates complex ideas effectively.	Organises ideas clearly and generally uses a variety of linking words effectively.	Generally uses complex vocabulary appropriately. Uses a satisfactory range of grammatical structures. Occasionally makes errors in the use of more complex forms but these do not cause difficulty for the reader.
2	A mix of bands 1 and 3			
1	May not provide all the necessary information or gives irrelevant information. Target reader is adequately informed.	Able to communicate simple ideas clearly.	Text is basically well organised but may occasionally be difficult to follow.	Uses a limited range of vocabulary appropriately. May use more complex vocabulary inaccurately. Simple grammatical forms are used appropriately with minimal errors. More complex forms are attempted with some success.
0	No relevant information provided.			

Speaking

Band	Grammatical Resource	Lexical Resource	Discourse Management	Pronunciation	Interactive Communication
5	Has good control of complex grammatical forms.	Uses a varied range of vocabulary effectively.	Able to speak fluently and confidently with very little hesitation. Expresses ideas effectively using a varied range of linking words and discourse markers*.	Is easy to understand. Uses intonation and sentence and word stress to convey meaning effectively. Pronunciation of individual sounds is clear.	Able to initiate, negotiate and respond effectively.
4	A mix of bands 3 and 5				
3	Uses a range of simple and grammatical forms mainly accurately.	Uses a varied range of vocabulary mainly appropriately.	Able to produce extended speech with very little hesitation. Expresses ideas clearly using an appropriate range of linking words and discourse markers*.	Is easy to understand. Uses intonation and sentence and word stress appropriately. Pronunciation of individual sounds is clear.	Able to initiate, negotiate and respond appropriately.
2	A mix of bands 1 and 3				
1	Uses simple grammatical forms and a limited range of more complex forms mainly accurately.	Uses vocabulary appropriately when discussing familiar topics.	Able to produce extended speech with some hesitation. Uses a range of linking words and discourse markers*.	Is easy to understand. Intonation and sentence and word stress are generally appropriate. Pronunciation of individual sounds is generally clear.	Able to initiate, negotiate and respond appropriately with very little help.
0	Below band 1				

*Discourse markers are spoken words or phrases which help to make the meaning clear (e.g. *actually*, *basically*, *what I mean is*).

Practice test

Reading and Use of English

Part 1

For questions **1–8**, read the text below and decide which answer (**A**, **B**, **C** or **D**) best fits each gap. There is an example at the beginning (**0**).

Example:

0 **A** pioneer   **B** developer   **C** designer   **D** creator

0	**A**	**B**	**C**	**D**
	▬	☐	☐	☐

Ernest Shackleton

Ernest Shackleton was an early **(0)** .... of polar exploration, who led three British expeditions to the Antarctic.

Shackleton's first experience of the polar regions was with Captain Robert Scott and his team and they established a new record. However, much to his **(1)** ...., Shackleton was sent home due to **(2)** .... health, meaning that he had to **(3)** .... his dream of reaching the South Pole. During his second expedition, he and three companions set another record – this time for having made the greatest **(4)** .... to the South Pole in history. Members of Shackleton's team also climbed Mount Erebus, the Antarctic's most active volcano. For these achievements, Shackleton received official **(5)** .... from the British king.

In 1911, the race to the South Pole ended with Roald Amundsen's victory. Shackleton turned his **(6)** .... to the crossing of Antarctica from sea to sea, via the Pole. Disaster **(7)** ...., though, when his ship, *Endurance*, became trapped in ice and was slowly **(8)** ....

Shackleton returned to the Antarctic in 1921, but died shortly after his arrival. At his wife's request, he was buried there.

1	**A** rage	**B** disorder	**C** annoyance	**D** temper
2	**A** dissolving	**B** deteriorating	**C** damaging	**D** decaying
3	**A** withdraw	**B** concede	**C** vanish	**D** abandon
4	**A** revolution	**B** progress	**C** modification	**D** gain
5	**A** recognition	**B** awareness	**C** gratitude	**D** reception
6	**A** objective	**B** basis	**C** focus	**D** aim
7	**A** struck	**B** caused	**C** broke	**D** established
8	**A** demolished	**B** smashed	**C** extinguished	**D** crushed

Part 2

For questions **9–16**, read the text below and think of the word which best fits each gap. Use only one word in each gap. There is an example at the beginning (**0**).

Example: | 0 | M | A | Y |

Health and Fitness

If regular physical activity benefits the body, a sedentary lifestyle **(0)** ....may.......... well do the opposite. **(9)** .... only does it increase people's chance of becoming overweight, it also gives rise to a range of health issues. **(10)** .... despite the well-documented advantages of physical activity, only 30 percent of adults report doing regular exercise **(11)** .... their leisure time. Even **(12)** .... shockingly perhaps, studies that measure people's levels of physical activity suggest that these 'self-reports' are, in **(13)** .... probability, overestimates.

According to a recent study, it **(14)** .... appear that, even for people who do exercise regularly, there's a clear link between excessive television watching and obesity. It was found that, regardless **(15)** .... whether or not they were regular exercisers, for every two hours devoted to watching television, people have a 23 percent higher risk of becoming seriously overweight.

It has also been established that remaining seated for hours **(16)** .... end changes the rate at which people burn calories, which means that even when they do exercise, they find it harder to lose weight than people who opt for a more active lifestyle.

Part 3

For questions **17–24**, read the text below. Use the word given in capitals at the end of some of the lines to form a word that fits in the gap **in the same line**. There is an example at the beginning **(0)**.

Example: | 0 | G | L | O | B | A | L |

The United Nations

The United Nations (UN) is a **(0)** ....global........ organisation made up of almost 200 member states, whose mission and work are influenced by the principles agreed on when it was founded.   **GLOBE**

Through bodies and committees like the Security Council and the General Assembly, the UN makes **(17)** .... for its members   **PROVIDE**
to state their views on various issues. The UN works in areas such as the **(18)** .... of international peace and security, the   **MAINTAIN**
protection of human rights, the upholding of international law and the **(19)** .... of humanitarian aid. By facilitating dialogue   **DISTRIBUTE**
between its members and also by hosting **(20)** ...., the UN   **NEGOTIATE**
has become a mechanism for governments to work **(21)** ....   **COLLABORATE**
to find solutions to problems.

The accurate interpretation and translation of the UN's six official languages is fundamental to the work of the organisation. This unique multilingual environment encourages increased efforts by the
(22) ...., which results in more involvement by the member   **PARTICIPATE**
states, better outcomes and greater **(23)** .... To date, the   **EFFECT**
various agencies, programmes and staff of the UN have been awarded the **(24)** .... Nobel Peace Prize more than ten times for   **PRESTIGE**
their work.

Part 4

For questions **25–30**, complete the second sentence so that it has a similar meaning to the first sentence, using the word given. **Do not change the word given.** You must use between **three** and **six** words, including the word given. Here is an example **(0)**.

Example

0   Economists expect the price of oil to fall next year.

ANTICIPATED

It .... the price of oil will fall next year.

The gap can be filled with the words 'is anticipated that', so you write:

Example: | **0** | | IS ANTICIPATED THAT |

---

25   When she was promoted to project manager, Jana put a lot of effort and enthusiasm into her new role.

THREW

Jana completely .... as project manager.

26   Leo was able to understand what the letter said by using a dictionary to help him.

AID

Leo understood what the letter said with .... a dictionary.

27   Until Olivia explained the situation to him, the manager was unaware of what was happening.

PICTURE

Until Olivia .... , the manager was unaware of what was happening.

28   If it has to be postponed due to the weather, the match will be played at a later date.

EVENT

In .... due to the weather, the match will be played at a later date.

29   The passengers were warned that they should never leave their luggage unattended.

CIRCUMSTANCES

The passengers were told that .... leave their luggage unattended.

30   Cathy wondered how likely it was that she would win the competition.

CHANCES

Cathy asked herself what .... the competition.

Part 5

You are going to read part of an article about multitasking. For questions **31–36**, choose the answer
(**A**, **B**, **C** or **D**) which you think fits best according to the text.

Multitasking: myth or reality?

In one of the many letters he wrote to his son in the 1740s, the British statesman Lord Chesterfield offered the following advice: 'There is time enough for everything in the course of the day, if you do but one thing at once, but there is not time enough in the year, if you will do two things at a time.' To Chesterfield, singular focus was not merely a practical way to structure one's time; it conveyed something about a person, regardless of their educational background. 'This steady and undissipated attention to one object, is a sure mark of a genius; as hurry, bustle, and agitation, are the never-failing symptoms of a weak and frivolous mind.'

In modern times, hurry, bustle, and agitation are a regular way of life for many people – unfortunately so much so that we have embraced a word to describe our efforts to respond to the many pressing demands on our time: *multitasking*. Used for decades to describe the parallel processing abilities of computers, multitasking is now shorthand for the human attempt to do simultaneously as many things as possible, as quickly as possible, preferably marshalling the power of as many technologies as possible.

Massachusetts-based psychiatrist Dr Edward Hallowell, who specialises in the treatment of attention deficit/hyperactivity disorder (ADD) and has written a book with the self-explanatory title *CrazyBusy*, has been offering therapies to combat extreme multitasking for years. In his book he calls multitasking a 'mythical activity in which people believe they can perform two or more tasks simultaneously'. In a 2005 article, he coined the term 'Attention Deficit Trait' (ADT), a syndrome which he claims is rampant in the business world. ADT is 'purely a response to the hyperactive environment in which we live', writes Hallowell, and its hallmark symptoms mimic those of ADD. 'Never in history has the human brain been asked to track so many data points,' Hallowell argues, and this challenge 'can be controlled only by creatively engineering one's environment and one's emotional and physical health.' Limiting multitasking is essential.

To better understand the multitasking phenomenon, neurologists and psychologists have studied the workings of the brain. In 1999, Jordan Grafman used functional magnetic resonance imaging (fMRI) scans to determine that when people engage in 'task-switching' – that is, multitasking behaviour – the flow of blood increases to a region of the frontal cortex called Brodmann area 10. (The flow of blood to particular regions of the brain is taken as an indication of activity in those regions.) 'This is presumably the last part of the brain to evolve, the most mysterious and exciting part,' Grafman said.

This fact is also what makes multitasking a poor long-term strategy for learning. Other studies, such as those performed by psychologist René Marois, have used fMRI to demonstrate the brain's response to handling multiple tasks. Marois found evidence of a 'response selection bottleneck' that occurs when the brain is forced to respond to several stimuli at once. As a result, task-switching leads to time lost as the brain determines which task to perform. Psychologist David Meyer believes that rather than a bottleneck in the brain, a process of 'adaptive executive control' takes place, which 'schedules task processes appropriately to obey instructions about their relative priorities and serial order', as he described to the *New Scientist*. Unlike many other researchers who study multitasking, Meyer is optimistic that, with training, the brain can learn to task-switch more effectively, and there is some evidence that certain simple tasks are amenable to such practice.

Psychology professor Russell Poldrack found that 'multitasking adversely affects how people learn. Even if you learn while multitasking, that learning is less flexible and more specialised, so you cannot retrieve the information as easily.' His research demonstrates that people use different areas of the brain for learning and storing new information when they are distracted: brain scans of people who are distracted or multitasking show activity in the striatum, a region of the brain involved in learning new skills; brain scans of people who are not distracted show activity in the hippocampus, a region involved in storing and recalling information. Discussing his research, Poldrack warned, 'We have to be aware that there is a cost to the way that our society is changing, that humans are not built to work this way. We're really built to focus. And when we sort of force ourselves to multitask, we're driving ourselves to perhaps be less efficient in the long run even though it sometimes feels like we're being more efficient.'

31   According to Lord Chesterfield, concentrating solely on one thing

   A   took up an excessive amount of people's time.

   B   was essentially a mark of superior intelligence.

   C   led to tasks not being completed on time.

   D   suited some people better than others.

32   In the second paragraph, the writer suggests that the concept of 'multitasking'

   A   involves an over-reliance on specialised equipment.

   B   is only now being used in the field of technology.

   C   has become increasingly common in recent years.

   D   is not as new as we might think.

33   What point does the writer make about Dr Hallowell?

   A   He believes certain professionals find themselves multitasking more than others.

   B   He wrote a book about multitasking long before the term became fashionable.

   C   He has been responsible for the identification of a new condition related to multitasking.

   D   He has disputed the definition of the word 'multitasking'.

34   What is suggested by Jordan Grafman's research on multitasking?

   A   There is considerable overlap between the brain's zones.

   B   Activity is confined to a specific area of the brain.

   C   There has been a great deal of uncertainty surrounding brain development.

   D   Experts are in agreement about what happens in the brain.

35   Marois and Meyer differ in their opinion of how the brain responds to multitasking in terms of

   A   the processing of information.

   B   the most suitable subject for research.

   C   the types of tasks that are suitable for multitasking.

   D   the fact that some people respond more quickly.

36   What implication does Russell Poldrack's research have for students?

   A   They may soon have to use new techniques to remember what they have learnt.

   B   They should make a conscious effort to consider how efficiently they work.

   C   They actually engage in more multitasking than they are aware of.

   D   They are probably failing to retain as much information as they think.

Part 6

You are going to read four contributions to an online discussion about school uniforms. For questions **37–40**, choose from the contributors **A–D**. The contributors may be chosen more than once.

School Uniform

Four people comment on school uniforms.

A

Proponents of school uniforms say that they're favoured by most teachers and students, as they eliminate a variety of problems at school. A 'level playing field' is created for students, socio-economic disparities are reduced and learners are less pre-occupied with their appearance, they claim, when a uniform policy is in place. In theory, these are strong arguments in favour of uniforms though whether or not wearing one guarantees greater scholastic achievement still remains to be seen, and surely that's what school is all about? I myself am in two minds as to whether they're a force for good, not least because of the cost involved. As anyone who is a parent of teenagers knows, young people insist on having a full 'weekend' wardrobe in addition to their uniform, and this, in my experience, doesn't make for a healthy bank balance! Uniforms are a yearly expenditure I'd rather not have, if I'm honest.

B

Post holidays, in August each year, the purchasing of a school uniform becomes a drain on finances in any household. But if it's got to be done, it should be done with minimum complaint. Those against school uniforms say that they infringe upon a student's right to express their individuality, and it's easy to see how they come to this conclusion. Why should students have to look like clones just to satisfy outdated government policies? While I respect the need for rules, surely students should still have the liberty to demonstrate their character through what they wear? And to those who claim that students attending schools with a non-uniform policy do less well academically, I say that evidence shows the contrary is the case. Not only that, but when students see that they are trusted to dress appropriately to come to school each day, it seems to encourage them to act in an altogether more mature fashion.

C

School uniforms ensure there is less drama, less distraction and an increased learning focus. It's that simple. It stands to reason that when all students are wearing the same outfit, they are less preoccupied with what they look like and can thus better concentrate on their studies, self-development and expressing their individuality through the various creative outlets that schools provide. Indeed the statistics seem to support that: when it comes to official assessment, improved scores are the case. Regardless of the often considerable cost involved in purchasing uniforms, they've become what I would call a necessary evil. And to be fair, there is something nice about seeing students walking along the street smartly dressed in their uniforms, taking pride in their school and appearance and acting accordingly, rather than wearing the latest baggy jeans and trainers.

D

Opponents of school uniforms maintain that they have no discernible positive effect on behaviour, and only emphasise the economic disparities they're intended to disguise. However, it can't be denied that they promote a sense of conformity among students albeit at the expense of individuality. Is that such a bad thing nowadays? Young people will need to face a plethora of rules once they leave the confines of school and go out into the real world, so wearing a uniform helps pave the way for learning to comply with rules. While it's true that having to buy a full school uniform each year for a growing teenager is an extra economic burden for parents, it's money well spent in my eyes. Why? Well, if a sense of pride in wearing that uniform is instilled in students by their school, they then conduct themselves in an exemplary manner when not on the school premises. And that, surely, is a good thing.

Which contributor

has a different opinion to contributor B about the link between uniforms and a student's sense of identity?

| 37 | |

holds a different view to contributor C on whether school uniforms improve academic performance?

| 38 | |

shares an opinion with contributor D on the connection between school uniforms and behaviour?

| 39 | |

expresses a different view from the others on the financial implications of having a school uniform policy?

| 40 | |

Part 7

You are going to read an extract from a magazine article about the relationship between dolphins and humans. Six paragraphs have been removed from the extract. Choose from the paragraphs **A–G** the one which fits each gap (**41–46**). There is one extra paragraph which you do not need to use.

Dolphins and humans

Just how unique is the bond between the friendly marine species and people?

Recently on a beach on the Bahamian island of Bimini, I was approached by a young woman. I was there as part of my training with the Dolphin Communication Project, a U.S. research organisation that studies a resident population of Atlantic spotted dolphins just offshore. The woman was a massage therapist, and she wanted my opinion. She had a plan to establish a dolphin resort at an undisclosed location in the Bahamas.

41

But the therapist didn't see it like that. 'You don't understand,' she said. 'Dolphins want to help people – they'll want to be with us at the resort. Humans and dolphins share a special bond, don't you know?' At the time, I'd never heard of a dolphin–human bond. As a novice dolphin researcher, I didn't know enough about dolphin behaviour to say whether she was talking science or science-fiction.

42

Science goes some way to clarifying this. It's clear that wild dolphins of some species are noted for seeking out social encounters with humans. The phenomenon of *lone sociable dolphins* – for whom human contact appears to be a substitute for dolphin company – is documented extensively in scientific literature. Well-known examples are Pita from Belize, Davina from England and Filippo from Italy. One report describes no less than 29 lone sociable dolphins that were regularly observed by scientists.

43

In addition to the lone sociable dolphin, we can look at *provisioned dolphins*, also known to spend time in proximity to humans and essentially bribed with fish to interact with humans. Unlike lone sociable dolphins, they only seem interested in humans because they receive food. Visitors regularly report curious and amiable interactions. Aggression, however, remains a problem. Tourists in Florida, Louisiana and other American coastal areas regularly feed wild dolphins, with the predictable result that the humans are commonly bitten, while dolphins have suffered propeller strikes and other injuries.

44

Meanwhile, Monkey Mia, a Western Australian tourist destination famous for its provisioned dolphins, has introduced policies to dissuade people from feeding adult males, and the daily feeding encounters are regulated by local officials in order to minimise risks. Clearly, dolphin curiosity doesn't result in benevolent encounters. But then, if their primary motive is hunger, why should it?

45

Elsewhere, it might have been the dolphins who first initiated regular contact with humans. In the Florida Keys in the USA, local dolphins were systematically targeted in order to familiarise them with humans. Evidence of friendly inter-species interaction is abundant. The wild spotted dolphins found there undeniably behave in a curious and welcoming manner toward researchers and tourists.

46	

It seems inconceivable that any animal could be more excited to see a human than my childhood Dalmatian, who nearly fainted from waggly-tailed happiness whenever I returned home from school. Perhaps this friendly excitement results from the domestication process? Even wild animals can thrive in constant close contact with humans when tamed, and some species reportedly pursue human contact in a purely wild setting – just like dolphins. Do these wild species have more of an affinity for humans than wild dolphins? This is, I'm afraid, in the eye of the beholder.

A

Because they are so dangerous for both parties, the National Marine Fisheries Service and its partners have initiated an awareness campaign to discourage such encounters. The U.S. Marine Mammal Protection Act of 1972 prohibits giving anything to, or otherwise interacting with, wild dolphins and other marine mammals.

B

However, since there is no scientific way of telling whether dolphins are friendlier to humans than other animals, I'm forced to turn to anecdotal accounts and personal opinion. My instinct tells me that domestic animals such as cats and dogs are friendlier than dolphins.

C

Now, some time after that encounter, I'm finally familiar enough with the expert literature to pick up this discussion where it left off. What's the nature of the dolphin–human relationship? Do dolphins have a desire to seek out human contact?

D

If, on the other hand, we accept that we're only talking about a handful of species, we are still left with the problem of how to measure friendliness. Luckily extensive research has been carried out.

E

The idea was to capture dolphins from the wild and transfer them to swimming pools where they would be used in healing therapy. What did I think? Well, I wasn't keen on the idea. Why jeopardise the animals' welfare by removing them from their home? Why not just take people out to swim with the wild dolphins, as they already did in Bimini, and let them interact with people on their own terms?

F

In a number of regions around the globe it's possible to watch or swim with groups of wild dolphins that are accustomed to human swimmers, no bribery required. They can be found, among other places, in the Bahamas, Japan, New Zealand and Hawaii, where it's technically illegal to swim with wild dolphins.

G

There is no doubt that these animals exhibit inquisitive behaviour, which lends weight to the idea that dolphins do, in fact, look for human contact with some regularity. One could even say it constitutes undeniable evidence: apparently wild dolphins *can* have an affinity with humans.

Part 8

You are going to read an article about sleep. For questions **47–56**, choose from the sections (**A–D**). The sections may be chosen more than once.

In which section does the writer

speculate on a biological reason why some people sleep for longer than others?   **47** ▢

explain that going to sleep is an instinctive course of action?   **48** ▢

make reference to research carried out in the past on human sleeping patterns?   **49** ▢

refer to a mechanism/feature of the body that informs individuals they require further sleep?   **50** ▢

mention the role of sleep in defending the human body's ability to fight illness?   **51** ▢

refer to the significance of monitoring people's quantity of sleep?   **52** ▢

give an example of natural daily events which affect people's decisions regarding sleep?   **53** ▢

refer to a chemical in the body which triggers people's desire to asleep?   **54** ▢

state a common misconception about what happens to the body during sleep?   **55** ▢

highlight an association between state of health and the amount of sleep required by a person?   **56** ▢

Sleep

What happens when we sleep and how important is this rest period for the body?

A Sleep is often seen as time when the body is inactive. In fact, the opposite is true. Sleep is an active, involuntary though complex process during which our body undertakes a number of activities. It involves low awareness of the outside world, relaxed muscles, and a raised anabolic state which helps us to build and repair our bodies. Primarily, sleep is for the brain, allowing it to recover and regenerate. During our sleep, the brain can process information, consolidate memory, and enable us to learn and function effectively during daytime. This is why we are encouraged to get a good night's sleep in the run-up to a job interview rather than staying awake all night to prepare. Whilst we sleep, our brain is not only strengthening memories but it is also reorganising them, picking out the emotional details and helping us produce new insights and creative ideas. Sleep affects our ability to use language and sustain attention. If we compromise on our sleep pattern, we compromise on our performance, our mood, and our interpersonal relationships. Sleep has also been shown to protect the immune system. Sleep is an inconvenient, time-consuming process, but it is such a prerequisite for life that we have simply evolved to fit it in.

B A mechanism called the circadian timer regulates the pattern of our sleep and waking. Most living things have internal circadian rhythms, meaning they are adapted to live in a cycle of day and night. The French geophysicist Jean-Jacques d'Ortous de Mairan was the first to discover circadian rhythms in an experiment with plants in 1729. Two centuries later, Dr Nathaniel Kleitman studied the effect of circadian rhythms on human sleep cycles. These rhythms respond primarily to light and darkness, and the cycle is actually longer than 24 hours. The internal master clock which regulates our circadian rhythms is made of nerve cells in our brain called the suprachiasmatic nucleus (SCN). The SCN controls the production of melatonin, which is a hormone that makes us feel sleepy. During sleep, melatonin levels rise sharply. The SCN is located just above our optic nerves, which send signals from the eyes to the brain.

Therefore, the SCN receives information about the amount of light in the environment through our eyes. When there is less light, it tells the brain to create more melatonin.

C Another chemical that affects sleep is serotonin. Produced by the brain, insufficient levels of serotonin are also related to mental health problems such as anxiety. Serotonin levels are highest in the brain when we are awake and active, and the brain creates more serotonin when it is lighter outside. This is why people feel tired at nighttime, and why it is a good idea to turn off the lights when we are trying to sleep. The immune system also influences serotonin, and therefore influences sleep patterns, which may explain why we need to sleep more if we are feeling under the weather. As humans are mainly daytime animals, the period we choose to sleep is determined naturally by the level of light in the environment; principally due to the setting and rising of the sun. Nowadays, however, light levels can be manipulated through the use of artificial lights. People who work nightshifts may wish to reduce the level of light they are exposed to during the daytime in order to sleep. This can be done through the use of blackout curtains.

D In humans, the amount of sleep a person needs depends upon their age. Newborn babies sleep for an average of 16–18 hours per day. Adolescents tend to require more sleep than adults, possibly due to the physiological changes that are happening in the body during this period. On reaching adulthood, people tend to sleep 7–8 hours per day, with older adults sleeping roughly for 6–7 hours but taking more frequent naps. It is important for us to gauge the amount of sleep we need, and to ensure that we get the right amount to ward off negative consequences associated with sleep deficit. The sleep debt we build up whilst awake can only be repaid through sleeping. This is regulated by a mechanism in the body called the sleep homeostat, which controls our drive to sleep. If we have a greater sleep debt, then the sleep homeostat indicates to us that we need more sleep.

Writing

Part 1

You must answer this question. Write your answer in **220–260** words in an appropriate style.

---

1 Your class has attended a panel discussion on what role the government should play in keeping its country's citizens healthy. You have made the notes below.

> *The role the government should play in keeping its country's citizens healthy*
> - *introducing educational campaigns*
> - *regulating the cost of food*
> - *encouraging people to exercise*

> *Some opinions expressed in the discussion*
> *'The government is failing to educate young people about the hidden dangers of sugar.'*
> *'Taxes on unhealthy food should be introduced.'*
> *'Gym membership should be free.'*

Write an essay discussing **two** of the roles in your notes. You should **explain which role would be most effective**, **giving reasons** in support of your answer.

You may, if you wish, make use of the opinions expressed in the discussion, but you should use your own words as far as possible.

Part 2

Write an answer to **one** of the questions **2–4** in this part. Write your answer in **220–260** words in an appropriate style.

2   You see the following announcement on a website, *Useful Inventions*.

REVIEWS WANTED

Send us a review of a gadget that you couldn't live without.

Explain what the gadget is, how you use it and why you couldn't live without it.

Write your **review**.

3   You belong to a committee that helps to organise an annual music festival in your town. This year's event has just taken place and you have been asked by the committee chairman to write a report.

Your report should explain what you believe the highlights and weaknesses of this year's festival were, and include some recommendations for next year.

Write your **report**.

4   You have received an email from an English friend.

> You won't believe this, but I've just been offered a temporary role in the Head Office of the software company I work for, and it's in your country! I'd need to spend a year there.
>
> I'm not sure if I should accept the offer. Please can you tell me what life's like in your country, some enjoyable things to do there and if you think I should go.
>
> Thanks,
>
> Alex

Write your **email** in reply.

Listening

Part 1

▶ 53 You will hear three different extracts. For questions **1–6**, choose the answer (**A**, **B** or **C**) which fits best according to what you hear. There are two questions for each extract.

Extract One

You hear a physics undergraduate telling a friend about a competition he took part in.

1 What does he say about it?

   A He believed the team could have been better prepared.

   B He felt the end result had always been anticipated.

   C He was frustrated that he was unable to attend.

2 What does he say about the other competitors?

   A Many of them were relatively inexperienced at entering competitions.

   B It's unusual for undergraduates to be involved at such a high level.

   C The women outnumbered the men on this particular occasion.

Extract Two

You hear two friends discussing their TV viewing habits.

3 What does the man say about TV audiences?

   A They want to have more control over how they watch TV.

   B They hope their opinion about future TV programmes will be considered.

   C They are now intolerant of watching TV in the conventional way.

4 What does the woman say about soap operas?

   A Modern-day social issues need to be explored in more depth.

   B Many of their story lines are representative of the lives of ordinary people.

   C They use more effective techniques than traditional story-telling processes.

Extract Three

You hear two friends talking about running a marathon.

5 The man admits that prior to running the marathon,

   A he had trouble keeping his emotions under control.

   B he made a conscious effort to build up his stamina.

   C he experienced considerable physical discomfort.

6 What does the woman say about the marathon she ran?

   A She was worried she'd be unable to complete it.

   B She had a lack of energy at times on the day.

   C She felt extremely thirsty throughout it.

Part 2

▶ 54 You will hear a man called Leo Anderson giving a presentation about his work as a volunteer on a rhino conservation project in South Africa. For questions **7–14**, complete the sentences with a word or short phrase.

RHINO CONSERVATION PROJECT

On arrival at the project, Leo was immediately assigned to the **(7)** .... team.

One of Leo's first duties was the **(8)** .... of the young rhinos.

Leo was responsible for cleaning out the rhinos' **(9)** .... each day.

The ACG **(10)** .... informs volunteers how physically challenging specific experiences on the conservation project are.

Leo's administrative duties included recording data on the rhinos' **(11)** ....

Leo was pleasantly surprised by the standard of the **(12)** .... that the volunteers stayed in.

What made the whole experience unforgettable for Leo was the amazing **(13)** .... among the volunteers.

Leo thought experience of volunteering would help him with his application to study **(14)** .... at university.

Part 3

▶ 55 You will hear an interview in which two young fashion designers called Michelle Barnes and Oliver Grimshaw are talking about their work in sustainable fashion. For questions **15–20**, choose the answer (**A**, **B**, **C** or **D**) which fits best according to what you hear.

15 Michelle believes that a major issue facing today's fashion industry is
  A the amount of time that's needed to introduce change.
  B the language used to describe processes.
  C the attitude people have to fashion.
  D the reputation it has previously gained.

16 Oliver feels his company has made progress in how their collections are produced by
  A keeping the focus limited to their area.
  B paying workers above average wages.
  C sourcing a wide range of waste products.
  D following industry legislation.

17 Michelle thinks that awareness of the negative impacts of the fashion industry has been raised by
  A members of the general public speaking out.
  B complaints made by those working in fashion.
  C successful environmental campaigns.
  D statistics that have been made public.

18 What does Oliver say about today's fashion students?
  A They already have more than enough positive role models to follow.
  B They are excited about working with the designers of the future.
  C There is a sense of urgency among them to lead the way.
  D Large fashion chains have set them a poor example.

19 Michelle feels that in the future Ethion ought to
  A develop its brand name.
  B recruit more senior-level staff.
  C improve garment production times.
  D aim to reuse already existing pieces.

20 What do Michelle and Oliver agree about the fashion industry in the UK?
  A Old buildings should be re-opened to facilitate its development.
  B Over time, valuable skills have been lost from it.
  C The costs involved in it are typically too high.
  D More money needs to be invested in it.

Part 4

▲ 56 You will hear five short extracts in which people are talking about a job interview they attended.
While you listen, you must complete both tasks.

TASK ONE

For questions **21–25**, choose from the list (**A–H**) what
each speaker feels they could have done better.

A have a deeper understanding of the role

B listen more carefully   Speaker 1 ☐ 21

C prevent anxiety taking over   Speaker 2 ☐ 22

D ask more questions   Speaker 3 ☐ 23

E give sufficient detail in responses   Speaker 4 ☐ 24

F behave more formally   Speaker 5 ☐ 25

G emphasise key skills

H focus on future opportunities

TASK TWO

For questions **26–30**, choose from the list (**A–H**) what
each speaker feels helped them to get the job.

A creative ability

B previous experience   Speaker 1 ☐ 26

C inspiring leadership skills   Speaker 2 ☐ 27

D an original approach   Speaker 3 ☐ 28

E multilingualism   Speaker 4 ☐ 29

F good performance under pressure   Speaker 5 ☐ 30

G caring nature

H an interest in learning new skills

Speaking

Part 1

The Interlocutor will ask you and the other candidate some questions about yourselves.

▶ **57** Listen to the recording and answer the questions. Pause the recording after each bleep and give your answer.

Part 2

The Interlocutor will give you and the other candidate three different photographs and ask you to talk on your own about two of your photographs for about a minute. You will also have to answer a question about your partner's pictures.

▶ **58** Listen to the recording and answer the questions. When you hear two bleeps, pause the recording for a minute and answer the question. Then start the recording again. When you hear one bleep, pause the recording for thirty seconds and answer the question.

Candidate A

- Why might the people have chosen to relax in this way?
- How might they be feeling?

Candidate B

- Which sport would be most exciting and why?
- How could young people benefit from doing this sport?

Part 3

The Interlocutor will ask you and the other candidate to discuss something together.

▶ 59 Look at the task and listen to the Interlocutor's instructions. When you hear the bleep, pause the recording for two minutes and discuss the task.

After two minutes, start the recording again and listen to the Interlocutor's instructions. When you hear the bleep, pause the recording for one minute and complete the task.

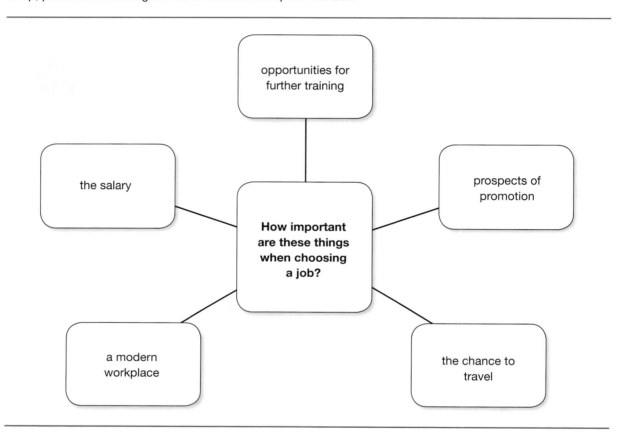

Part 4

The Interlocutor will ask you and the other candidate questions related to the topic of Part 3.

▶ 60 Listen to the recording and answer the Interlocutor's questions. Pause the recording when you hear each bleep and discuss the question with the other candidate.

Audio scripts

Unit 1

▶ 01

Ex = Examiner   K = Karl   El = Elena

Ex: Good morning. My name is Irene and this is my colleague, Deborah. And your names are?

K: Karl Weber.

El: Elena Calvi.

Ex: Can I have your mark sheets, please? Thank you. First of all, we'd like to know something about you. Where are you from, Karl?

K: I'm German. I live just outside Berlin now but I grew up in the centre of the city.

Ex: And Elena?

El: Italy.

Ex: What do you do there, Elena?

El: I work in a hotel.

Ex: Karl, what do you like most about the area where you grew up?

K: Well, there are so many things, really, but I suppose the one that really stands out for me is living so close to a great city like Berlin.

Ex: Elena, who has more influence on your life: your friends or your family?

El: My family.

Ex: Why?

El: I don't know, really. They just do.

▶ 02

For years I'd been telling all my friends that I wanted to get away from the hustle and bustle of London to somewhere quiet and peaceful. What I had in mind was a little cottage near the sea. Well, they do say you shouldn't wish too hard or your wish just might come true and that's exactly what happened. Out of the blue, I was offered a job managing a hotel in a remote part of Ireland. Suddenly, it seemed to me that I had, in fact, always been a real city person who could negotiate the complexities of urban life, the crowded underground trains, the roar of traffic, the millions of people – all of it – and without blinking. But the job offer was too good to turn down and a few weeks later I found myself in Castletownbere. In less than 24 hours I'd gone from a huge metropolis with a population of over 8 million to a quaint fishing village with barely 800 inhabitants. It was a huge change.

By the beginning of next month I will have been living here for exactly a year. I've been looking back, retracing my steps and coming to understand just how great a change it has actually been. I've got to know almost all of those 800 people and found a real sense of belonging, though I've also occasionally longed for the anonymity of city life. I've spent hours exploring the glorious countryside by bicycle and on foot, and have discovered a taste for silence and solitude I didn't know I had. I've also had great fun managing the hotel and getting to know some of its rather eccentric regular guests. By the time the first year comes to an end almost all my London friends will have been here to stay and they love it almost as much as I do. Of course, there are many things I miss, though in the end the crowded underground trains and the noisy London traffic I can easily do without.

▶ 03

1

I seemed to be always giving or throwing away things I'd bought but wasn't using. The only way to stop the cycle was to move into a much smaller place and really take downsizing and simplifying my life more seriously. It's going well so far though it's also been a challenge. There's less and less clutter and I now feel that my thinking is much clearer too. I spend more time outside, of course, because you can feel pretty hemmed in in such a small space. But there are some great places to walk literally outside my back door and I can even see the sea through my kitchen window, which is a real bonus. I don't think I could live here without that.

2

As soon as the prize money was in the bank I went out and bought this extraordinary 17th-century mansion. It was supposed to be my dream home but in some ways it's turned out to be a complete nightmare. I had no idea how edgy I was going to feel in a large and very ancient house. I have to be careful not to watch horror films on TV because I start to imagine every creak and groan from the rafters is actually someone lurking in one of the other rooms. Of course, it's glorious to have so much space. I've been able to accept my grandfather's gift of a grand piano because I've actually got somewhere to put it. Next step will be learning to play it.

3

I came to live in this part of town almost twenty years ago when I started university. My first home, if you can call it that, was a hall of residence just round the corner and then I lived in a series of shared flats. Finally I had enough money in the bank to get a mortgage and buy this place. I couldn't be happier living right in the centre of the city like this. Apart from the usual shops, there's a cinema, some rather pleasant cafés and even a really great arts centre round the corner. If I lived out of town, I know I'd really miss all that. I must admit I'm walled in by other buildings on all sides and that gets to me sometimes but it really doesn't outweigh the many advantages of inner-city living.

4

I tried to find something a bit bigger but everything I looked at was way outside my price range so I had to take this. I've had to leave a lot of my stuff at my parents' place. Perhaps one day I'll have enough room for more than a sofa bed and a desk! I tend to go out to eat – even for breakfast. The kitchenette is so tiny there's barely room to chop a carrot and it's difficult to get rid of the cooking smells afterwards. There are loads of cafés on this street and a lot of the people from round here hang out there in the mornings, so I've got to know them and find it to be a really vibrant neighbourhood. That's a real plus for someone living alone like me.

5

Where my partner and I lived before there were rooms we barely used, particularly after the children had all left home. That's one of the reasons I wanted to move. It's not at all cramped here but there's no excess either. I'm in and out of all the rooms every day. We both work from home and so we've each claimed one of the spare bedrooms as an office. It's great to have an office of my own, though it's right next to the room our neighbour, Tom, has set up as a gym and I can hear him working out. It reminds me that I'm living in close proximity to other people but it's sometimes a bit irritating.

▶ 04

I like to think I know most of my neighbours but perhaps I could get to know more of them or get to know the ones I do know a bit better. There is a neighbourhood association and they hold all sorts of social events, like barbecues and picnics and even run courses of various kinds, like yoga and language classes, but I somehow haven't managed to get involved in anything they offer apart from the annual street party, which is really great.

I read something interesting the other day that made me think. I read that the average American moves more than ten times in a lifetime. That sounds like a lot to me, but I bet if you move so often, you don't have much of a chance to get to know your neighbours at all. Apparently, that's the case, so someone has come up with the bright idea of creating an online forum so that neighbours can get to know each other. The publicity says it's like a town square where people can go to voice opinions and needs and even offer things for sale. It's a kind of social-networking site just for your neighbourhood. If it sounds a bit far-fetched to you for people to have to go online to get to know their neighbours, you might be surprised to hear how successful it has been. Apparently, in one small town where the forum was launched, almost two-thirds of the town's inhabitants had posted after the end of the first year. Perhaps if there was a forum like this for my neighbourhood, more busy people like me might get involved.

Personally, I'd like to see a local market place with stalls offering goods and services. I love markets and the idea of seeing what my neighbours have to offer really appeals to me.

Unit 2

▶ 05

1

I'm not saying I'm completely addicted but I would feel anxious if I didn't get a message every couple of minutes. I'm just used to talking to my friends pretty much all the time. I mean, obviously, there are exceptions – I do turn my phone off when I'm in class and I don't text when I'm having dinner with my family. But generally speaking, I like to be in contact twenty-four seven.

2

That totally depends on the situation – I'm sure some people would argue that not replying immediately shows a lack of interest or respect but the way I see it, there's more to life than texting. And I don't have a problem if my texts go unanswered for hours or even days.

3

I think that goes without saying. We all know people who've been dumped by text and that's a really mean and cowardly thing to do. Only the most insensitive person would even consider doing that.

4

I wouldn't go that far but yes, sometimes texting is preferable because you've got a bit more time to respond. I think it's fair to say that a lot of people are more outgoing and funny in their text messages than they are in a group situation.

▶ 06

This picture shows four friends sitting outside a café. They aren't talking to one another; instead they're all preoccupied with their phones. It could be that this photo captures a moment when they're all looking at the same message they've all just been sent and a few seconds before this was taken they'd all been chatting – but I imagine it's more likely that they're all looking at different messages because one of the boys looks very serious and one girl is laughing. I think this behaviour is quite typical among teenagers but it's not a good thing. People should really focus on the people they're with and ignore phone messages. There's no point going to a café with friends if you're just going to ignore them.

This picture also shows two friends. They're taking a selfie. It looks like they're on holiday somewhere cold. They're both wearing similar outfits – I don't know for sure but maybe they're wearing some sort of costume for a special event. They seem to be having a good time anyway.

▶ 07

1

A: I really related to the ideas on certain personality types in the book. I found it quite reassuring. Before I read this, I just thought I was weird because I didn't enjoy meeting new people or going to parties. I didn't realise I was an introvert and that there was actually absolutely nothing wrong with that at all.

B: Of course there isn't! In fact, I actually prefer introverts to extroverts. Extroverts are so attention-seeking and are only really interested in themselves. Introverts are much nicer people. Reading this book confirmed that for me.

A: The ideas were great but sometimes I found reading it a bit of a slog – especially all those long descriptions of studies on the brain and how that accounts for the way we behave. I found it all a bit boring, to be honest. A quick summary would have been enough. And, anyway, some of the results seemed to come to opposite conclusions.

B: Yeah, I'm always quite sceptical about that kind of thing. Most of those case studies are probably unreliable, so not worth devoting so many pages to them. It's a pity because she's good at making complicated scientific information quite accessible, which is a real achievement.

2

A: I'm not saying people shouldn't use social networking sites. It's just the online relationships with casual acquaintances I have a problem with – I mean, everyone presents a certain cultivated image of themselves online, which isn't always totally accurate. You know, the way people might admit to having a bad day in private, even if they'd never do so publicly online.

B: Exactly. And you can't blame them for that. I wouldn't dream of mentioning any of my insecurities online. The problem is that if all you see of someone is endless photos of parties and exciting holidays, it can be a bit annoying. It's the same as reading about celebrity lifestyles – all you see is a carefully edited version of their lives, which gives a totally false picture.

A: Absolutely. What gets me is people who insist on going on and on about their perfect life when they know you're going through a bad time.

B: Well, I suppose no one has to read anything they find boring or upsetting.

A: But we just can't resist. Everyone, including me, is so obsessed about staying in contact. I know I'd hate not to know what people are up to more than I hate all their shameless self-promotion!

3

A: I decided to see what it would be like to stay offline for a month, with no internet access at all, because I thought I was becoming too dependent on the internet.

B: Yeah, that was my motivation too. And how did you feel after the first week?

A: Well, I was finding it easier to distract myself with other activities, like phoning older relatives and reading. The problem was not that I was waiting to hear from anyone in particular – rather the feeling of being connected and available to the world. It was weird – almost like being invisible. I expect you'd get used to it eventually, though. But I think it's something everyone should consider trying.

B: Yes. Actually, I'd recommend it because it made me realise how easy it is to waste time doing basically nothing. So now I limit my internet time to an hour each day. I've had to learn to be strict with myself because I do really enjoy chatting online. It's interesting because I've still managed to maintain the online relationships I care about, without having to feel I need to be available to chat twenty-four seven.

▶ **08**

Research has shown that it's possible to identify a lot of information, such as people's socio-economic status and their emotional state, from their voice alone. It's also claimed that someone's age, height and weight can also be estimated just by listening to the way they speak.

Unit 3

▶ **09**

Chris should start planning his future right now. There's no sense in putting it off. First he needs to prioritise his career goals. He should picture what job within his current company he'd like to aim for and he should also consider any other companies he'd ideally like to work for in the longer term and in what capacity. He should think about how it feels to be doing that job. Then he should think about the steps he needs to take in order to get there. For example, are there any training courses he needs to do? Are there any extra responsibilities he could take on now? He should set monthly targets on the road to getting promoted and achieving his goals.

Deciding when to start a family is a big decision and isn't something you should take on lightly. Chris and his wife need to have a serious discussion about this. Money is an important factor, so it makes sense to plan ahead and start saving so that one or other of them can afford to stay at home and look after the baby if they want to.

Finally, I think Chris needs to dream a little. His plans for the future aren't that well defined and are a little unambitious.

▶ **10**

E = Examiner D = Daniela M = Martin

E: Now I'd like you to talk about something together for about two minutes. Here are some things that we often think make people mature and a question for you to discuss. First you have some time to look at the task. Now talk to each other about the extent to which these things make people consider themselves to be mature.

D: Shall we make a start?

M: OK.

D: Hmm … well, first of all, I really don't consider that we ever complete our education. What I mean is, it may be the case that you finish a university degree but nowadays a lot of people go on to do postgraduate courses or vocational training of some kind, even when they're quite old. It's more and more common for people to return to study throughout their lives.

M: I think that being financially independent is the key. If you are still reliant on your parents for money, you are never entirely free to make your own decisions, so in some senses you remain in the position that you were in when you were a child.

D: You mean, because you're having to ask your parents for money and possibly also having to justify what you spend it on?

M: Yes.

D: There's a lot to be said for that argument. In many cases I think it does make people less able to take responsibility for their own decisions and it often creates tensions in a family but it doesn't necessarily have to be like that. I read recently about someone who was over 40 and had to go back to live with his elderly parents. He was actually doing all sorts of things for them they needed done and couldn't do themselves, so there was a kind of balance in that case. And that brings me to another point. I don't think moving into your own flat or house necessarily makes you an adult either. A lot of people move out when they start university – I did, but although I probably thought of myself as very grown up, I wasn't, really.

M: Apart from earning your own living, I think the thing that really gives you adult status is having your own family. With children of your own, you grow up fast.

D: Yes, you're forced to mature by having to make sacrifices and by being responsible for other people, aren't you? For me that's the crucial thing: taking responsibility or being treated as if you are capable of taking responsibility. That's why the real transition from childhood to adulthood is being treated as an adult. Do you see what I mean?

M: Yes.

D: So, having your opinion sought by other adults is a real marker of maturity as I see it. It may be as a parent, as someone with professional skills and expertise or simply as someone who has accumulated enough knowledge of the world to justify their opinions.

E: Thank you. Now you have about a minute to decide which experience has the most effect on a person's maturity.

M: Well, for me it's being a parent.

D: I can't argue with the fact that people who are parents grow up fast – my older sister and brother-in-law certainly did – but I think having your opinions sought and respected is important too.

M: So which one shall we choose?

D: Mmm … being a parent, I suppose, because children often seek their parents' opinions. We'll settle for that.

▶ **11**

E = Examiner M = Martin D = Daniela

E: Thank you. Can I have the booklet, please? How important is it to continue to seek advice from older people throughout our lives?

M: Very. I think older people have a lot to offer, particularly on family matters.

D: Yes, indeed. All those years of experience of bringing up children are invaluable. But I think that there are a whole range of issues on which older people can offer advice and guidance.

M: Such as?

D: Well, I certainly wouldn't ask my grandmother how to delete an app from my phone but I do go to her for all sorts of other practical advice. She's a wonderful cook and she knows how to make things you don't find in recipe books, for example, but I also just consider her to be a wise person in general, with insights that I perhaps don't have.

E: Some people say we have stopped respecting older people. What do you think?

M: I think we have a bit because the world has changed so quickly and they haven't always been able to keep up with the changes – in technology, for example. This means we sometimes even make fun of them, something that certainly wouldn't have happened when they themselves were young.

D: No, it wouldn't – and it doesn't happen in traditional societies even today. The idea of older people as a source of wisdom is still very strong in those contexts.

E: Thank you. That is the end of the test.

▶ 12

I = Interviewer   D = Dan

I: My guest today is Dan Johnson, a scientist who does research into longevity – why some types of people tend to live longer than others. Thank you for joining us this morning, Dan. I'm going to start with a question about my own family background. Both my grandfather and great-grandfather were in their 90s when they died and I like to think I've inherited their long-life genes. What are my chances of making a century?

D: I wish I could look into a crystal ball and tell you the answer to that question. Sure, if I had a grandfather and a father who'd lived into their nineties, I'd be hoping science would tell me that I had a good chance of doing as well or better but in fact that's just wishful thinking. Sometimes I think that the appeal of the genetic explanation lies in our desire to see matters taken out of our hands. I'd go even further and say that many people use it as an excuse not to make basic lifestyle changes, preferring to rely on the belief that because they have family members who've lived into their 80s and 90s, they will too; regardless of whatever harmful habits they might have, such as smoking or not getting enough exercise, they live in the false hope that their genes will protect them. I hate to say it, but having family members who've lived long lives doesn't mean that you will too.

I: OK but my great grandfather is unusual, don't you think? Or am I wrong about that too?

D: Sorry but yes you are. I always tell people to take a good look at photographs from the late nineteenth and early twentieth centuries. There are plenty of elderly people in them so it really wasn't so very unusual to live a long life. I think I know where the confusion comes from because if we look at the average age at death it's much lower than it is today but that's because without antibiotics, everyone was more vulnerable to diseases, particularly babies and children. But if you did happen to make it into adulthood, you had almost as good a chance of living a long life as we do today.

I: And life was a lot less stressful then, so that would have helped too.

D: Do you think so? Granted, a miserable job you dislike causes the wrong kind of stress. Even those of us who have jobs we enjoy, comfortable homes and families who care about us, experience stress but much of that stress we experience comes from our own minds. As I see it, to a large extent, it's under our control. In the past, external factors were far more important. Think about all the wars, famines and epidemics. And the backbreaking work people had to do. An ordinary soldier in the First World War, or a young woman working as a maid in one of those big houses would have suffered far greater levels of stress than most of us do. Given the choice between the stresses of the past and contemporary stresses, I can tell you that I'd take the boring office job any day.

I: OK, but there's a common belief that stress is a factor and that laid-back people live longer. Is that true?

D: I wouldn't even go so far as to say that. What if you like your job, even if it is tough, and enjoy the challenges it presents? That's more likely to lead to a longer life than sitting round doing nothing and getting incredibly bored. But don't get me wrong, I'm not talking about being a success rather than being a loser. People who work hard tend to live longer but it's not because they are hugely successful and making a lot of money. What we've found is that there's a relationship between being hard-working and conscientious and being cautious and sensible about health. If you're responsible and reliable in your professional life, you'll have the same attitude to your health. For example, you'll probably avoid eating a lot of junk food and opt for healthier choices but you won't veer to the other extreme of starving yourself either. And that's another important part of the record that needs to be set straight: just because animals on a very low-calorie diet live longer, it doesn't necessarily mean that we do. Starvation dieting is disastrous for your health.

I: I seem to be getting all the factors wrong but, surely, being happily married does lead to a longer life, doesn't it?

D: It depends. Our research shows that for men, being married is closely related to being happy and healthy and if a man is happy with the relationship and healthy, his partner tends to be as well. I know I was more than a little disconcerted to discover that when the boot is on the other foot – that is, if a woman is happily married and her partner is not so happy – then it won't have such a positive impact on the length of her life. This strikes me as rather unfair – it doesn't matter how close they are in age, a woman always worries about her partner and feels responsible for him. The results of our study are really making me reassess my own relationships and behaviour.

I: What about widows? I've read they often live longer than women whose partners are still alive.

D: Yes, that's true. But the big question is why this should be the case. Let me tell you what I think could be an explanation. Women are fortunate in that they're often better at establishing and maintaining strong friendship networks than men are. Once women are on their own, they can enjoy and find support in these networks more than they could when their partners were still alive. This is just a theory, of course, but it's one that seems to make a lot of sense. I was in Japan last year and almost every tourist site I visited was full of happy groups of elderly women, who I assumed were widows. I saw men with their wives but I didn't see any groups of elderly men doing this kind of thing, I mean going on day trips together. This is just anecdotal evidence, of course, but I think it does give credence to my theory that women's friendships contribute to them living longer once they are widows.

I: Indeed! Well, thank you very much for joining us, Dan. I've been keeping track of all the beneficial factors and I don't think I'm doing too badly!

D: That's good to hear. Thank you for having me on the programme.

Unit 4

▶ **14**

Good morning. I'm Jon Hayes and for the last twenty years I've worked as a sports psychologist with top football teams, helping to prepare players mentally for important matches. People assume top footballers must be happy because of all their wealth and success. But they often forget that as well as all the benefits, the players are also under extreme pressure, and this is something that I think's got much worse in recent years. They're expected to perform at the highest level week after week. Of course, managers and fans always expect a lot from their team, which is OK, but a big problem for some players is that they expect perfection from themselves all the time.

A big part of my job is to help players cope when they don't perform their best. Players find being able to manage their frustration can make a big difference to their behaviour on the pitch and their enjoyment of the game.

I think sports psychology training is particularly helpful for the young players, many of whom are still teenagers. When they make mistakes, like missing a goal for example, they can sometimes get a lot of negative publicity and even abuse. So we also work on not taking criticism personally.

Sports psychologists like me give players a range of mental tools and techniques to help develop mental resilience. For example, footballers are taught to get rid of overly negative feelings through symbolic actions, such as wiping their hands on the grass or on their shirt to erase anything which might distract them from the game.

Many of the techniques we use are grounded in cutting-edge science, and all are designed to keep the mind clear and focused. Owing to improvements in neuroscience, we now know which area of the brain is used for decision-making – which is vital for improving performance. What we aim to do is to get the brain to release chemicals, such as dopamine, which have a positive effect and can increase our confidence. Just as nutritionists advise players not to eat junk food before matches, we help players to develop positive thinking skills to control their brains.

Even body language can be manipulated to project a positive frame of mind. If you have your head down and shoulders slumped, your brain chemistry changes for the worse. It's why I advise managers to look at players' body language to decide when to make a substitution. If they see a player with their head down and their eyes fixed on their feet, they'll know it's time for this player to come off the pitch.

I teach footballers to use memorised keywords to trigger appropriate mindsets or responses to certain situations. For example, a player might be trained to say 'ice' to remind him to stay cool when things get heated on the pitch. These keywords need to be simple, visual triggers that the brain can process quickly. Basically, all this training is aiming to give players more control and focus to enhance their performance on the pitch. But many of these techniques would work equally well in daily life.

▶ **15**

J = Jan   M = Marisol

J: In my opinion, the reason many people give up a sport or hobby is because of the costs involved.

M: I agree. It can be very expensive to join a gym, for instance. The monthly costs can be as high as 100 euros per month, which is too much.

J: Yes, and then what tends to happen is that people often join with the best of intentions but then find they don't have time to go often enough to justify the membership fee.

M: So you're saying lack of time and money are very significant reasons for people giving up sport?

J: Yes. I believe that goes a long way to explaining why people have to give up.

M: What about hobbies? Playing an instrument, for example?

J: I could be wrong but I imagine many people get demotivated because they realise they're never going to be an amazing pianist or guitar player.

M: Mmm … I know from my own experience that that's quite common. I gave up the piano after two years because I wasn't making enough progress, despite practising fairly often.

▶ **16**

1

I think there is a lot of value in having a hobby. I used to play the piano and now I've stopped, and I regret that. I used to hate practising for piano exams but, at the same time, I felt a sense of achievement. Perhaps I'll take it up again one day.

2

There's a lot of criticism of computer games but I think the people that criticise them have never played them. They're often criticised for being too violent and for stopping boys especially from doing other things, like going outside and playing football. But I think they can also develop your imagination and even social skills because often playing them is a shared experience.

Unit 5

▶ **17**

In this part of the test I'm going to give each of you three pictures. I'd like you to talk about two of them on your own for about a minute, and also to answer a question briefly about your partner's pictures.

It's your turn first. Here are your pictures. They show people who are very involved in what they're doing. I'd like you to compare two of the pictures and say why the people might be so involved in what they're doing, and how they might be feeling.

▶ **18**

Which person or people do you think looks happiest? Why?

▶ **20**

I = Interviewer   D = Donna   G = Graham

I: Good morning. In the studio this morning we're joined by Donna Marchant and Graham Donovan, two psychologists who've undertaken studies looking into some important questions: What makes us happy and does money have anything to do with it? Well, let's start with the second question. Donna?

D: The answer I get from reading other psychologists' research is a clear yes, though only to a limited extent. Other people's research tells me very clearly that if your income meets your basic needs, it will make you relatively happy, but – and it's a big but – if you have more than you need to make ends meet, you won't necessarily be any happier. The really interesting question is if you've reached that point, what should you do with the excess and how does that affect your happiness levels? That's what I've been looking into in my most recent research.

I: But how do we determine what excess income is? Is it everything that's left after we've covered basic needs like food, shelter, warmth? What do you think, Graham?

G: As I understand it, what Donna is saying – and she should know, she's the expert – is that without food and shelter, no one feels happy. But you also need safety. After that comes the need for relationships, a feeling of being appreciated and valued. In fact, as it's often said, without being able to achieve your full potential, you won't be completely happy.

I: So Donna, there's a kind of hierarchy of needs, is there?

D: Yes. Graham is drawing on a classic model or hierarchy developed by the American psychologist Abraham Maslow. I think I'm right in saying that this is where your research interests lie, don't they, Graham? But going back to your question, let me just say that fulfilling these higher-order needs takes money. And I would agree with Graham that none of the levels in the hierarchy are really extras. Money spent on your professional and personal development is money very well spent.

G: That's not my point, actually. Maslow's model is about the psychological development of the individual over time rather than what a person needs to be happy overall. The emphasis changes over different stages in a person's life. I'd add to that that after you've got food, shelter and safety, money doesn't really come into it so much. You can't buy friendship, self-esteem or fulfilment.

I: No, that's certainly not my experience. So Donna, what would you say is wrong with the way people spend their excess income?

D: There's a tragic paradox about money and happiness such that people often squander their wealth on the very things that are least likely to make them feel good, namely, consumer goods. What's more, the more they indulge in consumer goods, the more inclined they are to obsess about money and the less willing they'll be to use that money to help others. Obviously the implications of this are very serious indeed. Using money to help others – that's the key to happiness.

I: Graham, do you think the research on happiness supports Donna's position?

G: It's not quite that straightforward. There's a research study that tried to establish a link between altruistic spending and happiness but it's come in for quite a bit of criticism, much of which I would go along with. For what it's worth, the researchers got people to tell them how much they earned, how happy they felt, how much money they spent on themselves and how much went on 'social spending'; by that they meant gifts for others and donations to charity. They then looked at the relationship between income, happiness and the two types of spending. Because of the way they'd designed the study they couldn't prove it was the type of spending that made people happy or not but it was clear that spending seems to have more to do with happiness than income alone. I'm beginning to wonder if it's possible to look into this and come up with a definitive finding.

I: Donna, could you tell us more about the study you and your team conducted recently?

D: We took up the challenge. The more we know about the relationship between spending and happiness, the better able we will be to teach people the facts and perhaps change the emphasis on acquiring things in a vain attempt to make ourselves feel happier. I think that's a very important goal and one we've partially met in a paper the members of my team and I have just published. We're proud of having come up with a design that gets over the problems Graham mentioned. What we did, actually, was to ask people how happy they were before and after receiving a bonus at work. The bonuses varied in amount, I should add. After a few weeks we asked them how they had spent the money and how happy they felt. This time the relationship between social spending and happiness was much more clear-cut, so much so, in fact, that we feel confident in stating that the way people spent the bonus played more of a role in their happiness than the size of the bonus itself.

G: I don't want to quibble but how do you know that there were no other factors that might have intervened to make these people feel happy or unhappy? That said, rabid consumerism and fear about sharing our resources with others are social evils research needs to address and that's something you do seem to be doing. People should hear about your work.

I: I think so too and I hope that today's programme has helped in that regard but I'm afraid that's all we have time for. Thank you both, Donna and Graham, for being with us today.

Unit 6

▶ 21

1

A: Have you been down to the archaeological site recently?

B: Yes, the other day. It was really fascinating to see how much the archaeologists have unearthed already. I was amazed by it, really. I mean, it's a huge site and even with a sizeable team in place, they've only uncovered a fraction of it. It's going to be absolutely enormous when they've finished. I just can't believe that something like this can remain undiscovered for hundreds of years and only now come to light. And all of us locals virtually living on top of an important ancient settlement without having a clue that it's there!

A: I know. It makes you look at Saxton differently, doesn't it? I don't know about you but even though there are lots of more famous sites around, this feels more significant to me somehow.

B: I know what you mean. We're all familiar with the history of the town over the last few hundred years but this takes us back much further in time.

A: It's like the layers of centuries have been removed and I can actually understand much better how people lived over a thousand years ago.

B: And in some ways our lives haven't changed that much.

2

A: What did you think of the dinosaur exhibition then, James?

B: You know, I'd get more out of playing a computer game about dinosaurs than this exhibition.

A: Really? All the kids around us were absolutely loving it.

B: I know, but they were only young. Teenagers wouldn't be so impressed. You'd spend less on a computer game and could then relive the experience again and again. And the special effects would be far superior.

A: But I think you get more of an idea of the scale of dinosaurs from this exhibition and what the environment was really like.

B: I suppose so, and the other thing is I'm not sure how historically accurate games generally are.

A: Well, that's quite a big consideration! The museum obviously tried hard to recreate a real dinosaur experience and some of the dinosaurs were pretty terrifying but I felt I didn't really learn enough. I gave up trying to read those little information signs because there was always a large group of people around and I couldn't see them properly.

B: I just came away feeling confused about when the different dinosaur periods were and which dinosaurs were which.

3

A: That really old house in Wales is for sale – where we had that holiday – do you remember? It looks exactly the same.

B: Yes, of course. It was such a weird place, wasn't it? Great for playing hide-and-seek, though.

A: Yes. Brilliant, but freezing cold and mum was always complaining there was never any hot water. But what I mainly remember is being fascinated by its history and its occupants, wishing I could go back in time. I liked it when dad used to make up creepy stories about the people in the old paintings.

B: Which we never believed!

A: No – wouldn't it be awful if the person who buys it tries to update it unsympathetically – like get rid of all the original windows?

B: Mmm. I shouldn't think they'd be allowed to – it's bound to have a preservation order on it so they won't be able to turn it into flats or a hotel.

A: I expect you're right. I can't imagine all the furniture and paintings being auctioned off or ending up in a museum. I wish we could afford to buy it.

B: And take our kids there on holiday? Dream on!

▶ 22

Here are your pictures. They show people finding out about the past. I'd like you to compare two of the pictures and say why the people might be interested in this kind of information about the past, and how easy it might be for them to remember it.

▶ 23

What both these photos have in common is that they are of guided tours of historical places. The first picture looks as if it could be in a palace in Europe – possibly in the bedroom of a king or other important historical figure. The other picture is of an ancient monument in Egypt maybe. Whilst the people in the first picture look as if they live locally, the other group of tourists may have travelled a long way to get there and could be visiting many ancient sites. Neither of the groups looks as if they're very serious about remembering the information as they're not taking any notes. It may be a place they feel they should visit rather than having a particular interest in that period of history.

One significant difference in the pictures is the approach taken by the guides. The guide in the bedroom is wearing a period costume and could possibly be an actor. I think the aim of this is to make history come alive, which of course, makes it more memorable. Perhaps this is a more interesting approach as some of the people in the other picture look a bit bored – I doubt whether the tourists will remember very much about the talk given by the guide if they're just visiting the site for a few hours. Unless they've done a lot of reading beforehand and already know quite a lot about this site, it can be hard to imagine what the lives of the people who lived there thousands of years ago might have been like.

Unit 7

▶ 24

If you ask people to describe the archetypal salesperson, chances are the rug seller will come near the top of many lists. The pushy souk merchants tugging at every passing tourist begging, charming and then bullying customers to buy. Abdelmajid Rais El Fenni, known as Majid, is different. He runs one of the most successful boutiques in the kasbah of Tangiers, selling rugs, lamps, silverware and embroidery to clients from all over the world. He used to claw for business like his neighbours, who sell identical trinkets and rugs. But he soon realised that if he wanted to succeed, haggling would not get him anywhere. Instead he learnt to create value around his products, telling stories and selling the very best things he could find. 'You are like a beggar in sales, asking again and again all day,' he explains. 'My father used to say if you get upset, you lose the customer.' Businesspeople often talk about the importance of humility, of serving your customers and acknowledging the fickleness of the markets. For salespeople, humility is not an option but something that can be turned to their advantage. 'You look at everyone,' he says. 'You pay attention. Often customers don't even look at salespeople. They treat them like dirt. If I were a customer in someone else's shop, I would be friendly and polite. I tend to leave people alone to look at things. I turn the lights on, pay attention to what they're looking at, but I don't hassle them. If I see a salesman who interrupts and waves his hands about, I know he has another 20 years of learning to do.' Majid is a master at categorising the people who walk through his door and tailoring his approach. Majid explains his strategy after dealing with a tricky customer. 'Sometimes you need to be patient. At other times, you must treat the customer as a king. I made that man feel powerful by being so humble. He wanted to exercise his power. If I hadn't treated him so well, he would never have bought a carpet. Sometimes you need to teach, to establish your authority with customers who take you for a mere peddler.' He compares the different modes of selling to gears in a car. 'If the gear needs changing, you change it,' he says.

▶ 25

No business represents this marriage between traditional and modern selling as well as Apple. When it was planning its first stores in 2000–2001, it emphasised the importance of putting them in urban locations to attract passers-by, and letting visitors use the products, much as Majid lets his customers wander round his shop looking at the merchandise. Even if a potential customer would never have seriously considered switching from a PC to a Mac, the company knew that if they could get them into the store, they had a chance of converting them. That's why the stores were like latter-day cathedrals and why the company adopted a selling method akin to missionary work.

The stores were laid out with the new products up front, so customers who had never owned an Apple product could try them out. Next was a Red Zone, abuzz with staff and energy, where the conversion could take place in the form of a sale, and then a Family Room, where customers would be called by name and helped with service, support and lessons.

At a time when its rivals were trying to sell $2,000 computers in soulless big-box stores using cut-throat sales tactics, Apple went in the opposite direction. Ron Johnson, the former Apple executive charged with coming up with its retail offering, says that if the other companies had moved on from their aggressive shark-like approach to selling PCs, they would probably represent much stronger competition for Apple today. Apple sought 'not sharks, but … teachers, photographers and filmmakers'. In other words, converts themselves who sold out of enthusiasm, not just on commission.

Technology creates transparency and gives us more information. It should lead to better prospecting and franker negotiating. But so far it hasn't eliminated the ghost in the machine, which remains the human interaction.

▶ **26**

I = Interviewer   E = Elena   A = Adam

I: I have with me in the studio this morning Elena Vincent and Adam Carlisle, both of whom work in marketing, an industry which fascinates us all but one that also comes in for criticism from time to time. Elena, you started out in the industry when you were quite young, didn't you?

E: Relatively, yes. I was 22 when I got my first job as an administrative assistant with an advertising agency. It wasn't very exciting, but it was certainly a foot in the door. They were working on a campaign for a hotel that had once been a very popular holiday destination. Coincidentally, my grandparents had stayed there a couple of times. I did some research and discovered that a lot of famous people had also been regulars. I mentioned this to an account executive and they decided to theme the whole campaign around the idea of the past and the present. I didn't get to write any of the advertising copy, but I was really chuffed to see my idea made reality.

I: I understand that it was also a bit controversial because of some celebrities who were used in the campaign.

E: I wouldn't have called it controversial, although it did cause a bit of a stir. That was mainly because the celebrities disliked the images we used. I'd managed to find photographs of them at the hotel in the 70s and 80s. We put the old photographs alongside new ones taken in the same places and with the same posture and facial expressions. They'd all agreed to our using the photos, so I thought it was out of order to object after the event. They didn't like the sharp contrast between how they'd looked when they were young and how they look today.

I: But this campaign actually led to your being given a chance to do a marketing course, didn't it?

E: Yes, the agency wanted to move into marketing strategies aimed at services and they gave me a chance to do a course. I really put my heart and soul into it, though at the time I thought some of the techniques they presented on the course were a bit far-fetched. Now that I've seen how they work in practice I realise just how they can help marketers create very successful campaigns for services like hotels and restaurants. Through making use of the senses – visual appeal, sound and even smell – marketers can create a lasting positive impression. Smell is probably the most difficult sense to use successfully but we did a lot of activities where we actually saw how the various strategies could be applied. I still use what I learnt in my work, to great effect I must say.

I: Now that you've mentioned scent marketing, I'm going to bring Adam in here if I may. You started off researching the psychological effects of scents, didn't you?

A: Well no, not quite. My original dissertation topic focused on the way different perfumes are formulated but I got a bit bored with that. I had a girlfriend who was into aromatherapy and that led me into researching the way in which certain smells can change emotional

states. It's an area that's attracted a lot of attention from businesses using scents to enhance the appeal of their products and services. I knew my work would always find an audience and that I would see it applied in the marketing industry. That really gave me the incentive to go on doing research.

I: I understand scent marketing has come in for quite a lot of criticism though. Could you both give me your views on why you think that is?

E: No one has an issue with bread smelling like bread or coffee smelling like coffee. It's more complicated when smell is being used to manipulate people. I mean, when a powerful and irresistible scent is used to entice them into a shop only to find nothing identified with that smell actually on sale.

A: Yes, that's where problems arise. There's an advertisement aimed at getting people to drink more milk but milk is one of those smells that most people dislike. The marketing company opted, very cleverly in my opinion, for pumping out the smell of freshly baked cookies. They thought the cookie smell would make people want to eat some cookies and, by association, drink some milk. It worked but people did say it was manipulative.

I: I've heard that there are medical reasons why some people object to scent marketing.

E: The allergy lobby object very strongly. They don't like our environment being manipulated through pumping scented oils into the air – because it is potentially dangerous for this group, especially if the scent is so subtle that they would be potentially unaware of the danger. It's fair enough, really. If they start having breathing difficulties but can't actually smell whatever it is that is being pumped out, they won't realise they need to move away. This is a real problem because scents and aromas are being used in a whole range of contexts to market services: airlines, hotels and even, somewhat worryingly, casinos to encourage people to stay and keep gambling. They're really difficult to avoid.

A: Yes, allergy sufferers do have a problem. The gambling issue is an important one too; our motives are not always sinister though!

I: I'm sure they're not but there we must leave it. Thank you both … coming up now …

▶ **27**

A: What I think makes messages like these particularly effective is the fact that they're using anti-advertising slogans to attack the advertising industry.

B: Absolutely! It's a clever way of warning people not to be taken in by the power of advertising. Having said that, I do have some reservations. Some of these messages are a bit obvious, after all. I mean, we all know the whole point of advertising is to sell us things.

A: I can't argue with that but, as obvious as it may seem, we are still manipulated by the whole marketing industry. What campaigns like this do is make people stop and think. I especially like the use of humour – that's the key tool to changing hearts and minds.

B: Indeed it is. Poking fun at advertising robs it of some of its power. I do see that there is value in receiving an anti-advertising message from time to time but I do sometimes find things like this a bit patronising.

A: Patronising? I'm afraid I just don't see it like that at all. I'd really like to see at least one ad like this outside every shopping mall.

B: I can't think of anything worse! That would be the best way of ensuring that the message would lose its impact and its appeal.

A: Oh well, we'll just have to agree to differ on that one then.

▶ **28**

Now I'd like you to talk about something together for about two minutes. Here are some ways of promoting fashion products and a question for you to discuss. First you have some time to look at the task.

Now talk to each other about how effective these ways of promoting fashion products would be.

▶ **29**

Stealth advertising, or advertising you wouldn't even know is advertising, is coming to a living room, a college classroom or a blog near you. Here's how it works: imagine that you find your rather stylish friend is now looking more stylish than ever. Day after day she comes to college decked out in fantastic outfits that attract compliments from all and sundry. Then she lets slip that, in fact, what she is wearing is the new summer range from such and such a clothing company, available online or in-store and at the moment there happens to be a sale on, with some very attractive discounts. Would you smell a rat or would you think it was just normal chit-chat about clothes and where to get a bargain? Might it be the case that your friend is actually being paid to 'model' these fashion items and sing their praises so as to sell the brand to her classmates? I don't think anybody I know would do such a thing but if I were to learn that a friend was being paid to promote a product to me, I would be really angry.

As unlikely as this scenario might sound, this particular breed of stealth advertising is actually becoming more and more common. For the companies involved, it represents a huge saving on expensive campaigns but what's in it for people like my stylish friend? It sometimes starts with the person being offered the opportunity to trial a product – let's say a lip gloss. They get a year's supply of said lip gloss free and then, a few days later, someone contacts them to ask how they like it and then says, 'Hey, if you happen to be talking to your friends, can you just mention in passing that you use Lipluxe?' No pressure – after all, it's only if you happen to be talking to them. But you realise that you're being manipulated or your friends catch on and, outraged, contact the people who make Lipluxe to complain. In most cases they'll be fobbed off with one of those chillingly formal letters saying that it's normal practice, ending with the challenge, 'Should you wish to make a complaint, we suggest you contact the Advertising Control Board.' I say it's a challenge because nine out of ten times they know you won't.

But sometimes people do fight back. A friend of mine who is something of a fashionista has a blog where she writes about clothes and posts photos of herself wearing some of them. One day she was flicking through a magazine and she happened to see an ad for a brand of trainers in which the image was a lot of different pairs of feet wearing them … including hers! In tiny print at the bottom of the page were all the sources for the photographs, including her website. She was furious! Had the company asked my friend's permission to use her blog to promote the product, she would never have agreed to it. But a lot of bloggers wouldn't think twice about accepting money, though sometimes they're just given the clothes and encouraged to wear them. The really big bloggers demand high fees for this – sometimes as much as $50,000. I wonder what their friends would think if they knew.

Unit 8

▶ **30**

I'm Tim Cole, and as an experienced travel writer, I'm here to tell you not to believe everything you read in guidebooks because following some of the recommendations they give can result in the most bizarre situations. I'll never forget the night I arrived in Sydney, for example. I'd decided to check into a hotel recommended in my guidebook. My flight was late and I turned up at the address at 1a.m., exhausted and looking forward to a few hours' rest, but instead found myself at a comedy club, which at the time I didn't find at all funny. It turns out the hotel had moved to what was a department store, according to my useless guidebook.

The problem is that too many travellers are too trusting of their guidebooks and don't bother to research even the most basic facts before they set off. For example, many people don't think to check the publication date. Clearly, if this isn't within the last 12 months, you shouldn't buy it. Some guidebooks are only revised every couple of years, so it's no wonder the majority of guidebooks contain various inaccuracies and omissions.

This doesn't tend to apply as much to museums or other places of cultural interest, as this kind of information doesn't vary that much – so guidebooks are generally pretty dependable on these. But what I'm always extremely wary of are recommendations on restaurant prices, which can often come as a nasty shock. This can be a real problem for people on a budget. It wouldn't be such a disaster if other kinds of information were wrong, about the food or the ambience, for example – but these tend to be more or less OK.

Some people believe maps are now redundant in guidebooks because online versions are available – but I don't agree. Studying a real map is the best way to get to know a place. But some information I think is unnecessary. A special pet hate are those books which insist on including a multitude of photos. We already know what the Eiffel Tower looks like! Why not include more background information instead?

Of course, most guidebooks are also now available in a digital format and many travellers prefer using these because they're obviously not heavy to carry, so you can download as many as you like. But I avoid them because navigation is much harder than flicking through the index at the back of a book. Life's just too short and you can never guarantee you'll have internet access anyway. The only digital travel guide I'd consider using would have to be what you might describe as 'tailor-made' – specially designed for my individual trip. Otherwise, I'm happy to stick with the traditional form of guidebook.

However, on my trip to Hawaii last summer I experimented with a new way of getting good travel advice: an app called 'In-the-know'. This relies on insider advice from locals who have cool and interesting lifestyles – in Hawaii this didn't just include surfers – I actually got some really surprising tips from a sportswear designer. Without his advice I'd never have visited the unique Ukulele Festival or eaten spam sushi. But the thing I'll never forget was a ten-kilometre kayak expedition along the coast for a night-time swim with manta rays in a huge cave. A truly magnificent sight. And my top tip for anyone visiting Hawaii!

▶ **31**

Matt: Mia, you went to Thailand last year, didn't you?

Mia: Yes, I did. It was amazing! You have to go there, Matt!

Matt: Well, I'm already planning to go there. In the summer, hopefully. I was wondering if you can recommend a guidebook.

Mia: Well, the guidebook I used was so out of date I really wouldn't recommend it. In fact, I don't think I'll ever use one again. I'm thinking of just relying on Twitter recommendations next time I'm travelling. I've heard they're a much more reliable way to get advice.

Matt: That sounds like a great idea..

Mia: I'll show you my photos if you like. Are you free this evening?

▶ **32**

Here are your pictures. They show people on holiday buying souvenirs. I'd like you to compare two of the pictures and say why the people might want to buy these items and how useful each item might be as a reminder of their holiday.

▶ **33**

In both pictures the people are interested in buying local products or crafts but in one picture a man is selling typical baskets and hats from his bicycle, whereas in the other one the people are at an expensive airport shop, which looks as if it's mainly selling food products. Um … I would imagine that most people who travel to a new country that they may never visit again are interested in buying souvenirs that are typical of that area. But I doubt whether most tourists actually check to see if that item is actually locally made. I think some of these things are often mass-produced in countries like China. I'd be surprised if the street seller had actually made these things. It's not certain in either picture whether the people are actually going to make any purchases. I couldn't say if they're buying presents or not. Often these kinds of products are bought as gifts but they could just be shopping for themselves. The people talking to the street seller may just want to give the man some business and the people at the airport may just be trying to pass the time. In all likelihood they'll buy something that'll never be used and will be a waste of money.

▶ **34**

New York City's population in April 2000 stood at just over eight million – the highest it had ever been since records began. However, while the city's population grew substantially in the first half of the 20th century, it dropped from nearly 7.9 million in 1950 to 7.1 million in 1980. This was despite the baby boom and the surge in immigration from Europe, which started in the 1950s and continued through the 1970s. It was during this period that many families left New York City for the suburbs. But this trend was reversed over the next two decades as parts of the city were regenerated and a rise in immigration from Asia boosted the population to a peak of eight million by the year 2000.

It is unlikely that population growth will reach the levels seen in the first part of the 20th century, when the city's population went up by 38 percent between 1900 and 1910, but sharp declines are also unlikely. A period of relative stability in population levels seems likely during the first few decades of the 21st century. Moderate growth is expected, although it will be sufficiently high to push the population up to nine million by 2030.

▶ **35**

1
I hate to admit it but I've got no choice. I have to leave here to find work.

2
Don't worry, Mum. I'm not lonely. I've made loads of friends here already.

3
I wish I hadn't left. I think I would have had a better chance of starting my own business at home.

4
The government hasn't done enough to create jobs – that's why so many people are leaving.

5
Listen, Son, I really think you should stay in Australia. You've got lots more opportunities there.

6
I don't regret emigrating for one minute. It's the best decision I've ever made.

Unit 9

▶ **36**

Babies and small children pass a number of developmental milestones as they grow. Only weeks after a child is born she knows a smile for what it is and may even smile back, though she is not yet able to actually recognise the important people in her life. This comes a little later, when, at four months, the baby can identify her mother and begins to know who's who among all the people she encounters regularly. Mind you, names don't mean much to her at this stage but at ten months she will begin to recognise her own name and react to it appropriately. It's at this age also that she'll start to get a real kick out of the game of *peekaboo*. The adult hides his face behind his hands or some other object and then reveals it. This usually gets a laugh from the baby and is early evidence of a burgeoning sense of humour. She will begin to display helpful behaviour when she is little more than a year old but bear in mind that the child might actually be more of a hindrance than a help. Still, it's the thought that counts, so don't discourage her. It won't be long before she'll also get the hang of dressing herself – usually at around two. Once again, don't crush the child's enthusiasm as this may actually be slowing down her development and hanging on to an extra responsibility an adult can actually share with her.

▶ **37**

In this part of the test I'm going to give each of you three pictures. I'd like you to talk about two of them on your own for about a minute and a half, and also to answer a question briefly about your partner's pictures.

It's your turn first. Here are your pictures. They show people doing things on their own. I'd like you to compare two of the pictures and say why people might be doing these things on their own and what reactions they might get from other people.

▶ **38**

Both these photographs show people doing things alone that we often do with others. Apart from that similarity, they are in some ways rather different from one another. In the first picture there is a young boy by himself watching a film in a cinema. He seems completely engrossed in whatever it is he's watching and perfectly happy to be there without anyone else. What's more, he's got a huge container of popcorn all to himself. In the second picture a man is having a solitary meal in a restaurant and although he too seems quite engrossed in what he's doing, I have the impression that he's reading a magazine because he's feeling a bit self-conscious about being a lone diner. A woman on her own in a restaurant might attract a bit of attention, but a man on his own, on the other hand, probably wouldn't attract very much attention at all. It depends on the kind of restaurant of course. In a fast food restaurant people probably wouldn't even notice whether people dining were unaccompanied or with friends. Even if they did, I don't think they would think anything of it.

▶ 39

E = Examiner   C = Candidate

E: Who do you think is happiest doing these things on their own? Why?

C: It strikes me that the woman playing solitaire may actually be quite content even if she's not smiling or laughing. Perhaps she would prefer not to have someone across the table playing against her.

▶ 40

1

It was Saturday, so the multi-storey car park was jam-packed. I had to drive around for ages to find a space. I locked the car, headed for the lift and got out at ground level where the shops are. It was only then I realised I hadn't registered which row I'd parked in or even which floor I was on. I think I've finally got it through my own thick skull that the secret is to make a mental note of where I am. Everyone kept staring at me hanging around in the car park on my own. I could feel myself blushing. When most of the other cars had gone, I finally found mine.

2

I've always had trouble remembering my girlfriend's cousin's name. What pops into my head first is 'Antoinette' and then I think it's 'Brigitte'. I usually avoid calling her anything, which was what I did last time we met. I don't think she noticed but my girlfriend certainly did and she was not impressed. She would barely speak to me for the rest of the afternoon which made me feel pretty uneasy I have to say. Boy did she ever give me a talking to when we got home. There's actually an old song about a girl called Bernadette and the experts say using a song or poem sometimes does the trick. I'll give it a go.

3

I was actually really looking forward to our wedding anniversary, but I was so busy I put it right out of my mind. By the time I remembered, all the decent shops were closed and I ended up downloading a couple of new albums I thought he'd like on iTunes when I got home. He'd bought me some pearl earrings. I could tell he was thinking our anniversary was so unimportant to me I'd let it slip my mind. He looked miserable and I felt terrible. Apparently, there's some kind of anniversary alert app you can get and they'll send you messages with suggestions for gifts. I'll have to go for that next year instead of relying on my memory.

4

My sister used to put these little sticky notes all over the house with things she was trying to commit to memory. You'd find them on packets of cornflakes and on the bathroom mirror – everywhere you'd least expect them to be. That's what I should have done because even if I put things down on paper, if there are lots of facts and figures and so on, I get them all muddled up. For this subject there were heaps of dates and place names. I knew that if I didn't get them straightened out in my mind, my chances of getting a good mark in the final exam were out of the window, and it turned out that I was right.

5

There I was in a busy station in the middle of France and I needed to get some change for the ticket machine and get to the airport or I was going to miss my flight. I studied French for about seven years but I've let it get really rusty. I was desperately racking my brains for the phrase 'I need change' but all that came into my head were words in Spanish. Apparently, if you conjure up an image of the person who told you something, you sometimes remember it. So just when I was beginning to panic I thought of my old French teacher and suddenly a complete sentence popped into my head. I got my change.

Unit 10

▶ 42

1

I did this magazine quiz called 'How well does your partner know you?' I don't usually bother with this kind of thing because I think they're a waste of time. You had to grade statements and then give the same quiz to your partner to answer about you.

There was a huge discrepancy between my results and my partner's, and the analysis said something like, 'You should have spent more time getting to know each other.' Some of our answers really shocked me because they showed that we're actually quite incompatible. It's made me start to question a lot of things in our relationship. I did the quiz for a laugh but I rather wish I hadn't now.

2

I'd already had an interview and had actually been working for the company for a couple of weeks when they said I had to do a personality test. I was kind of surprised as I thought this was only used for recruitment purposes but I didn't really mind as it was actually quite interesting – but they must have got my results mixed up with someone else's because they said I wasn't good at handling pressure. I've never felt so insulted in my life. Me? Not handle pressure? I complained to my boss and she said not to worry about it. Now she realises just how wide of the mark the results were.

3

I'm not generally a big fan of personality tests but I basically had nothing else to do at work so I thought I'd give it a go. I honestly didn't expect to learn much ... I mean how could choosing colours say anything about your personality? You had to click on eight colours in order of preference, then wait a few minutes and repeat the same test. When I read the results I could hardly believe it. My attitudes, my worries, my problems with my partner, my work habits – it was all absolutely spot on. It didn't tell me anything I didn't already know about myself though.

4

The psychology department at my university were asking for student volunteers to do a personality test. They made us wait for ages in this really stuffy room with only three seats and there must have been at least 15 of us. Some people were getting really impatient. We were all a bit stunned when they explained that the point of the test had been to study our behaviour in the overcrowded room. I was quite proud of myself when they said I'd scored highly for tolerance and resilience, just because I hadn't lost my temper. I'd always wanted to get to the bottom of how these tests work, which is why I volunteered. I found it fascinating.

5

I've got my own translation business but I wasn't getting enough commissions. I decided to see if one of those life coaches could get to the bottom of whatever was going wrong and we both thought it would be useful for me to do a personality test. I was a bit taken aback when she said my test results showed that I needed to work in collaboration with others. It's weird as I've always seen myself as a bit of a loner and as not taking too kindly to people telling me what to do. But this new way of working might be just what I need to inspire me and will actually make a refreshing change.

▶ **43**

N = Nadia   A = Adam

N: Personally, I'm all in favour of robots doing as much work as possible. But I suppose the key issue here is to decide which tasks a robot is capable of doing as well as a human. I think they'd be just as good, if not better, at flying a plane. Would you go along with that?

A: I would, up to a point. I mean, most planes already depend on an automated system but pilots are still needed to make decisions in an emergency and I'm not sure I'd trust a robot to do that instead. Also, I think passengers feel reassured when the pilot talks to them.

N: Sure. But don't you think having a robot instead of a human pilot would remove the possibility of human error?

A: Possibly, but I think most people would still rather have a real person in charge. I think tasks with less responsibility are more appropriate for robots.

N: I suppose so. I hadn't thought of that. How would you feel about a robot looking after your grandmother? There are some practical tasks that a robot could do to help look after the elderly. For example, helping them to get washed and dressed.

A: Mmm. Maybe – as long as they'd also have some human interaction. It would be terrible to only have a robot as a companion.

N: Oh yes, absolutely. That would be terrible. I wouldn't mind having my meals cooked by a robot.

A: Simple meals would be OK. I can't see there'd be a problem with robots preparing things like pizzas. In a pizza restaurant, all they'd have to do is to put the right toppings on and put the pizza in the oven for the correct amount of time. But I just wonder how useful robots would be in a high-class restaurant where the cooks need to be able to taste the food!

N: So we're saying that a robot could cook effectively in certain circumstances.

A: Right.

Unit 11

▶ **44**

P = Presenter   M = Mark   D = Diana

P: Welcome to the *Review Show*. Joining me today are Diana Abel and Mark Shaw. The first book we'll be discussing is Robert Provine's *Laughter: a scientific investigation*. Mark, what did you make of it?

M: Well, he talks a lot about the idea that laughter is not primarily a response to humour but a social lubricant – something used to smooth interaction between people – interesting but I don't think Provine is the first psychologist to make this claim. But he is the first to popularise this theory. I think a lot of people will reject the notion that we don't just laugh because we find something funny and that laughter actually has a much more complex role. But what I found really disturbing is that, according to a recent study in the UK, we're laughing much less than we used to.

P: Indeed … Diana, I know you were particularly struck by the comparisons between male and female laughter in the book.

D: Yes, that's right. While researching the book, Provine found that one of the key qualities women look for in a potential partner is a good sense of humour – something sought after much less commonly by men.

That was certainly news to me. It seems women want a man who will make them laugh, while men like women who laugh at their jokes. Men may even feel threatened by a woman who's funny, which goes a long way to explain why until relatively recently there were so few female comedians around.

P: Provine does stress the importance of increasing laughter in our lives and gives some advice on how to achieve this. Were you persuaded by any of his suggestions, Diana?

D: Well, while Provine thinks we should all try to laugh more, he's not advocating attending laughter workshops or anything like that in order to be able to tell an amusing anecdote. His message is really quite simple. If you want to laugh more or better still make other people laugh, rather than trying to learn to play the clown, engage with people who have a humorous outlook and avoid those who are always gloomy – which makes sense to me. One thing I'm in favour of, which Provine neglected to mention, is that people should lighten up and laugh at themselves more.

P: Did either of you find your own attitude to laughter had changed after reading the book?

M: I certainly started noticing when people actually laughed and found it confirmed Provine's theory, that is, people were laughing at things that weren't remotely funny and also in odd places during a conversation.

D: The effect it had on me was to monitor my own impulses to laugh – it made me less spontaneous in a way.

M: … analysing what made you want to laugh instead of reacting naturally – I experienced that too. And it also made me aware of how little I actually laugh. I've found I am making more of an effort to be funny.

P: So did you find the book answered everything you ever wanted to know about laughter?

M: It was pretty comprehensive, especially the parts on how humour and comedy work. He also focuses on how humour can be abusive and cruel – anyone who's experienced this in the playground will be able to relate to that. The section on the mechanics of breathing and laughing I could have done without.

D: I was drawn to the social aspects of laughter. Provine argues that laughter existed long before comedy and I wish he'd gone into more depth about how the need for laughter may have been triggered.

M: That was the most informative section of the book, so that could have been expanded in my view. The descriptions of how laughter may have started with chimpanzees tickling each other are wonderful.

P: But, overall, would you recommend this to someone who hasn't got a professional or academic interest in laughter?

M: Without question, yes. There were some bits where I felt my lack of a background in neuroscience was a disadvantage but you can just skip those bits and move on to some of the lovely anecdotes about the research – some of the accounts of the contagious nature of laughter are really amazing. In some places people couldn't stop laughing for days.

D: Yes, incredible.

P: And do you think the book will help people?

M: Well, if you just want to find out about the benefits of laughter, there are more appropriate self-help guides. This is more wide-ranging than that.

P: I see. So, moving on to another book about comedy …

▶ 45

They did an experiment recently which shows that people are able to tell how a dog is feeling by reading its facial expressions. They showed volunteers photos of a dog expressing different feelings and the funny thing was it wasn't dog owners who were able to identify the different emotions best – people who'd never owned a dog were just as good. The researchers think people may have a natural empathy with dogs. But they're not sure why – it may be because humans and dogs have evolved with each other over thousands of years. I think they should do more research to find out if people can read other animals' emotions as well.

▶ 46

In this part of the test I'm going to give each of you three pictures. I'd like you to talk about two of them on your own for about a minute, and also to answer a question briefly about your partner's pictures.

It's your turn first. Here are your pictures. They show people creating an image. I'd like you to compare two of the pictures and say how successful the people are at creating the image and how people might react to them.

▶ 47

E = Examiner   C = Candidate

E: Which image do you think is the most powerful?

C: Well, it's quite hard to say because these can all be extremely influential; they can make us decide to buy a product or vote for a politician – but I suppose the most powerful might be the image created by the fashion shoot because it's more subtle, while the others are more direct. These kinds of images can help to sell thousands of products and can change people's attitudes to the way they dress or whatever.

Unit 12

▶ 48

Hi, I'm Max Bignall. When I arrived in New York six months ago to study physics at university, I was interested to hear about something called the Secret Science Club. It really is quite something. I knew that the club was started by two science writers, but not that the third founder was a radio producer. He did have a scientific background too, though.

The club started as a small informal gathering held in a Brooklyn bar but soon outgrew this venue and is now held at The Bell House, which is a popular Brooklyn venue for weddings and other private events. But most nights during the week what you can see are the types of acts you would expect from a trendy New York bar, namely performances by musicians – usually up-and-coming bands. And somewhat bizarrely, once a month you'll find a friendly scientist lecturing in down-to-earth language about a topical scientific issue. The lectures often include experiments at the end, which go down well with the crowd, especially if they involve audience participation.

The talks cover all kinds of issues: they've had a climate scientist talking about super-storms, an evolutionary biologist on the elusive animals that live in our cities, an astrophysicist talking about black holes – which was the highlight for me – and last time we had a mathematical sociologist explaining how ideas spread. The lectures themselves are generally very entertaining and accessible – even for non-scientists – but where I sometimes get lost is at the end, when people ask questions which can be quite specialised. And then there's a chance for everyone to listen to music and talk about the lecture. What's really invaluable for science students like me is the opportunity to network with some of the best experts in their field.

Nobody can agree about the precise origins of clubs like the Secret Science Club but they seem to have started in universities at the end of the 1990s. Of course, the idea itself is much older. In the 18th century people used to meet up in coffee houses in Britain and France to discuss the affairs of the day, including scientific discoveries.

I could be wrong, but I think the majority of people who attend the Secret Science Club aren't academics, just people with an interest in science. The appeal for people like this is that the lectures help them to understand the relevance of science in their daily lives. I like the fact that the Secret Science Club is inclusive and wants to share ideas beyond the scientific community. Scientists have a responsibility to help people see how science continues to shape the way we see the world and the future.

▶ 49

E = Examiner   G = Gustave   M = Maria

E: Good afternoon. My name is Pam Nelson and this is my colleague, Stephanie Mason. And your names are?

G: Gustave Jansen.

M: Maria Fernández Lourido.

E: Can I have your mark sheets, please? Thank you. First of all, we'd like to know something about you. Gustave, where are you from?

G: I'm from Germany.

E: What do you do there?

G: I'm a student.

E: Maria, how long have you been studying English?

M: Well, I started learning English in primary school, so I suppose I must have been studying it for about fifteen years now.

E: Gustave, what do you enjoy most about learning English?

G: The fact that I can watch films and TV series and understand quite a lot.

E: What did you like most about the area where you grew up, Gustave?

G: There are a lot of interesting, old buildings. I really like architecture.

E: Maria, do you ever wish you were rich and famous?

M: To be perfectly honest, not anymore, no. I used to when I was younger, of course, but I now think that there are so many responsibilities and problems that come with having money and fame and that sometimes they actually destroy the person's happiness. I would have to say that I don't enjoy my job because of the money. It's more because it gives me a lot of satisfaction.

▶ 50

E = Examiner   M = Maria   G = Gustave

E: In this part of the test I'm going to give each of you three pictures. I'd like you to talk about two of them on your own for about a minute and also to answer a question briefly about your partner's pictures.

Maria, it's your turn first. Here are your pictures. They show people doing research. I'd like you to compare two of the pictures and say why people might choose to do research like this and what problems they might have.

M: Both these photographs show women scientists carrying out research but they are actually quite different from one another. In the first photograph the woman seems to be doing some kind of … umm …

chemistry experiment – she has a whole lot of … umm … small glass … umm … containers in front of her on a bench and she is holding a notebook or perhaps a tablet. Perhaps she is making notes of the results of her experiment. The second woman is obviously doing something quite different. Instead of working in a lab she is outside doing some kind of fieldwork. I think she is probably a biologist. I imagine her work involves examining plants in their natural habitat, like the plant she's looking at. While the first woman could have the problem of an unexpected reaction of some kind, in which an explosion or perhaps some kind of poisonous gas is produced, the other woman is outside in the open air or perhaps in a hothouse and probably has to deal with extreme temperatures. They're both wearing lab coats to protect their clothing and possibly to prevent the chemicals and plants they're working with from becoming contaminated.

E: Thank you. Gustave, who do you think is most involved in what they are doing?

G: The woman in the laboratory.

E: Why?

G: She's looking at the slide very closely.

▶ 51

E = Examiner   M = Maria   G = Gustave

E: Now I'd like you to talk about something together for about two minutes. Here are some ways that good ideas sometimes spread from one person to another and a question for you to discuss. First you have some time to look at the task.
Now, talk to each other about how effective these ways are for spreading good ideas.

M: OK, let's make a start. I actually think good ideas often spread because one person tells another person about them. Do you agree?

G: I think more good ideas are spread through online communication than by means of face-to-face interaction. The point I'm trying to make is that a lot of conversation is quite trivial but if someone has something important to say, they're very likely to put it in a blog or perhaps record a podcast.

M: It could actually just be telepathy as well, now I come to think of it. I mean, someone has an idea somewhere and then by coincidence it turns out someone else in a completely different country has the same idea.

G: If you look at a lot of nineteenth- and early-twentieth-century inventions, it's quite difficult to say who was the real originator of the idea because it often seems to have been invented by two or more people simultaneously.

M: Hmm … And in the past there were books and magazines, of course, but nowadays Twitter is a really important way of spreading ideas. As I see it, it's far more important than anything else, at least for young people. People are constantly tweeting things they've read or just thought about.

G: It's amazing how quickly an idea or just a rumour of some kind can spread through a medium like that. I do have a few reservations about whether these things could actually be called good ideas, though.

E: Thank you. Now you have about a minute to decide which method would reach the largest number of people.

G: For me it would have to be online resources like blogs or even online newspapers and magazines. Almost everyone has an internet connection and potentially has access to good new ideas because of that.

M: Yes I suppose so, but I still tend to think that Twitter reaches more people.

G: There are loads of people who don't have a Twitter account.

M: That's true, so perhaps we could say that the internet is our first choice because of its almost universal appeal.

▶ 52

E = Examiner   G = Gustave   M = Maria

E: How important is it for people to learn about the history of science at school?

G: It's very important. People should study history.

E: Maria, what do you think about studying history?

M: History is an important subject and history of science especially. It's fascinating to learn about when discoveries were made and under what circumstances. I mean, often scientists had such passion for their work that they were willing to make huge sacrifices in terms of their health and their relationships to other people. Of course, many were rather eccentric as well so their stories make fascinating reading. Would you agree?

G: Sometimes scientists solved an important problem completely by chance. I always enjoyed learning about that kind of research. They often ended up getting ill as a result of their work. I mean people like Marie Curie.

E: Some people say they don't see the point of scientific research. Why do you think this is?

M: Well, in some cases I think it is because they don't actually know very much about it. There are reports on science research in the better newspapers but not everyone reads them and they may not be aware of the important contribution research can make to things like curing disease or warning us of dangers like global warming.

E: Gustave, do you think people are well informed about the value of scientific research?

G: No, and in my opinion it's up to scientists to inform them.

E: Why scientists?

G: They know more about it.

M: Yes, but they can inform the press about their work and then it can be presented to the public in an entertaining way. The problem is that it's not easy for people to get access to research reports directly. My father is a scientist and he says that unless your university or research institute subscribes to a journal you have to pay to read the articles and it can be very expensive.

G: If it's taken out of scientists' hands there will inevitably be distortion. There's a lot of false news on social media and so on, offering cures for diseases.

M: So maybe it's a question of educating people so that they can tell the difference between real scientific reporting and false news.

E: Gustave, what do you think about other media like television?

G: There are some pretty good science documentaries on TV but I think the universities themselves should have YouTube channels and so on to publicise research.

M: A lot of them do, actually. The university where my father works gives researchers the opportunity to make a kind of mini-documentary about their research for the YouTube channel. My father has made one on his research.

G: That sounds like a good idea I guess. But how do people know the YouTube channel exists?

M: Yes, that can be a problem and the other issue is talking about science in a way that's interesting and relevant for the general public.

E: Thank you. That is the end of the test.

Practice Test

Part 1

 53

1

A: How did it go at the Physics competition in the Netherlands?

B: I couldn't stay for the duration unfortunately … due to a family crisis … but the rest of my group did and the guys did incredibly well. We had lots of resources at our disposal, and that paid off. Anyway, despite being up against some of the best physicists in the world, we came second in the problem-solving category, which was no mean feat considering the opposition! We also won the Best Presentation award for our presentation on string theory. Well, at the risk of sounding smug, I think that was pretty much a given all along.

A: What were the other competitors like? Were they from a similar background?

B: Well, there seemed to be a good balance of males and females this year. Mind you, that's hardly unexpected … that gender gap in physics has been closing for a while now and that's refreshing. It's usually PhD students who enter … I suppose they've got the necessary expertise, so we were unique in that we're not PhD students! And obviously many of them were competition veterans … they've been doing this for years.

2

A: I think that since people have started watching several episodes of programmes back-to-back, they're becoming more demanding. Hence the decision, I suppose, by many TV conglomerates to dump entire series of certain shows online at a time, rather than drip-feed us episode by episode. I suppose it's all about instant gratification for the viewer. And there's a growing distaste for commercials too, which is bad news for the advertising industry. Research shows that one of the things people most enjoy about streaming shows is that they can either mute or fast-forward through the ads, as opposed to waiting them out when watching a live show.

B: That makes sense. It does seem that we're in the golden age of TV. For me, soap operas have never been better. They really do seem to touch on the rhythms of contemporary life. I would say, though, that scriptwriters should remember that effective story-telling has to follow certain principles … you know … add some surprise into the mix without being phoney about it. There's a love of the bizarre twist nowadays that often isn't even really based on the characters themselves – there's no clear connection. That's a low-grade form of story-telling, I think. Classic story-telling's about people facing some sort of dilemma and dealing with it.

3

A: How did you rise to the marathon challenge?

B: Well, the night before the marathon I thought I was starting to come down with something dreadful but thankfully it turned out to be nothing more than a few stomach cramps. I fully expected to have a bit of a wobble before it, but I managed to stay composed. Anyway, I thought back to the half-marathon I ran last year and I remembered that feeling of being sure I'd underperform when the day came. And this particular marathon really stirred up a lot of self-doubt too. I think it was a mixture of concern about endurance as well as a fear of the route itself, which is notoriously tough.

A: I know what you mean. When I ran my first marathon, I found it hard going at times for several reasons. Even though I'd followed all the rules about what to eat and drink beforehand, I just couldn't shake off the craving for cold drinks. I was well prepared though, and managed to get the pace just right, so I didn't burn out after the first couple of hours … something that many novice marathon runners do. Then they're so disheartened at not making the finish line.

Part 2

 54

Good afternoon everyone. I'm Leo Anderson and I'm here to talk to you about my work with rhinos in South Africa. I was with an organisation called the African Conservation Group, the ACG.

Several other volunteers arrived in Johannesburg at the same time I did, and we were put into teams such as the maintenance team that's responsible for the upkeep of the centre or the game ranger team. They'd decided I'd be best in the wildlife capture team, which mainly focuses on tagging animals so that their movements can be monitored, but has other duties too.

The first job I had was with the infant rhinos, so I wasn't exactly thrown in at the deep end! I was asked to assist with bottle-feeding these cute animals. We didn't have to prepare the formula – that was done for us – and then we were usually asked to feed them.

Another of my daily duties was clearing the enclosures. Well, that was really hard work to begin with, but I got used to it. I remember there was a huge panic one day as one of the animals almost escaped. That meant that the fences around the site had to be checked and reinforced.

To give volunteers an idea of how physically demanding working on a rhino conservation project is, the ACG established a rating system which is clearly displayed on their website. It's goes from one to five, and the more rhinos you see, the more challenging the experience is. One rhino, for instance, means suitable for all levels of fitness and physical ability but five rhinos means you need to be in excellent health as volunteers will often be on their feet from dawn to dusk.

The centre also does a lot of research on rhino behaviour … things like observing the interaction between adolescent rhinos, though that's not something that I was involved in … and monitoring the sleeping patterns of both males and females. Logging information on the central database about that was something I was regularly required to do.

Accommodation-wise, the centre has some beautiful bungalows where many of the permanent staff live, and where we often got together in the evenings. They're astonishingly luxurious. The rest of us had wooden huts, which we had to share. And though I expected them to be pretty basic, they were actually far from it.

Overall, my experience at the ACG was superb. It was fantastic to work with a group that has such a strong commitment to the rhinos, and in particular to the rehabilitation of orphaned rhinos. And the remarkable chemistry between all of us who'd gone there to help was especially memorable.

So how and why did I get involved? Well, back when I was applying for a place at university I knew there'd be a lot of competition for certain courses, like wildlife management and zoology. And as veterinary medicine, the degree I'd hoped to do, is particularly competitive, I was sure that my experience on a conservation programme would help make my application stand out.

Now if you have any questions, please feel free to come up and have a chat …

Part 3

 55

I = Interviewer   O = Oliver   M = Michelle

I: On *Business Matters* today I'm talking to two young fashion designers, Michelle Barnes and Oliver Grimshaw, who run a very successful start-up company in sustainable fashion called Ethion. Michelle, generally speaking, what do you think of the fashion industry today?

M: It needs to change, doesn't it? I mean the industry needs to evolve. To put it simply, environmentally and socially, the way fashion's produced isn't working. It's damaging. But I think we've come some way in recognising this so that there's been a definite shift throughout both the fashion and textile industries towards more sustainable practices that consider the impact on our planet, for instance. The word 'transparency's has become a buzz word for many companies that are really beginning to include sustainable solutions and want the public to know about it. The shift's towards change, but change takes time and comes with its own challenges. You know, we're still dealing with resistance and misinformation along the way on the part of some companies, and consumer scepticism.

I: I see. Oliver, your company's considered to be a pioneer when it comes to sustainable design … by which we mean fashion that can be supported indefinitely in terms of human impact on the environment and social responsibility. Do you feel that progress has been made when it comes to the way fashion collections are produced?

O: Well, we always wanted to just use pre-existing materials, originally for what it meant to us artistically rather than environmentally, but the more we became involved in the industry, the more we felt the urge to break all the rules. We've only ever used waste from designer products that didn't actually get to market, and we've always produced locally with a social conscience, by making a conscious effort to rehabilitate the long-term unemployed through a cooperative.

I: I see. Michelle, do you feel customers are becoming more aware of the negative impacts of the fashion industry?

M: Without a shadow of a doubt! Too many stories have been told … too much awareness of polluted rivers because of chemicals being dumped, for example, and widespread malpractice in terms of breaking the law have appeared for consumers not to have become aware of this issue. And consumers that were aware of this all along are now more outspoken in demanding change. Despite the relatively slow response from the industry itself, consumers are beginning to ask relevant and increasingly more meaningful questions on how the industry operates. And it's that which has had a significant impact.

I: Many believe that it's up to the next generation of designers to make a radical difference. Do students have good role models at the moment? Oliver?

O: If there were too many role models, students would react against them … as they're reacting against the so-called 'fast fashion' companies, and the social and environmental exploitation which means workers are not treated well. It's precisely because there are so few role models that there's this sense that we need to do something about it pretty quickly. Some of my most exhilarating moments are spent among students and very young designers. The role of the designer's changing profoundly in terms of ethics, and I strongly sense that the next generation will relish the chance to collaborate on finding sustainable solutions.

I: Michelle, you founded Ethion … a platform for designers with ethical and sustainable standards, which is a very noble concept. What direction do you think your company should move in?

M: Well, it's taken time for us to get established and I wouldn't say we're there yet, but step-by-step we're heading where we want to be. Top of our agenda is upcycling. In a world still churning out trendy, throw-away fashion pieces at breakneck speed, the idea of recycled, refashioned clothing can be an anomaly. But it's the way to go as far as we're concerned. We've got a good structure in place now and have come up with some solid plans for growth.

I: Sounds good. And finally, what do you both think about the state of the fashion industry here in the UK at the moment? Michelle?

M: Well, for years now, we've seen more and more of our local manufacturers being abandoned for production facilities much further afield, simply because it's cheaper. It's a shame really because all that expertise we had has been greatly diminished. Perhaps the government needs to provide more of an incentive for entrepreneurs to start new fashion companies in an attempt to get back to where we were …

O: … and when you think about the number of buildings dedicated to fashion that there used to be throughout this country too … you know, linen factories, woollen mills and so on. It's a disgrace that we've practically killed our home industry. We've ended up gradually industrialising the globe without keeping our own artisanal skills alive.

I: Indeed … well, Michelle and Oliver, thank you for talking to us today …

Part 4

 56

1

Interviews are not really my thing … I get so worked up. Anyway, I have to say the panel at the last interview I had was superb. They asked me all the usual stuff about where I saw myself in a few years' time, but I was well prepared for that! But I wish there'd been a bit more depth to my answers when they asked for examples of my innovation. I got the job because I reckon I ticked a lot of their boxes, especially in terms of international communication … I suppose it has come in handy that I'd lived in rural places in different countries where English wasn't widely spoken, and mixed with the locals.

2
My last interview was no picnic, I can tell you! It's almost like the panel wanted me to fail! The way they worded one question about the role meant that I got the wrong end of the stick and went on about *their* role as employers instead of mine! Still … it was my own fault, I suppose. But I kept my cool and answered the other questions as best I could. I did a good job hiding my nerves and I did my absolute utmost to show that I'd a long way to go in terms of professional development, honing my creative skills, etc. … I mean nobody likes a wise guy. Unbelievably, I got the job!

3
I love interviews! I thrive in demanding situations where there's that time pressure. My last interview was with a large energy company. In hindsight, I probably should've spent a little more time stressing my plans for career progression. At least I'd done a fair bit of background reading on the organisation, so that obviously went down well because I've now joined the company. Another thing that I feel the interview panel liked hearing about was my experience of training the customer services team … no mean feat I can tell you after what they'd been through with the last manager, but the team members have turned things around and can now operate entirely self-sufficiently.

4
Looking back at my last interview, I think it's a shame I wasn't a bit more on the ball when it came to highlighting the one thing that should have made me stand out head and shoulders above the other candidates … and that's my language skills. It completely slipped my mind! I suppose it's just as well then that I was able to speak knowledgeably about company performance. Anyway, to cut a long story short, I was offered the job and have just started. I think it's important to demonstrate to the interview panel that you can think outside the box. And I think that's possibly where I shone at my last interview.

5
Well, I know looking the part's important for a job in a law firm because lawyers, as you know, tend to be pretty conventional dressers. My black suit did nicely, I think. On reflection though, I could've done a better job in turning the tables on them by getting them to talk more. Anyway, that said, my one chance to come into my own was when they asked me about working in stressful situations. My background in the Tokyo stock market, and also that year that I spent in New York, meant I had more than enough examples to give them. They must've been happy with what they heard because they offered me the role!

Speaking Part 1

 57

First of all, we'd like to know something about you.
Where are you from?
What do you do here?
How long have you been studying English?
What do you enjoy most about learning English?
If you could live in any city in the world, which one would you live in? Why?
Who do you think is the most influential person in your country? Why?
What was the most interesting TV programme you've watched recently about?
If you had more free time, what would you like to learn to do? Why?
Who do you enjoy spending your free time with? Why?

Speaking Part 2

 58

In this part of the test, I'm going to give each of you three pictures. I'd like you to talk about two of them on your own for about a minute, and also to answer a question about your partner's pictures.
Candidate A, it's your turn first. Here are your pictures. They show people relaxing outdoors. I'd like you to compare two of the pictures, and say why the people might have chosen to relax in this way, and how they might be feeling. All right?
Thank you. Candidate B, in which situation do the people seem most relaxed?
Thank you. Now, Candidate B, here are your pictures. They show young people doing sports. I'd like you to compare two of the pictures, and say which sport would be most exciting and why, and how young people could benefit from doing this sport? All right?
Thank you. Candidate A, do you think it's important for young people to take part in sport while they're studying?

Speaking Part 3

 59

Now I'd like you to talk about something together for about two minutes. Here are some things people often have to consider when applying for a job and a question for you to discuss. First you have some time to look at the task.
Now, talk to each other about how important these things are when choosing a job. All right? Could you start now, please?
Thank you. Now you have about a minute to decide which of these things older people might feel is more important when choosing a job.

Speaking Part 4

▶ 60

Is it best for people to find a job close to their home or in another town/city? Why?
Why do you think some people prefer to live and work in another country?
Some people say it's better to work from home than work in an office. Do you agree?
What are the advantages of working in teams?
Some people say it's not a good idea to stay in the same job for life. What's your opinion?
Thank you. That is the end of the test.

Pearson Education Limited
KAO Two, KAO Park, Harlow,
Essex, CM17 9SR, England
and Associated Companies throughout the world

www.pearsonELT.com/gold

© Pearson Education Limited 2019

Coursebook: Sally Burgess and Amanda Thomas
Practice Test: Imelda Maguire-Karayel

The right of Sally Burgess, Amanda Thomas and Imelda Maguire-Karayel
to be identified as authors of this Work has been asserted by them in
accordance with the Copyright, Designs and Patents Act 1988.

New Edition first published 2019
Seventh impression 2023

ISBN: 978-1-292-39448-0 (Gold C1 Advanced New Edition Coursebook
and MyEnglishLab pack)

ISBN: 978-1-292-39636-1 (Gold C1 Advanced New Edition Coursebook)

Set in Frutiger Neue LT Pro Thin
Printed in Slovakia by Neografia

Acknowledgements
The publishers would like to thank the following people for their
feedback and comments during the development of the materials:
Agnieszka Adamowska (Poland); Mehroo Bhoori (Italy); Marc Broderick
(Spain); Begona Coral (Spain); Oliver Hutchison (Spain); Karen Shaw
(Switzerland); Rowena Smith (Italy); Chris Thirlaway (Brazil).

The authors would like to thank the whole Pearson team for their
expertise, support and encouragement.

We are grateful to the following for permission to reproduce
copyright material:

Text
11 From the *Financial Times* 21 October 2016. The endless city: how
satellites changed the way we see the streets by Edwin Heathcote © The
Financial Times LTD 2018, All Rights Reserved; 15, 52, 65 © Telegraph
Media Group Limited 2018; 21 From the *Financial Times* 10 March 2012,
How to have a conversation by John McDermott © The Financial Times
LTD 2018, All Rights Reserved; 40 From the *Financial Times* 25 May
2012, Recipe for success by Natalie Graham © The Financial Times LTD
2018, All Rights Reserved; 43 This is an edited extract from *The Antidote:
Happiness For People Who Can't Stand Positive Thinking*, by Oliver
Burkeman, published by Farrar, Straus & Giroux Inc.; 105 Dr Christopher
Scanlon is Associate Director of the Learning Transformations Unit at
Swinburne University of Technology; 188 Christine Rosen, "The Myth of
Multitasking," *The New Atlantis*, Number 20, Spring 2008, pp. 105–110;
192 This essay was originally published in *Aeon*, https://aeon.co/; 194
Mental Health Foundation.

Photos
The publisher would like to thank the following for their kind permission
to reproduce their photographs:

123RF.com: Claudiodivizia 145, Foodandmore 75, Ion Chiosea 105,
Kzenon 131, Luckybusiness 45, Michael Simons 27, Serezniy 25, Tatyana
Tomsickova 90, Wavebreak Media Ltd 136, carbo82 66, hafakot 139,
sdimitrov 205; **Alamy Stock Photo:** AF archive 134, Andrew Aitchison
49, Bill Crump 145, Chris Willson 32, Cliff Hide News 89, Contraband
Collection 86, Cultura RM 122, D. Hurst 65, David Grossman 85, Enigma
Images 139, France Chateau 61, Gina Kelly 51, ITAR-TASS News Agency
106, ITAR-TASS Photo Agency 16, IanDagnall Computing 127, Image
Source 137, Ingemar Magnusson 48, John Kellerman 11, Leon Werdinger
93, Mark Richardson 145, Mauritius images GmbH 33, PJF Military
Collection 143, Park Dale 143, Paul Fearn 100, RubberBall 22, Selwyn
136, Shutterstock.com 60, Takatoshi Kurikawa 147, Thomas Trutschel /
photothek images UG 141, Travelscape Images 55, UrbanImages 145,
Valera197615 26, Victor Watts 145, WENN Ltd 40, Washington Imaging
59, Wavebreak Media ltd 141, Witthaya Khampanant 147, World History
Archive 58, iPhone 136, imageBROKER 70, third cross 147, topz 76;
Getty Images: Adam Gault 142, Artiga Photo 116, Brendan Smialowski /
AFP 118, Cultura RM Exclusive / Seb Oliver 61, DAJ 38, David Epperson 8,
Inti St Clair 44, JRLPhotographer 139, Jeff Greenberg 83, Joe Polillio 138,
Johnny Haglund 21, Jupiterimages 82, Klaus Vedfelt 16, Last Resort 43,
Lonely Planet Images 80, Luca Sage 92, Maskot 61, Mike Pont 57, Paul
Morigi 118, PeopleImages 88, Quang Vu 83, RUNSTUDIO 142, Richard
Elliott 93, Sam Edwards 142, SensorSpot 115, Tanakorn Pussawong 112,
Tribune New Agency 73, VCG 109, ZhangKun 41, alvarez 120, whitemay
63, winhorse 83; **Shutterstock.com:** Africa Studio 118, AnnaTamila 6,
Ardelean Andreea 134, Benerys 139, Blazej Lyjak 18, Borysevych.com
96, CANARYLUC 124, ESB Professional 30, Everett Historical 126, Fresnel
16, Halfpoint 141, Have a nice day Photo 136, Hlemeida Ivan 139,
Iakov Filimonov 139, Ipatov 205, Ivanko80 111, Jaromir Chalabala 137,
Jonny89 147, Joshua Resnick 140, Kantoh 107, Karramba Production 93,
Life science 95, Maksim Shmeljo 205, Maria Savenko 138, Martin M303
10, Mojca Odar 136, Monkey Business Images 205, Monkey Business
Images. 140, Ober-art 19, PT Images 28, Peter Bernik 140, Photographee.
eu 49, Prasit Rodphan 119, Rex 125, 125, Rido 35, Ron Ellis 9, S_L 53,
Sathaporn Sumarai 99, Savvapanf Photo 15, StockphotoVideo 141,
SuxxesPhoto 13, TDway 140, Theera Disayarat 142, Tyler Olson 142,
Viktor1 113, Vladimir Melnikov 123, Wavebreakmedia 134, elwynn
141, fotoinfo 143, garagestock 138, gpointstudio 140, hanohiki 205,
kurhan 137, kuruneko 147, lightpoet 121, liza1979 79, maradon 333
102, melnikof 141, nobeastsofierce 64, pathdoc 77, photodonato 76,
tankists276 205, turtix 80, wavebreakmedia 136, 140, 72, withGod 142.

All other images © Pearson Education

Illustrated by Oxford Designers & Illustrators Ltd